T0305235

Robust Equity Portfolio Management + Website

The Frank J. Fabozzi Series

How to Select Investment Managers and Evaluate Performance by G. Timothy Haight, Stephen O. Morrell, and Glenn E. Ross

Bayesian Methods in Finance by Svetlozar T. Rachev, John S. J. Hsu, Biliana S. Bagasheva, and Frank J. Fabozzi

The Handbook of Municipal Bonds edited by Sylvan G. Feldstein and Frank J. Fabozzi

Subprime Mortgage Credit Derivatives by Laurie S. Goodman, Shumin Li, Douglas J. Lucas, Thomas A Zimmerman, and Frank J. Fabozzi

Introduction to Securitization by Frank J. Fabozzi and Vinod Kothari

Structured Products and Related Credit Derivatives edited by Brian P. Lancaster, Glenn M. Schultz, and Frank J. Fabozzi

Handbook of Finance: Volume I: Financial Markets and Instruments edited by Frank J. Fabozzi

Handbook of Finance: Volume II: Financial Management and Asset Management edited by Frank J. Fabozzi

Handbook of Finance: Volume III: Valuation, Financial Modeling, and Quantitative Tools edited by Frank J. Fabozzi

Finance: Capital Markets, Financial Management, and Investment Management by Frank J. Fabozzi and Pamela Peterson-Drake

Active Private Equity Real Estate Strategy edited by David J. Lynn

Foundations and Applications of the Time Value of Money by Pamela Peterson-Drake and Frank J. Fabozzi

Leveraged Finance: Concepts, Methods, and Trading of High-Yield Bonds, Loans, and Derivatives by Stephen Antczak, Douglas Lucas, and Frank J. Fabozzi

Modern Financial Systems: Theory and Applications by Edwin Neave

Institutional Investment Management: Equity and Bond Portfolio Strategies and Applications by Frank J. Fabozzi

Robust Equity Portfolio Management + Website

Formulations, Implementations, and Properties Using MATLAB

WOO CHANG KIM
JANG HO KIM
FRANK J. FABOZZI

WILEY

Published by John Wiley & Sons, Inc., Hoboken, New Jersey.
Published simultaneously in Canada.

For general information on our other products and services or for technical support, please contact our Customer Care Department within the United States at (800) 762-2974, outside the United States at (317) 572-3993 or fax (317) 572-4002.

Wiley publishes in a variety of print and electronic formats and by print-on-demand. Some material included with standard print versions of this book may not be included in e-books or in print-on-demand. If this book refers to media such as a CD or DVD that is not included in the version you purchased, you may download this material at http://booksupport.wiley .com. For more information about Wiley products, visit www.wiley.com.

Library of Congress Cataloging-in-Publication Data

Names: Kim, Woo Chang. | Kim, Jang-Ho. | Fabozzi, Frank J.
Title: Robust equity portfolio management + website : formulations,
    implementations, and properties using MATLAB / Woo Chang Kim, Jang Ho Kim,
    Frank J. Fabozzi.
Description: Hoboken : Wiley, 2015. | Series: Frank J. Fabozzi series |
    Includes index.
Identifiers: LCCN 2015030347 | ISBN 9781118797266 (hardback) |
    ISBN 9781118797303 (epdf) | ISBN 9781118797372 (epub)
Subjects: LCSH: Porffolio management. | Investments–Mathematical models. |
    Investment analysis–Mathematical models. | BISAC: BUSINESS & ECONOMICS /
    Investments & Securities.
Classification: LCC HG4529.5 .K556 2015 | DDC 332.60285/53–dc23 LC record
    available at http://lccn.loc.gov/2015030347

Cover Design: Wiley
Cover Image: © Danil Melekhin/Getty Images, Inc.

Printed in the United States of America

10 9 8 7 6 5 4 3 2 1

WCK
To my daughter, Joohyung
JHK
To my wife, Insun Jung
FJF
To my sister, Lucy

Contents

Preface

The mean-variance model for constructing portfolios, introduced by Harry Markowitz, changed how portfolio managers analyze portfolios, especially for managing equity portfolios. The model provides a strong foundation for quantifying the return and risk attributes of a portfolio, as well as mathematically forming optimal portfolios. Following the 1952 publication of Markowitz's mean-variance model, there have been numerous extensions of the original model, particularly starting in the 1990s, that have sought to overcome criticisms of the original model. In this book, we focus on one of these extensions, the construction of robust portfolios for equity portfolio management within the mean-variance framework. We refer to this approach as robust equity portfolio management.

The book will be most helpful for readers who are interested in learning about the quantitative side of equity portfolio management, mainly portfolio optimization and risk analysis. Mean-variance portfolio optimization is covered in detail, leading to an extensive discussion on robust portfolio optimization. Nonetheless, readers without prior knowledge of portfolio management or mathematical modeling should be able to follow the presentation, as basic concepts are covered in each chapter. Furthermore, the main quantitative approaches are presented with MATLAB examples, allowing readers to easily implement portfolio problems in MATLAB or similar modeling software. An online appendix provides the MATLAB codes presented in the chapter boxes (www.wiley.com/go/robustequitypm).

Although this is not the only book on robust portfolio management, it distinguishes itself from other books by focusing solely on quantitative robust equity portfolio management, including step-by-step implementations. Other books, such as *Robust Portfolio Optimization and Management* by Frank J. Fabozzi, Petter N. Kolm, Dessislava Pachamanova, and Sergio M. Focardi, also introduce robust approaches, but we believe that readers seeking to learn the formulations, implementations, and properties of robust equity portfolios will benefit considerably by studying the chapters in the current book.

Woo Chang Kim
Jang Ho Kim
Frank J. Fabozzi

CHAPTER 1

Introduction

The foundations of what is popularly referred to as "modern portfolio theory" is attributable to the seminal work of Harry Markowitz, published more than a half a century ago.[1] Markowitz provided a framework for the selection of securities for portfolio construction to obtain an optimal portfolio. To do so, Markowitz suggested that for all assets that are candidates for inclusion in a portfolio, one should measure an asset's return by its mean return and risk by an asset's variance of returns. In the selection of assets to include in a portfolio, the Markowitz framework takes into account the co-movement of asset returns by using the covariance between all pairs of assets. The portfolio's expected return and risk as measured by the portfolio variance are then determined by the weights of each asset included in the portfolio. For this reason, the Markowitz framework is commonly referred to as *mean-variance portfolio analysis*. Markowitz argued that the optimal portfolio should be selected based on the trade-off between a portfolio's return and risk. While these concepts are considered the basis of portfolio construction these days, the development of the mean-variance model shaped how investment managers analyze portfolios and sparked an overwhelming volume of research on the theory of portfolio selection.

Once the fundamentals of modern portfolio theory were established, studies addressing the limitations of mean-variance analysis appeared, seeking to improve the effectiveness of the original model under practical situations. Some research efforts concentrated on reducing the sensitivity of portfolios formed from mean-variance analysis. Portfolio sensitivity means that the resulting portfolio constructed using mean-variance analysis and its performance is heavily dependent on the inputs of the model. Hence, if the estimated input values were even slightly different from their true values, the estimated optimal portfolio will actually be far from the best choice. This is especially a drawback when managing equity portfolios because the equity market is one of the more volatile markets, making it difficult to estimate values such as expected returns.

In equity portfolio management, there has been increased interest in the construction of portfolios that offer the potential for more robust performance even during more volatile equity market periods. One common approach for doing so is to increase the robustness of the input values of mean-variance analysis by adopting estimators that are more robust to outliers. It is also possible to achieve higher robustness by focusing on the outputs of the mean-variance model by performing simulations for collecting many possible portfolios and then finally arriving at one optimal portfolio based on all the possible ones. There are other methods that are based on the equilibrium of the equity market for gaining robustness.[2]

Although various techniques have been applied to improve the stability of portfolios, one of the approaches that has received much attention is robust portfolio optimization. Robust optimization is a method that incorporates parameter uncertainty by defining a set of possible values, referred to as an uncertainty set. The optimal solution represents the best choice when considering all possibilities from the uncertainty set. Robust optimization was developed for addressing optimization problems where the true values of the model's parameters are not known with certainty, but the bounds are assumed to be known. In 1973, Allen Soyster discussed inexact linear programming; in the 1990s, the initial approach expanded to incorporate a number of ways for defining uncertainty sets and addressing more complex optimization problems. When robust optimization is extended to portfolio selection, the inputs used in mean-variance analysis—the vector of mean returns and the covariance matrix of returns—become the uncertain parameters for finding the optimal portfolio. Since the turn of the century, there have been numerous proposals for formulating robust portfolio optimization problems. Much of the focus has been on mathematical theories behind uncertainty set construction and reformulations resulting in optimization problems that can be solved efficiently; and, as a result, there are many formulations that can be used to build robust equity portfolios.

Even though there has been considerable development on robust portfolio management, most approaches require skills far beyond perfecting mean-variance analysis. For example, it is not an easy task for a portfolio manager without extensive background knowledge in optimization and mathematics to understand robust portfolio optimization formulations. More importantly, being able to interpret robust formulations is only the first step. The second step requires solving the optimization problem to arrive at the optimal decision. Programming expertise, in addition to optimization and mathematics, is necessary in the second step because most robust formulations require complex computations. Thus, while the need and the value of robust portfolio management are apparent, only those with appropriate training will be equipped to explore the advanced methods for improving portfolio robustness.

This book is aimed at providing a step-by-step guide for using robust models for optimal portfolio construction. It is not assumed that the reader has prior knowledge in portfolio management and optimization. In this book, the basics of portfolio theory and optimization, along with programming examples, will allow the reader to gain familiarity with portfolio optimization. Once the fundamentals of portfolio management are outlined, robust approaches for managing portfolios are explained with an emphasis on robust portfolio optimization. Details on robust formulations, implementation of robust portfolio optimization, attributes of robust portfolios, and robust portfolio performance will prepare the reader to utilize robust portfolio optimization for managing portfolios. In this book, we not only review theoretical developments but provide numerous programming examples to demonstrate their use in practice. The programming examples that appear throughout the book illustrate the details of implementing various techniques including methods for constructing robust equity portfolios.

1.1 OVERVIEW OF THE CHAPTERS

The book is divided into three parts. The first part, Chapters 2 through 4, introduces the mean-variance model, discusses its shortcomings, and explains common approaches for increasing the robustness of portfolios. The second part, Chapters 5 and 6, contains an overview of optimization and details the steps involved in formulating a robust portfolio optimization problem. The third part, Chapters 7 through 10, focuses on analyzing robust portfolios constructed from robust portfolio optimization by identifying attributes and summarizing performances.

Chapter 2 begins by describing how portfolio return and risk are measured, which leads to formulating the mean-variance portfolio problem. Mean-variance analysis finds the optimal portfolio from the trade-off between return and risk, and the framework also explains the benefits of diversification. Chapter 3 investigates shortcomings of the mean-variance model, which limit its use as a strategy for managing equity portfolios; improvements can be made with respect to measuring risk, estimating the input variables, and reducing the sensitivity of portfolio weights. In particular, the combination of estimation errors in the input values and high sensitivity of the resulting portfolio is a major issue with the mean-variance model. Therefore, in Chapter 4, practices for reducing the sensitivity of portfolios are demonstrated, including robust statistics, simulation methods, and stochastic programming.

Chapter 5 presents a comprehensive overview of optimization, including definitions of linear programming, quadratic programming, and conic optimization. The chapter also discusses how robust optimization transforms basic optimization problems so as to incorporate parameter uncertainty. The discussion is extended to applying robust optimization to portfolio selection in Chapter 6. While concentrating on the uncertainty caused by estimating expected returns of stocks, two robust formulations are shown with specific instructions provided as to their implementation.

Chapters 7, 8, and 9 analyze portfolio attributes that are revealed when portfolios are formed from robust portfolio optimization. In Chapter 7, we provide empirical evidence that indicates that some uncertainty sets lead to portfolios that favor skewness but penalize kurtosis. The high factor exposure of robust portfolios at the portfolio level is addressed in Chapter 8, and Chapter 9 examines portfolio weights allocated to individual stocks for comparing the composition of robust portfolios with mean-variance portfolios that assume no uncertainty. Chapter 10 illustrates the robustness of robust portfolios by observing their historical performance.

The final chapter, Chapter 11, discusses software packages that can help solve robust portfolio optimization and provides examples for finding robust portfolios.

1.2   USE OF MATLAB

Financial modeling often requires computer programs for solving complex computations. The use of powerful computing tools is inevitable in portfolio management because portfolio selection problems are mathematically expressed as optimization problems. Thus, tools that efficiently solve optimization problems give portfolio managers a great advantage; the tools are more valuable for robust portfolio management because approaches such as robust portfolio optimization involve more intense computations.

Therefore, in this book we discuss various aspects of robust portfolio management with examples on how to implement models in MATLAB, which is a programming language and interactive environment primarily for numerical computations.[3] MATLAB is widely used in academic studies as well as research in the financial industry, especially for computations that involve matrices such as portfolio optimization. The examples presented use MATLAB mainly because the language provides a straightforward approach for executing portfolio optimization. This high-level language with an extensive list of built-in functions allows beginners to easily perform various computations and visualize their results. Furthermore, the syntax for writing a script or a function is so intuitive that the reader can quickly become familiar with MATLAB even without prior experience. Hence, the MATLAB examples throughout the book will not only supplement understanding the theoretical concepts but will also let the reader apply the examples to construct optimal portfolios that reflect their investment goals.

While MATLAB features an add-on toolbox for financial computations, the examples in this book use built-in functions for solving optimization and not the functions in the financial toolbox that are customized for certain types of financial decision problems. For example, the *quadprog* function in MATLAB is used for implementing portfolio problems that are formulated as quadratic programming. This gives the reader flexibility since the examples will show how the function parameters can be modified based on different investment assumptions and portfolio constraints. Becoming familiar with the built-in optimization functions is also crucial because robust formulations are not included in the financial toolbox and therefore must be solved with the optimization functions. We also include examples that use CVX, which is a modeling system for convex optimization that runs in the MATLAB environment.[4] CVX enhances MATLAB, making it more expressive and powerful for solving optimizations like the mean-variance portfolio problems that are formulated as convex optimization problems. Many examples in this book present MATLAB codes that use the built-in functions of MATLAB as well as CVX in order to demonstrate two approaches for obtaining robust portfolios for a given problem. Since CVX is MATLAB-based, the reader will gain exposure to an additional tool without having to learn a new programming environment.

NOTES

1. Harry M. Markowitz, "Portfolio Selection," *Journal of Finance* 7, 1 (1952), pp. 77–91.
2. An example of improving the robustness of inputs is to use shrinkage estimators, introduced in Philippe Jorion, "Bayes-Stein Estimation for Portfolio Analysis," *Journal of Financial and Quantitative Analysis* 21, 3 (1986), pp. 279–292. Using simulation to gain robustness is illustrated in Richard Michaud and Robert Michaud, "Estimation Error and Portfolio Optimization: A Resampling Solution," *Journal of Investment Management* 6, 1 (2008), pp. 8–28. The Black–Litterman model is an equilibrium-based approach that incorporates an investor's views; it was proposed in Fischer Black and Robert Litterman, "Asset Allocation: Combining Investor Views with Market Equilibrium," *Goldman, Sachs & Co., Fixed Income Research* (1990). Various robust approaches including the ones mentioned here are detailed in Chapter 4.
3. MATLAB documentations and a list of functions with examples are available at http://www.mathworks.com/products/matlab/
4. A CVX user's guide and download details can be found at http://cvxr.com/cvx/

CHAPTER 2

Mean-Variance Portfolio Selection

Before we begin our discussion on robust portfolio management, we briefly review portfolio theory as formulated by Harry Markowitz in 1952. Portfolio theory explains how to construct portfolios based on the correlation of the mean, variance, and covariance of asset returns. The framework is commonly referred to as *mean-variance*. Despite its appearance more than half a century ago, it is also referred to as *modern portfolio theory*. The theory has been applied in asset management in two ways: The first is in allocating funds across major asset classes. The second application has been to the selection of securities within an asset class. Throughout this book, we apply mean-variance analysis to the construction of equity portfolios.

Mean-variance analysis not only provides a framework for selecting portfolios, it also explains how portfolio risk is reduced by diversifying a portfolio. Robust portfolio optimization builds on the idea of mean-variance optimization. Thus, the topics introduced in this chapter provide an introduction to the advanced robust methods to be explained in the chapters to follow. Specifically, in this chapter we describe how to:

- Measure return and risk of a portfolio within the mean-variance framework
- Reduce portfolio risk through diversification
- Select an optimal portfolio through mean-variance analysis
- Utilize factor models for estimating stock returns
- Apply the mean-variance model through an example

2.1   RETURN OF PORTFOLIOS

In modern portfolio theory, a portfolio that is composed of N assets is expressed as weights that add to one in order to represent the proportion of total investment allocated to each asset,

$$\omega_1 + \omega_2 + \cdots + \omega_N = \sum_{i=1}^{N} \omega_i = 1$$

where ω_i is the weight allocated to asset i. The rate of return of an asset is the change in the value of the asset in terms of percentage change or proportion of the initial value,

$$r = \frac{P_{final} - P_{initial}}{P_{initial}}$$

where $P_{initial}$ and P_{final} are the initial and final values of the asset. For simplicity, rate of return is often referred to as *return*. From the above definition of an asset's return, the portfolio return can be expressed as

$$r_p = \omega_1 r_1 + \omega_2 r_2 + \cdots + \omega_N r_N = \sum_{i=1}^{N} \omega_i r_i$$

where asset i has a return of r_i. In matrix form, portfolio return r_p is written as

$$r_p = \omega' r$$

where ω and r are vectors in $\mathbb{R}^N$.

Then, the *expected return* of a portfolio, or the *mean* of portfolio returns, is

$$E(r_p) = E(\omega_1 r_1 + \omega_2 r_2 + \cdots + \omega_N r_N),$$

and the linearity of expected value allows writing the expected return as a weighted average of expectations,

$$E(r_p) = \omega_1 E(r_1) + \omega_2 E(r_2) + \cdots + \omega_N E(r_N) = \sum_{i=1}^{N} \omega_i E(r_i). \qquad (2.1)$$

In matrices, it is expressed as

$$E(r_p) = \omega' \mu$$

where $\mu \in \mathbb{R}^N$ is a vector of expected returns of assets,

$$\mu = \begin{bmatrix} E(r_1) \\ \vdots \\ E(r_N) \end{bmatrix}.$$

The expected returns of assets are typically estimated from historical data. For example, the expected value of the past 10 monthly returns may be used as the expected return for the following month. We include a simple MATLAB demonstration in Box 2.1.

Box 2.1 FUNCTION THAT COMPUTES RETURN AND RISK OF A PORTFOLIO

```
% ================================================================
% portfolioreturnrisk.m
%
% Computes the return and risk of a portfolio given return data
%
% Input:
%    returns: T-by-N matrix with T period returns for N assets
%    portfolio: weights of a portfolio
% Output:
%    ret: return of the portfolio measured by mean
%    risk: risk of the portfolio measured by standard deviation
% ================================================================
function [ret, risk] = portfolioreturnrisk( returns,...
  portfolio )
    % Compute the mean vector and covariance matrix
    mu = mean(returns)';
    sigma = cov(returns);

    % Compute return and risk based on expected return and
    % covariance
    ret = mu' * portfolio;
    risk = sqrt(portfolio' * sigma * portfolio);
end
```

2.2 RISK OF PORTFOLIOS

The risk of a portfolio is measured by the *variance* of returns. The variance of asset returns measures the variability of possible returns around the expected return and is computed as

$$\sigma_i^2 = \text{var}(r_i) = E\left(\left(r_i - E\left(r_i\right)\right)^2\right)$$

where r_i is the return for asset i. Higher variability results in higher uncertainty and, thus, is considered to expose an investor to more risk. The *standard deviation* of asset returns is simply the square root of the variance and basically reflects the same information as the variance:

$$\sigma_i = \sqrt{\text{var}(r_i)}.$$

The variance of a portfolio is not as straightforward as the expected portfolio return; the variance of portfolio returns is not simply the weighted sum of individual asset variances. Instead, recall the property of the variance,

$$\text{var}\left(\sum_{i=1}^{n}\alpha_i X_i\right) = \sum_{i=1}^{n}\sum_{j=1}^{n}\alpha_i\alpha_j\text{cov}(X_i, X_j)$$

where X_i's are random variables and $\text{cov}(X_i, X_j)$ is the covariance between X_i and X_j. Therefore, for a portfolio with two assets, the portfolio variance is

$$\text{var}(\omega_1 r_1 + \omega_2 r_2) = \omega_1^2\,\text{var}(r_1) + \omega_2^2\,\text{var}(r_2) + 2\omega_1\omega_2\text{cov}(r_1, r_2),$$

and for N assets, it becomes

$$\text{var}(r_p) = \sum_{i=1}^{N}\sum_{j=1}^{N}\omega_i\omega_j\text{cov}(r_i, r_j) \tag{2.2}$$

where $\omega_i\omega_j\text{cov}(r_i, r_j) = \omega_i^2\,\text{var}(r_i)$ when $i = j$.

The extra term with covariance is one of the most important findings of modern portfolio theory, providing a major breakthrough in computing portfolio risk. *Covariance* measures how much two random variables move together:

$$\sigma_{i,j} = \text{cov}\left(X_i, X_j\right) = E\left((X_i - E(X_i))(X_j - E(X_j))\right).$$

More generally, *correlation* is quoted to show how closely two assets move up or down at the same time. Correlation is computed by dividing the covariance by the product of the individual standard deviations:

$$\text{corr}\left(X_i, X_j\right) = \frac{\text{cov}\left(X_i, X_j\right)}{\sigma(X_i)\sigma(X_j)}.$$

Correlation is more frequently cited because it takes values between positive one and negative one, where positive one indicates a perfect co-movement in the same direction. Furthermore, since the standard deviation is non-negative, the correlation is negative only when the two random variables have negative covariance.

In matrix form, portfolio variance is equivalent to

$$\text{var}\left(r_p\right) = \omega'\Sigma\omega$$

where $\Sigma \in \mathbb{R}^{N \times N}$ is the covariance matrix:

$$\Sigma = \begin{bmatrix} \sigma_{1,1} & \cdots & & & \sigma_{1,N} \\ & \ddots & & & \\ \vdots & & \sigma_{i,j} & & \vdots \\ & & & \ddots & \\ \sigma_{N,1} & \cdots & & & \sigma_{N,N} \end{bmatrix}.$$

Since $\sigma_{i,j} = \sigma_i^2$ when $i = j$, the diagonal elements of Σ are the variances of each asset. Computing the covariance matrix and portfolio variance from return data is shown in Box 2.1.

We conclude this section by mentioning that there are legitimate criticisms of using variance to represent risk. First, variance counts both upside and downside volatility toward risk, whereas most investors will be pleased with upside deviation. Another shortcoming is that variance alone does not completely measure variability when portfolio return is not symmetric. Nonetheless, as mentioned previously, the use of covariance changes the perception of portfolio risk. An example is its contribution to understanding portfolio diversification.

2.3 DIVERSIFICATION

We often hear the saying, "Don't put all your eggs in one basket." The same applies when investing in stocks. Even though the concept is intuitively understandable, it was difficult to quantify the benefits until the establishment of modern portfolio theory. Keep in mind how portfolio return and risk are formulated while we consider the following example.

An investor decides to invest in either Twitter, Inc. (TWTR) or Tesla Motors, Inc. (TSLA), or both. The investor believes that the daily returns of the first six months in 2014 are a reasonable estimate for future short-term movement. The stock prices of Twitter and Tesla Motors for this period are shown in Exhibit 2.1. While Tesla Motors' stock has positive expected daily return, both stocks have at least 3% daily volatility, measured by standard deviation. Let us now look into what happens if the investor holds a portfolio with both stocks. According to the formula for expected return and variance of portfolios given by equations (2.1) and (2.2), respectively, a portfolio that allocates half in Twitter and the other half in Tesla Motors has estimated values as shown in Exhibit 2.2. The 50-50 portfolio has positive expected return and, more importantly, has a standard deviation less than investing only in either one of the two stocks,

$$\mathrm{var}\left(r_p\right) = 0.5^2 \cdot 0.0018 + 0.5^2 \cdot 0.0012 + 2 \cdot 0.5 \cdot 0.5 \cdot 0.00019 \approx 0.084\%.$$

Diversifying between two stocks indeed reduces portfolio risk.

Exhibit 2.1   Daily stock price of Twitter and Tesla Motors from January to June 2014

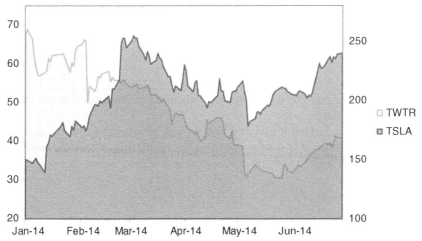

	TWTR	TSLA
Mean	−0.26%	0.44%
Variance	0.18%	0.12%
Standard Deviation	4.20%	3.49%
Correlation	0.13	

Exhibit 2.2   Portfolio with 50-50 allocation in Twitter and Tesla Motors

	TWTR 50%, TSLA 50%
Mean	0.087%
Variance	0.084%
Standard Deviation	2.89%

The reduction in risk is due to the low correlation between the two stocks. In fact, if the correlation between the stock movements of Twitter and Tesla Motors were lower, the investor will be able to enjoy an extra decline in the overall portfolio risk. As presented in Exhibit 2.3, the standard deviation of portfolio returns becomes less than 2% when the two stocks have negative correlation. In most cases, it is extremely difficult to find stocks with negative correlation. But stocks in different industries or sectors have low correlation. Moreover, dividing the investment among various asset classes, such as fixed income instruments and commodities, is a better approach to

Exhibit 2.3 Risk of the 50-50 portfolio for three correlation levels

Correlation betweenTWTR and TSLA	Standard Deviation
0.5	3.33%
0	2.73%
−0.5	1.94%

expand diversification benefits since they normally reveal less co-movement than the stock market.

In Exhibit 2.2, we looked at a simple case of dividing the investment equally between the two stocks. But do all combinations of the two stocks reduce risk? Exhibit 2.4 demonstrates what happens when the portfolio

Exhibit 2.4 Portfolio return and risk for various proportions

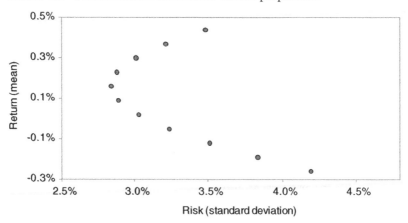

Allocation			
TWTR	TSLA	Mean	Standard Deviation
100%	0%	−0.26%	4.20%
90%	10%	−0.19%	3.84%
80%	20%	−0.12%	3.51%
70%	30%	−0.05%	3.24%
60%	40%	0.02%	3.03%
50%	50%	0.09%	2.89%
40%	60%	0.16%	2.84%
30%	70%	0.23%	2.89%
20%	80%	0.30%	3.01%
10%	90%	0.37%	3.22%
0%	100%	0.44%	3.49%

is composed of different proportions between the two stocks. The figure included in Exhibit 2.4 is the mean-standard deviation plane, where each portfolio is located as a point based on its level of expected return and standard deviation. Even with two stocks, the portfolio can have a wide range of return and risk levels as the points on the mean-standard deviation plane form a curve. In general, investors desire higher return and lower risk, so a portfolio on the upper left is preferred. The process of computing and selecting optimal portfolios becomes more complex as the number of candidate stocks increase. Mean-variance analysis presents a framework to help the decision making of investors.

2.4   MEAN-VARIANCE ANALYSIS

Modern portfolio theory is based on some assumptions about the market and its participants. As previously stated, investors seek lower risk and higher return. Investors also make decisions based on the expected return and variance, and all investors have the same information. Finally, the theory assumes that investment decisions are made for a single period. Because investors only analyze the mean and variance of returns, the approach is known as mean-variance optimization.[1]

The portfolio selection problem is formulated as a minimization problem,

$$\text{minimize (risk)}$$

$$\text{subject to } \left(\text{expected return} = r_p\right)$$

where r_p is the target level of portfolio return. By substituting the formulas from sections 2.1 and 2.2, the portfolio problem is written as

$$\min_{\omega} \frac{1}{2} \sum_{i=1}^{N} \sum_{j=1}^{N} \omega_i \omega_j \text{cov}(r_i, r_j)$$

$$\text{s.t. } \sum_{i=1}^{N} \omega_i E(r_i) = r_p$$

$$\sum_{i=1}^{N} \omega_i = 1$$

where $\frac{1}{2}$ in the first line is added for calculation convenience, and the last line guarantees full allocation of investment principal. Conventionally, the optimization problem is written in matrix form:

$$\min_{\omega} \frac{1}{2}\omega' \Sigma \omega$$

$$\text{s.t. } \omega'\mu = r_p \qquad\qquad (2.3)$$

$$\omega'\iota = 1$$

where $\mu \in \mathbb{R}^N$ and $\Sigma \in \mathbb{R}^{N \times N}$ are the expected return vector and covariance matrix, respectively, and $\iota \in \mathbb{R}^N$ is a vector of ones. The optimal solution for this problem is found by writing the Lagrangian function,

$$L(\omega, \lambda, \gamma) = \frac{1}{2}\omega' \Sigma \omega - \lambda \left(\omega'\mu - r_p\right) - \gamma(\omega'\iota - 1)$$

where λ and γ are Lagrange multipliers, and solving the first-order condition,[2]

$$\frac{\partial L}{\partial \omega} = \Sigma \omega - \lambda \mu - \gamma \iota = 0$$

$$\frac{\partial L}{\partial \lambda} = \omega'\mu - r_p = 0$$

$$\frac{\partial L}{\partial \gamma} = \omega'\iota - 1 = 0.$$

Many variations exist for constructing the optimal portfolio. The formulation for minimizing portfolio risk is also written as the following:

$$\min_{\omega} \frac{1}{2}\omega' \Sigma \omega$$

$$\text{s.t. } \omega'\mu \geq r_p$$

$$\omega'\iota = 1$$

by only providing a lower bound on expected portfolio return. Instead of searching for the optimal portfolio with minimum risk for a given level of return, the optimal allocation can be found by providing the upper-bound on risk while maximizing portfolio return,

$$\max_{\omega} \omega'\mu$$

$$\text{s.t. } \omega' \Sigma \omega \leq \sigma_p^2$$

$$\omega'\iota = 1.$$

Furthermore, a trade-off function between risk and return can be used to reach the optimal portfolio,

$$\min_{\omega} \lambda \omega' \Sigma \omega - \omega' \mu$$

$$\text{s.t. } \omega' \iota = 1$$

where λ is the risk-averse coefficient because larger values of λ result in stronger focus on the risk term.

By solving the problem given by equation (2.3) with various levels of r_p, portfolios with minimum variance for each level of expected return are found and produce a curve such as the one in Exhibit 2.5. For each level of return, minimum-variance portfolios are optimal because investors prefer lower risk when other conditions are the same. This set of minimum-variance portfolios may contain more than one portfolio for the same level of risk. Since higher return is favored for equivalent levels of risk, investors are only interested in the upper part of the curve, known as the *efficient frontier*. Portfolios on the efficient frontier, which is shown in bolded black in Exhibit 2.5, are the *mean-variance efficient portfolios*. The leftmost point where the efficient frontier begins is the *global minimum-variance portfolio*, and investors seeking an investment with the lowest risk will hold this portfolio.

The strength of the portfolio problem such as the one given by equation (2.3) is that it is in the form of a quadratic program, and there are known algorithms for efficiently solving this type of problem. The formulation also allows implementing additional constraints. Constraints such

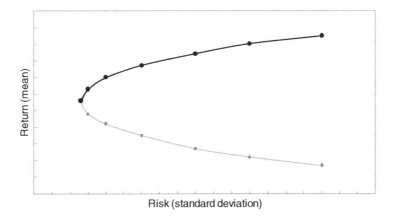

Exhibit 2.5 Minimum-variance set and the efficient frontier

as no-shorting or limiting maximum exposure can be inserted into the
original form and still be solved as a quadratic programming problem.
We show a simple MATLAB function for finding mean-variance efficient
portfolios in Box 2.2, which uses the *quadprog* function. We will continue
our discussion on formulating and solving portfolio problems along with
MATLAB examples in Chapter 5.

Box 2.2 FUNCTION THAT FINDS THE OPTIMAL MEAN-VARIANCE PORTFOLIO FOR VARIOUS RETURN LEVELS

```
% ================================================================
% meanvariance.m
%
% Find the optimal mean-variance portfolio for the below
% problem with various levels of portfolio return (r_p) and
% plot the efficient frontier
%
%     min  1/2*(w'*sigma*w)
%     s.t. mu'*w >= r_p,  w'*ones = 1
%
% Input:
%   returns: matrix of stock returns (each column represents
%            a single stock)
%   retMin: minimum level of portfolio return (optional)
%   retMax: maximum level of portfolio return (optional)
%   retInterval: interval between retMin and retMax (optional)
% Output:
%   ret: vector of portfolio returns
%   risk: vector of portfolio risk (standard deviation)
% ================================================================
function [ret, risk] = meanvariance( returns, retMin, ...
  retMax, retInterval )

    % Set minimum and maximum levels for portfolio return
    % unless they are provided by the user
    if (nargin == 1)
        retMin = 0;
        retMax = 0.5;
        retInterval = 0.1;
    end

    % Retrieve the inputs of the mean-variance model
    mu = mean(returns)';
    sigma = cov(returns);
    n = size(returns,2);
```

```
    % Save portfolio return and risk for each return level
    retLevels = retMin:retInterval:retMax;
    numPfo = length(retLevels);
    ret = zeros(numPfo, 1);
    risk = zeros(numPfo, 1);

    % Find the optimal portfolio for each return level
    for i = 1:numPfo
        pfo = quadprog(sigma, [], -mu', -retLevels(i), ...
            ones(1,n), 1);
        ret(i) = mu' * pfo;
        risk(i) = sqrt(pfo' * sigma * pfo);
    end

    % Plot the portfolios on the mean-standard deviation plane
    plot(risk, ret);
end
```

2.5 FACTOR MODELS

One difficulty in using mean-variance analysis is estimating the input values of the model. When solving the mean-variance problem for N candidate stocks, a total of $2N + \frac{N(N-1)}{2}$ values are required as inputs,

$$(N \text{ mean values}) + (N \text{ variances}) + \left(\frac{N^2 - N}{2} \text{ covariances} \right).$$

An optimal portfolio with 100 candidate stocks demands 5,150 esti-mated values and 125,750 values are needed with 500 candidate stocks. Accurately estimating all the necessary estimates is definitely challenging, even for the most experienced investors and portfolio managers.

Individual asset movements can be described by large movements in the financial markets. This also applies to the stock market since there are under-lying elements known as *factors* that affect the major price movements for stocks. From factor models, expected returns, variances, and covariances of stocks are estimated by analyzing the movement in factors, which are far less in number compared to the total number of stocks.

The *single-factor model* with a random return of a factor f for a return of stock i is written as

$$r_i = \alpha_i + \beta_i f + \varepsilon_i \tag{2.4}$$

where α_i and β_i are constants and ε_i is the error term with $E(\varepsilon_i) = 0$.[3] Moreover, the error term is assumed to be uncorrelated with factor returns, and errors between stocks are also assumed to be uncorrelated. The β_i, referred to as the *beta* of stock i, is also called the *factor loading* because it reflects the sensitivity of the stock return to the factor. Based on the factor model given by (2.4), the inputs of mean-variance analysis are expressed from the factor return as

$$\mu_i = \alpha_i + \beta_i \mu_f \qquad (2.5)$$

$$\sigma_i^2 = \beta_i^2 \sigma_f^2 + \sigma_{\varepsilon_i}^2$$

$$\sigma_{i,j} = \beta_i \beta_j \sigma_f^2$$

where μ_f is the expected factor return, and $\sigma_{\varepsilon_i}^2$ and σ_f^2 are the variances of ε_i and f, respectively. According to the equations in (2.5), μ_f and σ_f^2 along with α_i and β_i for each stock are required. In other words, the optimal portfolio is found with a total of $2 + 3N$ estimates. The use of factor models significantly reduces the estimated values for forming the covariance matrix.

A similar derivation applies when assuming that there is more than one factor in the market. Writing the *multifactor model* in matrix form results in the following:

$$r = \alpha + \beta f + \varepsilon$$

where $r \in \mathbb{R}^N$, $\alpha \in \mathbb{R}^N$, $\varepsilon \in \mathbb{R}^N$, $\beta \in \mathbb{R}^{N \times M}$, and $f \in \mathbb{R}^M$ for M factors. Then the expected return vector $\mu \in \mathbb{R}^N$ and the covariance matrix $\Sigma \in \mathbb{R}^{N \times N}$ are given by

$$\mu = \alpha + \beta \mu_f$$

$$\Sigma = \beta \Sigma_f \beta' + \Sigma_\varepsilon$$

where $\mu_f \in \mathbb{R}^N$ is the expected return of factors, $\Sigma_f \in \mathbb{R}^{M \times M}$ is the covariance matrix of factors, and $\Sigma_\varepsilon \in \mathbb{R}^{N \times N}$ is a diagonal matrix with error variances. A MATLAB function that finds the values of α and β through linear regression is shown in Box 2.3.

The selection of factors is certainly important, and the strength of the factors will decide the accuracy of return estimates. One candidate is to use macroeconomic factors such as gross domestic product, unemployment rate, and inflation. These factors explain economic conditions and hence affect movement in financial markets. Within the stock market, employing firm characteristic factors is a common choice. Firm characteristic factors,

---

Box 2.3 FUNCTION THAT FINDS VALUES OF ALPHA AND BETA FOR A STOCK GIVEN FACTOR RETURNS

```
% ================================================================
% factormodel.m
%
% Find values of alpha (a) and beta (b) from the factor model:
%     r = a + b*f + e
%
% Input:
%   returns: vector of returns for a stock
%   factorReturns: matrix of factor returns (each column is a
%                  single factor)
% Output:
%   alpha: value of alpha from factor model
%   beta: value of beta from factor model
% ================================================================
function [alpha, beta] = factormodel( returns, factorReturns )

    % Perform linear regression
    coeffs = regress(returns, [ones(size(returns)), ...
        factorReturns]);
    alpha = coeffs(1);
    beta = coeffs(2:end);
end
```

referred to as *fundamental factors*, include, as examples, price–earnings ratio, book-to-market equity ratio, leverage ratios, and industry.[4] Finally, statistical factors are also adopted for identifying factors. A statistical method such as principal components analysis finds vectors that maximally explain the variance of a given data.

2.6 EXAMPLE

Before we conclude this chapter, we demonstrate the use of the mean-variance model using historical returns in the U.S. stock market. In this example, an investor decides to form a stock portfolio composed of the following 10 firms:

1. Alcoa Inc.
2. Devon Energy Corporation

3. eBay Inc.
4. Ford Motor Co.
5. FedEx Corporation
6. General Electric Company
7. The Home Depot, Inc.
8. Hewlett-Packard Company
9. JPMorgan Chase & Co.
10. The Procter & Gamble Company

The investor believes that stock returns during 2011 to 2013 provide acceptable estimates, and collects monthly returns for the 10 stocks for the 3-year period. In MATLAB, the investor creates a 36-by-10 matrix of returns where each column contains monthly returns for a single firm. Then, the function for finding mean-variance optimal portfolios defined in Box 2.2 is called, as shown below:

```
[ret, risk] = meanvariance(returns, 0.01, 0.03, 0.001);
```

where `returns` represents the matrix of returns.

By plotting the outcomes on the mean-standard deviation plane, the investor arrives at a set of efficient portfolios as shown in Exhibit 2.6. From the list of mean-variance efficient portfolios, the investor can select the one with the desired level of risk and return and further analyze its composition to make the final investment decision.

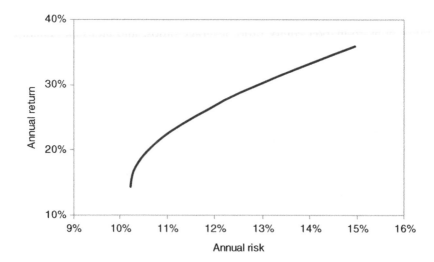

Exhibit 2.6   Mean-variance efficient portfolios

KEY POINTS

- The mean-variance model is the basic framework for portfolio selection.
- Portfolio return is expressed as the expected value, and portfolio risk is measured by the variance or standard deviation of returns.
- The inclusion of covariance between asset returns for computing portfolio risk is a major contribution of modern portfolio theory, and explains the benefit of diversification.
- The mean-variance portfolio problem is written as a mathematical program with a quadratic objective function, and the problem can be solved efficiently.
- Factor models assume that individual stock returns can be expressed using the returns of factors, and the use of factors reduces the number of required values that must be estimated for solving the mean-variance problem.

NOTES

1. The approach was first introduced in Harry M. Markowitz, "Portfolio Selection," *Journal of Finance* 7, 1 (1952), pp. 77–91; and also in Harry M. Markowitz, *Portfolio Selection: Efficient Diversification of Investments* (New Haven, CT: Yale University Press, 1959).
2. Finding the optimal solution of an optimization problem is discussed in detail in Chapter 5.
3. In his 1959 book, Markowitz suggested the use of a single index that could be used as a proxy for the covariance to make the computation of the efficient portfolio easier for computers at that time. The single index would be the "underlying factor, the general prosperity of the market as expressed by some index." (See Markowitz, *Portfolio Selection Efficient Diversification of Investments*, pp. 96–101.) A single index model was then tested and proposed by Sharpe in 1963 (William F. Sharpe, "A Simplified Model for Portfolio Analysis," *Management Science*, 9, 2 (1963), pp. 277–293), followed by proposed multi-index models to better capture the covariance structure (see, for example, Kalman J. Cohen and Gerald A. Pogue, "An Empirical Evaluation Of Alternative Portfolio Selection Models," *Journal of Business* 40, 2 (1967), pp. 166–193.)
4. The two models widely used are the three-factor model by Eugene F. Fama and Kenneth R. French, "Common Risk Factors in the Returns on Stocks and Bonds," *Journal of Financial Economics* 33, 1 (1993), pp. 3–56; and the four-factor model by Mark M. Carhart, "On Persistence in Mutual Fund Performance," *Journal of Finance* 52, 1 (1997), pp. 57–82.

CHAPTER 3

Shortcomings of Mean-Variance Analysis

As illustrated in the previous chapter, mean-variance analysis is powerful for figuring out the optimal allocation of investments. The framework is straightforward, as it uses mean, variance, and covariance of asset returns for finding the trade-off between return and risk. Unfortunately, the simplicity of the mean-variance model comes at a cost. Several shortcomings have been documented by academics and practitioners. Before discussing ways to improve the framework, we focus on the following key issues in this chapter:

- Limitations of the use of variance for measuring risk
- Difficulty in estimating the inputs of the model
- Sensitivity of the resulting portfolios

3.1 LIMITATIONS ON THE USE OF VARIANCE

The concept of variance is easily understood, and so is its formula. Nonetheless, using variance of returns for measuring investment risk raises questions. The most apparent reason is because variance reflects both upside and downside deviations. The variance of returns is written as:[1]

$$\frac{1}{T}\sum_{i=1}^{T}(r_i - \bar{r})^2$$

where $\bar{r}$ is the mean return, and T is the total number of returns. Thus, regardless of whether r_i is a positive or negative return, it is accounted for when computing the variance. But it is fair to say that most investors will not consider a large positive return as *risk*. For example, suppose the monthly returns of assets A and B during a year were as shown below, where the two assets had identical returns every month except December:

	Jan	Feb	Mar	Apr	May	Jun	Jul	Aug	Sep	Oct	Nov	Dec
A	−2%	−3%	−2%	−3%	−3%	−2%	−3%	−2%	−3%	−3%	−2%	−10%
B	−2%	−3%	−2%	−3%	−3%	−2%	−3%	−2%	−3%	−3%	−2%	10%

The sample standard deviations which is the (square roots of sample variances, also referred to as volatility) of the two assets is 2.2% and 3.7%, respectively. Even though asset B had the same monthly returns except for the +10% return in December, as opposed to asset A's −10% return, asset B still has higher volatility than asset A. It is true that asset B is more volatile by definition because the returns are more dispersed, but many may not consider asset B to be riskier as an investment instrument. Similarly, suppose assets C and D had the following returns also during a one-year period:

	Jan	Feb	Mar	Apr	May	Jun	Jul	Aug	Sep	Oct	Nov	Dec
C	5%	8%	8%	7%	6%	10%	9%	8%	5%	6%	9%	8%
D	−2%	1%	1%	0%	−1%	3%	2%	1%	−2%	−1%	2%	1%

In this case, the sample standard deviations of the two assets are identical, meaning the two assets have comparable risk when variance (or standard deviation) is used as the measure for risk. An investor holding asset C will strongly disagree because asset C collected at least 5% return each month, whereas asset D only recorded a maximum monthly return of 3% and many months with negative returns.

One of the explanations for the choice of variance is the assumption that stock returns are normally distributed. Variance becomes more appropriate in this case because a normal distribution is always symmetric. In fact, since the first two moments fully define a normal distribution, the normality assumption provides an explanation for mean-variance analysis.[2] But the assumption is challenged when historical stock market returns are examined. As presented in Exhibits 3.1 and 3.2, the overall stock market return and individual stock returns are not exactly normally distributed; historical returns tend to have fat-tails (i.e., more extreme values), especially on the negative side. Hence, comparing portfolio risk based on variance may be a naïve approach. It may be more appropriate to measure the risk by only observing the unfavorable events or the events that result in investment losses. There have been many attempts to capture the worst returns and we will continue this discussion in section 3.4 where we introduce additional measures of risk.

3.2 DIFFICULTY IN ESTIMATING THE INPUTS

Another shortcoming of mean-variance analysis is the difficulty in estimating the inputs: means, variances, and covariances of stock returns. Unless the true parameters are given, the values must be approximated, and it is realistically impossible to avoid estimation error. A common approach is to estimate

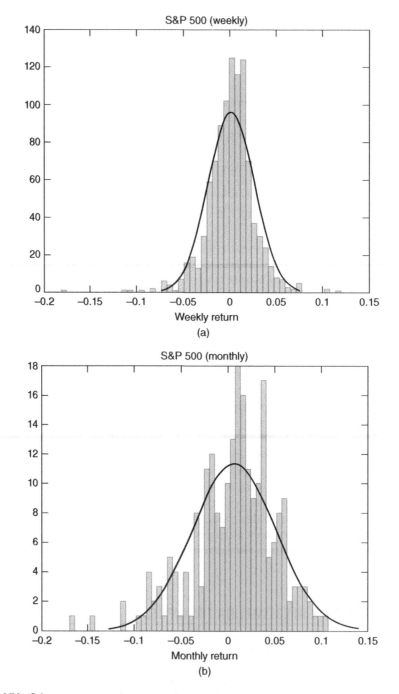

Exhibit 3.1 Histogram of S&P 500 returns from 1995 to 2013 and estimated normal distribution

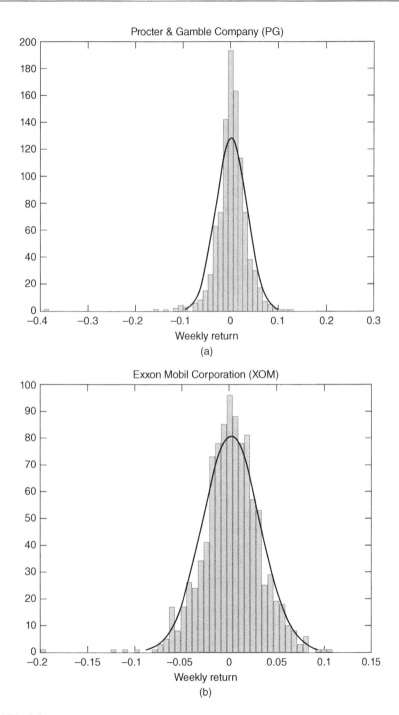

Exhibit 3.2 Histogram of weekly returns from 1995 to 2013 and estimated normal distribution

the input values based on recent historical returns. In this case, sample estimators of mean, variance, and covariance are used as the input parameters. If the mean-variance model is used to find the best portfolio allocation for the next investment period in the future, the inputs must properly represent the stock returns for the next period. But since this requires forecasting future stock behavior, it is a difficult task to estimate the inputs. This is no surprise because the case is similar for other models that aim at predicting future events, but it is still a general concern that should be advised when using the mean-variance model.

To demonstrate a simple example, consider portfolios that invest in the following 10 companies from the U.S. stock market.

1. Alcoa Inc.
2. Devon Energy Corporation
3. eBay Inc.
4. Ford Motor Co.
5. FedEx Corporation
6. General Electric Company
7. The Home Depot, Inc.
8. Hewlett-Packard Company
9. JPMorgan Chase & Co.
10. The Procter & Gamble Company

Suppose we are given historical monthly returns up to the end of 2013 for the 10 stocks and our task is to find the optimal allocation for 2014. Among many ways to utilize the given data, two common approaches would be to either use the returns during the two most recent years or the three most recent years. Exhibit 3.3 shows two efficient frontiers where one is constructed using stock returns for 2012 and 2013 (two years), and the other is constructed from returns for 2011, 2012, and 2013 (three years). The exhibit clearly shows how the optimal portfolio for the two cases differ, especially when investors are interested in low-risk portfolios. Before observing the actual stock performances in 2014, it is nearly impossible to know whether two or three years in the past is a better choice. Since the output is directly affected by the inputs, estimating the input parameters is always a great challenge.

The importance of accurate inputs is further demonstrated by comparing estimated frontier, actual frontier, and true frontier.[3] The *estimated frontier* is an efficient frontier plotted based on estimated data where the efficient portfolios are also found from the same estimated data. For example, the frontiers in Exhibit 3.3 are estimated frontiers; the efficient frontier in gray estimates parameters from returns in 2012 and 2013

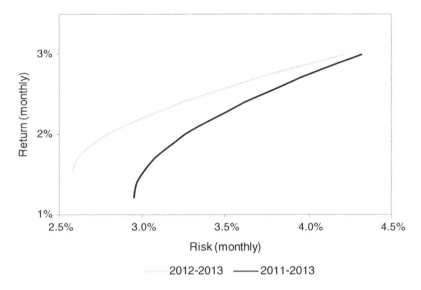

Exhibit 3.3   Two efficient frontiers from different sets of data

for finding efficient portfolios, and portfolio return and risk are calculated
based on stock returns in 2012 and 2013. The *actual frontier* is an efficient
frontier plotted based on true parameters for the investment period, but
where the efficient portfolios are constructed from estimated parameters.
In other words, portfolio weights are derived from estimation, but portfolio
return and risk are computed from true parameters. The frontiers in
Exhibit 3.3 would be actual frontiers if the portfolios were plotted on
the mean-standard deviation plane by measuring portfolio return and risk
with true parameter values in 2014. Actual frontiers reflect real investment
situations where the data used for estimation and data used for evaluation
are different. Finally, the *true frontier* represents an ideal situation where
estimation and evaluation are both carried out from the true parameters.
However, this would be an unrealistic case because, in practice, portfolios
are constructed without knowing the true values. In summary, an estimated
frontier represents estimated performance of portfolios formed from
estimated parameters, an actual frontier represents true performance of
portfolios formed from estimated parameters, and a true frontier represents
true performance of portfolios formed with true input values.

   We examine the effect of estimation error on portfolio return and risk
based on the concepts of the three frontiers. For our illustration, we use two
nonoverlapping periods, estimation period and evaluation period; returns
during the estimation period provide the estimated parameters, and returns

during the evaluation period are assumed to give us the true parameters. The three frontiers are presented in Exhibit 3.4 for portfolios that invest in the same 10 stocks as in the previous experiment. Here, the estimation period is 2011 and 2012, the evaluation period is 2013, and input values are calculated from weekly stock returns during the period.

The estimated frontier and true frontier show considerable discrepancy, and this is no surprise because the two frontiers use different input values in portfolio construction using the mean-variance method. More importantly, it is found that the estimated frontier often lies far above the true frontier, which means that errors in estimating input values result in overestimating portfolio performance. This optimistic outlook will definitely be a concern for investors. Furthermore, the actual frontier appears to frequently lie far below the true frontier, showing the inefficiency of portfolios when using estimated parameters. In short, unless the true values are known, mean-variance analysis will likely overestimate portfolio performance and end up far underachieving. Hence, even when the model is convincing, it lacks value without proper inputs.

The three frontiers in our experiment can be plotted using MATLAB, as shown in Box 3.1. The function *threefrontiers* takes returns for an estimation period and an evaluation period as inputs for drawing the frontiers on the mean-standard deviation plane. Again, instead of providing the estimated input parameters and true input parameters, the function extracts the estimated parameters from estimation period returns and true parameters from evaluation period returns.

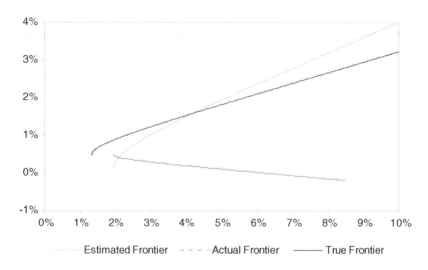

Exhibit 3.4 Estimated, actual, and true frontiers for investing in 10 stocks

Box 3.1 FUNCTION FOR PLOTTING ESTIMATED, ACTUAL, AND TRUE FRONTIERS

```
%  ================================================================
%  threefrontiers.m
%
%  Plot three efficient frontiers:
%    1. Estimated frontier
%    2. Actual frontier
%    3. True frontier
%
%  The optimal mean-variance portfolio is found from the below
%  problem with various levels of portfolio return (r_p),
%
%       min  1/2*(w'*sigma*w)
%       s.t. mu'*w >= r_p
%             w'*ones = 1
%
%  Input:
%    estReturns: matrix of estimated stock returns used for
%       estimation (each column represents a single stock)
%    trueReturns: matrix of true stock returns used for
%       evaluation (each column represents a single stock)
%    retMin: minimum level of portfolio return (optional)
%    retMax: maximum level of portfolio return (optional)
%    retInterval: interval between retmin and retmax (optional)
%  ================================================================
function threefrontiers( estReturns, trueReturns, retMin,...
   retMax, retInterval )

     % Set minimum and maximum levels for portfolio return unless
     % they are provided by the user
     if (nargin == 2)
         retMin = 0;
         retMax = 0.5;
         retInterval = 0.1;
     end
     retlevels = retMin:retInterval:retMax;
     numPfo = length(retlevels);

     % Number of assets
     n = size(estReturns,2);
```

(Continued)

```
% Estimated inputs for the mean-variance model
estMu = mean(estReturns)';
estSigma = cov(estReturns);

% True inputs for the mean-variance model
trueMu = mean(trueReturns)';
trueSigma = cov(trueReturns);

% Find the optimal portfolio from estimated data and save
% the estimated and actual frontiers
estRet = zeros(numPfo,1);
estRisk = zeros(numPfo,1);
actRet = zeros(numPfo,1);
actRisk = zeros(numPfo,1);
for i = 1:numPfo
    pfo = quadprog(estSigma, [], -estMu', -retlevels(i),...
      ones(1,n), 1);
    estRet(i) = estMu' * pfo;
    estRisk(i) = sqrt(pfo' * estSigma * pfo);
    actRet(i) = trueMu' * pfo;
    actRisk(i) = sqrt(pfo' * trueSigma * pfo);
end

% Find the optimal portfolio from true data and save the
% true frontier
trueRet = zeros(numPfo,1);
trueRisk = zeros(numPfo,1);
for i = 1:numPfo
    pfo = quadprog(trueSigma, [], -trueMu', -retlevels(i),...
      ones(1,n), 1);
    trueRet(i) = trueMu' * pfo;
    trueRisk(i) = sqrt(pfo' * trueSigma * pfo);
end

% Plot the three frontiers
plot(estRisk, estRet, ':', actRisk, actRet, '--', trueRisk,...
  trueRet, '-');
end
```

3.3   SENSITIVITY OF MEAN-VARIANCE PORTFOLIOS

We have shown how errors in estimating mean, variance, and covariance
of stock returns affect the composition of optimal portfolios. Studies show
that the effect of even small deviations in the input values of mean-variance
analysis on the resulting portfolios are notably large.[4] In other words,

mean-variance efficient portfolios are highly sensitive to the inputs. Furthermore, among the inputs of the mean-variance model, shifts in expected returns are observed to cause the most concern.[5]

We illustrate the sensitivity of mean-variance portfolios to changes in mean returns by focusing on the 10 stocks listed in section 3.2. We begin by finding the optimal allocation for the 10 stocks for a portfolio with an expected monthly return of 2%. We use the monthly stock returns from 2011 to 2013 to construct the mean vector and the covariance matrix of returns. The 10 companies along with their expected returns based on 2011 to 2013 data are shown in the first three columns of Exhibit 3.5. Once we find the optimal portfolio allocation from these data, we then observe a change in the portfolio weights by shifting the expected return of stocks one by one. In particular, we increase the magnitude of initial expected returns (in the third column of Exhibit 3.5) by 5% (i.e., multiply the initial value by 1.05), which are shown in the last column of Exhibit 3.5. Note that this shift does not increase a 10% expected return to a 15% return, but rather to a 10.5% expected return. Also, a −10% expected return would become a −10.5% return because we only increase the magnitude.

The results of the sensitivity analysis are presented in Exhibit 3.6. Each graph shows how the optimal allocation for a stock changes as the expected returns of the 10 stocks are shifted one by one. For example, the first graph in Exhibit 3.6 shows that 14.2% was originally allocated to Alcoa Inc., but the optimal portfolio shows only a 13.9% allocation, when only the expected return of Alcoa Inc. is shifted 5% from −0.57% to −0.60%. Moreover, the optimal weight in Alcoa Inc. is the highest at 15.1%, when only the expected return for Home Depot Inc. is shifted 5% from 2.38% to 2.49%.

Exhibit 3.5 Expected return of 10 stocks

Index	Company	Expected Monthly Return (2011–2013)	Expected Return Shifted 5%
1	Alcoa Inc.	−0.57%	−0.60%
2	Devon Energy Corporation	−0.65%	−0.69%
3	eBay Inc.	1.77%	1.86%
4	Ford Motor Co.	0.29%	0.31%
5	FedEx Corporation	1.36%	1.42%
6	General Electric Company	1.07%	1.12%
7	The Home Depot, Inc.	2.38%	2.49%
8	Hewlett-Packard Company	−0.41%	−0.44%
9	JPMorgan Chase & Co.	1.20%	1.26%
10	The Procter & Gamble Company	0.88%	0.93%

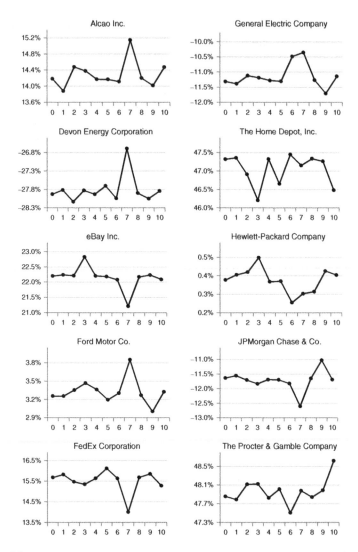

Exhibit 3.6   Portfolio weights given to each stock when expected return of a single stock is shifted (horizontal-axis: index of stock with change in expected return; 0: no change)

The 10 graphs in Exhibit 3.6 clearly demonstrate how a small shift in a single expected return causes a change in portfolio weight allocated to each stock in the portfolio. Most noticeably, a deviation in the expected return of Home Depot Inc. drastically changes the amount of investment in many stocks, including Alcoa Inc., Devon Energy Corporation, eBay Inc., and

FedEx Corporation. The sensitivity of mean-variance portfolios may be the biggest concern for investors because even a small change in the model inputs can greatly affect investment decisions.

3.4 IMPROVEMENTS ON MEAN-VARIANCE ANALYSIS

We conclude this chapter by discussing ways to resolve the three short-comings reviewed in this chapter. We begin with the limitations that arise from measuring risk using variance. Since stock returns are not necessarily symmetric and risk should focus on *bad* (or negative) returns, several new measures of risk have been proposed in the literature.

One variation of variance is semivariance, which only considers deviation in one direction. *Semivariance* is defined as

$$\frac{1}{T}\sum_{i=1}^{T}(\min(0, r_i - \bar{r}))^2$$

where $\min(a, b)$ is the minimum value between a and b. The formula is almost identical to variance except that values of r_i that are greater than the mean return are ignored, or, more precisely, considered as having zero deviation.

Sometimes the mean value is replaced with a target value to find the deviation below the target. For example, when the target value is set to 0%, the target semivariance becomes

$$\frac{1}{T}\sum_{i=1}^{T}(\min(0, r_i))^2$$

which finds the deviation of negative returns. By setting the target rate appropriately, semivariance will be able to capture the deviation in returns that an investor considers *risk*.

Another approach for measuring risk is to probabilistically describe the worst returns. An example would be to express the returns during the worst $p\%$ of the cases. These measures focus on the worst losses, and investors generally require this information to fully understanding the risk associated with an investment.[6] The most common measure is *value-at-risk*, often written as VaR.[7] This risk measure provides a minimum level of loss that is exceeded with a small probability. VaR of v with a probability level of p means that v is the smallest value, such that the probability of a loss exceeding v is at most p. VaR has three components: the value of minimum loss, a probability level associated with the minimum loss, and a time interval.[8] Note that the value of minimum loss is likely a positive value, since a negative return is a positive loss. Correspondingly, VaR is conventionally specified as a positive value. For example, "the VaR at 5% level (or 95% level) during a year is 10%" is equivalent to saying that "there is at most 5% probability that loss will exceed 10% in a year." Similarly, it can also be interpreted as "there is a more than 95% probability that loss will be less than 10% during a one year period." The loss can be expressed as an investment amount (e.g., in U.S. dollars) or as a rate of return, and thus VaR can also be written in both ways.

One advantage of VaR is that it does not necessarily assume a specific type of return distribution and does not assume returns are symmetric. In addition, VaR can be easily estimated from historical data or from simulation by measuring quantiles.[9] Even with the wide popularity of this measure, there are drawbacks that cause concerns. Since VaR represents a certain level of loss, it fails to fully reflect the extreme events beyond that level. For example, the VaR at the 5% level (or, equivalently, 95% level) for an investment does not tell us how bad the worst 1% of returns can be. Exhibit 3.7 demonstrates this limitation through a histogram of 100 returns. We assume that these 100 returns characterize the distribution of investment returns. Since there are 100 returns plotted on the histogram, the worst return does not affect the VaR at the 5% level. Thus, even though the two cases in Exhibit 3.7 have different worst possible returns, they have the same VaR at the 5% level. In fact, the two have the same VaR for probability levels greater than 2% according to the two histograms.

An important criticism of VaR is that it is uninformative about the extreme losses beyond it. This is because the only information provided is the probability of losing more than VaR which is equal to the tail probability level 5%. However, should any such loss occur, there is no information about its possible magnitude. Conditional VaR, also known as CVaR or expected shortfall and average value at risk, is a risk measure that overcomes this drawback of VaR. CVaR at $p\%$ level is the expected return of the worst $p\%$ of the cases. In other words, it is the expected value of the returns beyond the VaR level. The extreme cases are included in the calculation for CVaR because the average value is taken.

VaR and CVaR can be easily calculated for a given set of data by sorting the returns in ascending order when each data point is assumed to occur with equal probability. As a simple example, if historical returns for the past 100 days are collected, VaR at the 5% level is estimated as the fifth smallest return; and CVaR at the 5% level is estimated as the mean of the five smallest returns. Box 3.2 shows a MATLAB function that computes the two risk measures from a vector of returns.

There are several variations of the classical mean-variance analysis that replace variance with other risk measures.[10] Nonetheless, the

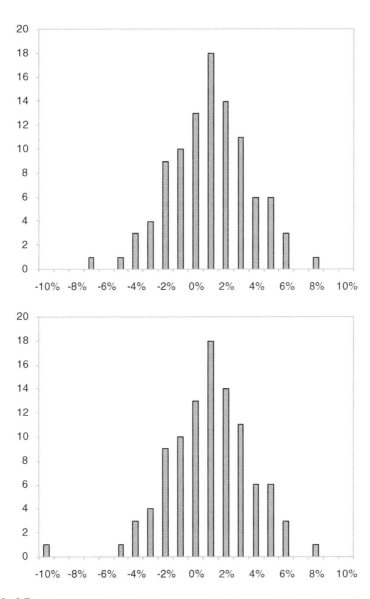

Exhibit 3.7 Histograms of portfolio returns with the same VaR at 5% level

Box 3.2 FUNCTION FOR COMPUTING VAR AND CVAR

```
% ================================================================
% varcvar.m
%
% Find the value-at-risk and conditional value-at-risk from the
% provided returns (e.g., historical returns)
%
% Input:
%    returns: a column vector of returns
%    prob: probability level between 0 and 1 for VaR and CVaR
%          (prob = 0.05 : finds VaR and CVaR for the worst 5% of
%           the cases)
% Output:
%    var: value-at-risk
%    cvar: conditional value-at-risk
% ================================================================
function [var, cvar] = varcvar( returns, prob )

    % Sort the returns in ascending order
    returnsSorted = sort(returns);

    % Total number of returns
    num = size(returns,1);

    % Index of the sorted return that represents desired VaR
    returnIndexVaR = floor(prob * num);

    var = -returnsSorted(returnIndexVaR);
    cvar = -mean(returnsSorted(1:returnIndexVaR));
end
```

mean-variance model is still widely used, and it is generally agreed that the model provides informative guidelines to investors. A greater concern arises when mean-variance analysis is used to produce investment guidelines using estimated parameters such as estimations for means, variances, and covariances of returns.

The shortcoming mentioned in sections 3.2 and 3.3 are closely tied to each other. It is difficult to accurately estimate the inputs of the mean-variance framework, but the sensitivity of the model exacerbates the situation because even a small estimation error causes a major discrepancy in the resulting portfolios. Many developments address this issue and introduce ways to increase the robustness of the portfolios constructed. Some studies introduce estimators that make the input values less sensitive to changes in data, and others propose advanced optimization models that increase the robustness of the framework (i.e., the process of forming efficient portfolios). Increasing the robustness of portfolios formed from the mean-variance model is the emphasis in this book, and we will discuss this topic in much detail in the following chapters.

KEY POINTS

- Mean-variance analysis has several shortcomings that should be investigated in order to fully understand the model and the portfolios that are produced.
- One possible improvement to mean-variance analysis is using an alternative measure for risk because variance increases not only when there are deviations in the negative direction but also in the positive direction.
- Since stock returns are empirically asymmetric, risk measures such as semivariance, VaR, and CVaR emphasize losses and portfolio optimization models that use these measures have been developed.
- Another limitation of the mean-variance model is the difficulty in estimating the input parameters. This is especially a concern when the goal is to provide an investment outlook because it requires the true parameters that represent future behavior.
- Empirical analyses indicate high sensitivity of mean-variance portfolios to inputs parameters, which implies that even a small estimation error can greatly affect the resulting portfolios.
- The combination of estimation errors in the inputs and high sensitivity of the output is a major issue with mean-variance analysis, and there have been many extensions of the model that increase portfolio robustness.

NOTES

1. Note that the sample variance divides by $T-1$ instead of T, and the sample variance should be used when estimating the variance from historical or simulated data.
2. Markowitz explains mean-variance analysis in relation to the normality assumption by discussing expected utility maximization in Harry M. Markowitz and Kenneth A. Bay, *Risk-Return Analysis: The Theory and Practice of Rational Investing*, Vol. 1 (McGraw-Hill Education, 2014).
3. The effect of errors in parameter estimation on mean-variance portfolios was investigated using the three frontiers by Mark Broadie, "Computing Efficient Frontiers Using Estimated Parameters," *Annals of Operations Research* 45 (1993), pp. 21–58.

4. The effect of a small increase in a single asset on portfolio weights is studied by Michael J. Best and Robert R. Grauer, "On the Sensitivity of Mean-Variance-Efficient Portfolios to Changes in Asset Means: Some Analytical and Computational Results," *Review of Financial Studies* 4, 2 (1991), pp. 315–342.

5. Errors in estimating expected returns are found to be at least 10 times more important than errors in estimating variances and covariances in Vijay K. Chopra and William T. Ziemba, "The Effect of Errors in Means, Variances, and Covariances on Optimal Portfolio Choice," *Journal of Portfolio Management* 19, 2 (1993), pp. 6–11.

6. VaR and CVaR, introduced here, are further covered in Chapter 7.

7. VaR was first proposed by J. P. Morgan, *RiskMetrics Technical Documents*, 4th ed. (New York: J.P. Morgan, 1996).

8. The probability level for VaR describing the worst $p\%$ of the cases is denoted as VaR at $p\%$ level, or VaR at $(100-p)\%$ level. In other words, VaR at the 5% level and VaR at the 95% level both refer to the same value. Regardless of its notation, the worst $p\%$ of the cases are represented where $p\%$ is less than 50%.

9. Several approaches for computing VaR are summarized in John L. Maginn, Donald L. Tuttle, Dennis W. McLeavey, Jerald E. Pinto, and Dennis W. McLeavey, *Managing Investment Portfolios: A Dynamic Process*, 3rd ed. (John Wiley & Sons, 2007), pp. 598–613.

10. Portfolio optimization using semivariance, VaR, and CVaR are discussed in Harry M. Markowitz, *Portfolio Selection: Efficient Diversification of Investments* (New Haven, CT: Yale University Press, 1959); Gordon J. Alexander and Alexandre M. Baptista, "Economic Implications of Using a Mean-VaR Model for Portfolio Selection: A Comparison with Mean-Variance Analysis," *Journal of Economic Dynamics and Control* 26, 7 (2002), pp. 1159–1193; and R. Tyrrell Rockafellar and Stanislav Uryasev, "Optimization of Conditional Value-at-Risk," *Journal of Risk* 2 (2000), pp. 21–42.

CHAPTER 4

Robust Approaches for Portfolio Selection

In the previous chapter, we summarized the major weaknesses of the mean-variance model, noting that the most illustrated shortcoming in implementing the model is the sensitivity of the portfolio constructed to changes in inputs. Since the turn of the century, there have been many portfolio selection models proposed for improving the model's robustness. The purpose of this chapter is to describe the robust approaches that can be used for constructing portfolios. We begin the chapter by describing the concept of robustness and then introduce the most widely recognized robust approaches for portfolio construction:

- Robust statistics
- Shrinkage estimation
- Monte Carlo simulation (portfolio resampling)
- Constraining portfolio weights
- Bayesian approach (Black-Litterman model)
- Stochastic programming

4.1 ROBUSTNESS

The definition of robustness can be derived from the main drawback of the mean-variance model: Robust models are approaches with results that are insensitive to small deviations from the model's assumptions. A robust version of the mean-variance model will construct portfolios whose weights for the candidate stocks are relatively stable, regardless of small changes in the expected returns and the covariance matrix of returns. Robust results could mean either robust portfolio weights, which is the output of the optimization problem, or robust performance, which determines investors' wealth. However, the two cannot be separated, because robust performance requires robust portfolio weights when considering measures such as turnover (which measures fluctuation in weights because substantial changes can amount to large transaction costs). Robustness in portfolio selection is especially important because in practice, the true distribution of returns is never known (we simply cannot predict future stock returns). Even if past stock returns perfectly follow a multivariate normal distribution and the risk of a portfolio is computed using the variances and covariances of returns, the uncertainty in portfolio returns still exists because there is no guarantee of the future distribution of returns. To further explain the need for robustness, we first explain how risk and uncertainty can differ in their meaning.

Uncertainty Aversion

The distinction between risk and uncertainty can be made by defining measurable uncertainty as *risk* and unmeasurable uncertainty as the true *uncertainty*.[1] For example, rolling a die contains risk but not uncertainty because we know exactly that each of the six sides can face upwards with a probability of one in six. Likewise, aversion to risk and aversion to uncertainty may represent two different preferences. A risk-averse investor will construct minimum-variance portfolios whereas an uncertainty-averse investor will seek robust portfolios. To explain uncertainty aversion, let us consider the following situation of drawing balls from two urns.[2]

Consider two urns containing red and green balls. Urn A contains a total of 100 balls, but the ratio between red and green balls is unknown. For urn B, it is known that it contains 50 red and 50 green balls. One ball is drawn from each urn at random (i.e., one ball from urn A and one from urn B). You are asked to select between two choices A_R and B_R, where the rewards are as shown below:

	Urn	(Color of the ball drawn from urn)	
		Red	Green
Choice A_R:	A	$100	$0
Choice B_R:	B	$100	$0

For example, you are given $100 if a red ball is drawn from urn A when choosing A_R and similarly given $100 if a red ball is drawn from urn B when selecting B_R. Furthermore, you are given another choice between A_G and B_G with the following rewards for the two urns:

	Urn	(Color of the ball drawn from urn)	
		Red	Green
Choice A_G:	A	$0	$100
Choice B_G:	B	$0	$100

If one thinks that urn A contains less red than green balls (less than 50 red balls), one would prefer to bet on B_R rather than on A_R. However, since this means that one believes there are over 50 green balls in urn A, one should prefer to bet on A_G rather than on B_G. Similarly, if one thinks that urn A contains more red than green balls, one should prefer B_G to A_G but not B_R to A_R. Surprisingly, most people prefer B_R to A_R and B_G to A_G, as we explain later. Let us look at another situation, this time with only one urn.

Now consider an urn C that contains 30 red balls and 60 green and yellow balls, where the proportion of green and yellow balls is not known. One ball is drawn at random from urn C. You are given an option between the following two choices, C_R and C_G:

	(Color of the ball drawn from urn C)		
	Red	Green	Yellow
Choice C_R:	$100	$0	$0
Choice C_G:	$0	$100	$0

Similarly, under the same circumstances, you are given another choice between C_{RY} and C_{GY}:

	(Color of the ball drawn from urn C)		
	Red	Green	Yellow
Choice C_{RY}:	$100	$0	$100
Choice C_{GY}:	$0	$100	$100

Notice how choices C_{RY} and C_{GY} are identical to C_R and C_G except for the additional $100 reward if a yellow ball is drawn from the urn. Between C_R and C_G, most people choose to bet on C_R over C_G. However, the same decision makers frequently prefer C_{GY} to C_{RY}, even though the only difference from the first set of choices is that both C_{RY} and C_{GY} receive $100 for a yellow ball. Intuitively, if one believes that there are less than 30 green balls (more than 30 yellow balls), one will decide to bet on C_R rather than C_G and also on C_{RY} rather than C_{GY}. Likewise, if one believes that there are more than 30 green balls (less than 30 yellow balls), one will prefer C_G to C_R and C_{GY} to C_{RY}.

We can observe from the previous examples how rational decision makers may be averse to uncertainty. For the first example with two urns, the majority of decision makers always prefers urn B over urn A because they are certain that they have a 50-50 chance of winning by selecting urn B;

whereas they do not have the slightest clue of the chances of winning if urn A is selected. This behavior cannot be explained by attaching probability distributions to the number of red balls because it does not express the decision maker's aversion to uncertainty. Uncertainty aversion also explains the frequent behavior in the second example with one urn as well.

Of course, the analogy of betting on the color of balls does not directly show why robustness is important in portfolio selection, but we introduce these examples to show how uncertainty aversion plays an important role. The classical mean-variance problem with the risk-return trade-off as the objective function is written as:

$$\min_{\omega} \lambda \omega' \Sigma \omega - \omega' \mu$$

$$s.t. \ \omega' \iota = 1$$

where $\mu \in \mathbb{R}^N$ is the expected returns, $\Sigma \in \mathbb{R}^{N \times N}$ is the covariance matrix, $\omega \in \mathbb{R}^N$ is the portfolio weights, $\iota \in \mathbb{R}^N$ is a vector of ones, $N \in \mathbb{N}$ is the number of stocks, and $\lambda \in \mathbb{R}$ is the risk coefficient. This formulation allows investors to represent their level of risk aversion by calibrating the risk-averse coefficient; small values of λ represent investors seeking risk whereas very large values will result in the construction of minimum-variance portfolios. Even though this formulation requires the level of risk aversion as one of the parameters, it still does not reflect the level of uncertainty aversion of investors; the risk coefficient does not protect investors from errors in estimating the expected return and covariance. The remainder of the chapter covers techniques to increase portfolio robustness.

4.2   ROBUST STATISTICS

For portfolio selection problems, the uncertainty comes from estimating the mean and covariance of stock returns. Therefore, the first obvious improvement for achieving robust portfolios would be to make these estimates robust. This approach could be understood intuitively: Robust inputs will result in robust outputs. In fact, sample mean and sample covariance are known to be extremely sensitive to outliers. However, there are estimators available that give meaningful estimates with or without the presence of outliers. In other words, we often assume the distribution of key variables, but these *robust estimators* provide valuable stock return information even when the realized distribution deviates from the assumed distribution (i.e., the assumed distribution is not an accurate representation of the realized distribution). Since robust statistics include a broad range of estimators even outside the domain of portfolio selection, we only introduce primitive examples that are often used to express the risk and return of portfolios.[3]

Mean vs. Median

We begin by looking at the sensitivity of the sample mean and show how the median provides a more robust metric. Let us analyze the daily returns of a hypothetical stock for a trading period of 20 days as shown in Exhibit 4.1. The bar graph clearly displays one return that stands out from the rest on March 12. We assume that this sharp decline of more than 7% was due to a false report on the company's earnings.[4] The *sample mean* for the 20-day trading period is

$$\bar{x} = \frac{1}{N}\sum_{i=1}^{N} x_i = \frac{1}{20}((-1.48\%) + (-1.42\%) + \cdots + (-2.08\%)) = -0.21\%.$$

Exhibit 4.1   Daily returns of a stock for 20 trading days

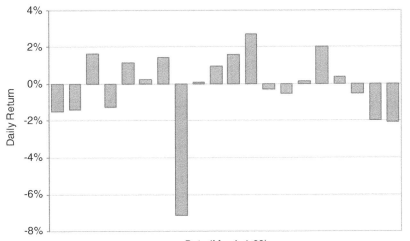

Date	Return	Date	Return
March 1	−1.48%	March 15	1.58%
March 4	−1.42%	March 18	2.72%
March 5	1.64%	March 19	−0.27%
March 6	−1.27%	March 20	−0.53%
March 7	1.16%	March 21	0.14%
March 8	0.26%	March 22	2.03%
March 11	1.42%	March 25	0.36%
March 12	−7.16%	March 26	−0.53%
March 13	0.12%	March 27	−1.96%
March 14	0.97%	March 28	−2.08%

Next, since we know that the return on March 12 was due to a false report, we may discard this data point as it gives false information. In this case, the sample mean (using only 19 daily returns) becomes 0.15%. Even though the difference between -0.21% and 0.15% might not seem like much, it may decide whether this stock will have a positive or negative estimated return when making future investment decisions.

As shown, the sample mean can be very sensitive to even one outlier. On the other hand, the *sample median* of the 20-day period can be computed by sorting the daily returns:

$$(-7.16\%, -2.08\%, -1.96\%, -1.48\%, -1.42\%, -1.27\%, -0.53\%,$$

$$-0.53\%, -0.27\%, 0.12\%, 0.14\%, 0.26\%, 0.36\%, 0.97\%,$$

$$1.16\%, 1.42\%, 1.58\%, 1.64\%, 2.03\%, 2.72\%).$$

Since there are an even number of returns, the median is the average between the 10th and the 11th data point, $\frac{0.12\% + 0.14\%}{2} = 0.13\%$. It is easily observed that the sample median is close to the sample mean without the outlier. In fact, the value of the sample median would not have changed even if the return on March 12 was -8%, -10%, or even -20%. (Note that a change in one observation can have an unbounded effect on the sample mean.) The sample median is a robust estimator because it finds the *middle* of the distribution and is not affected by how far the tail events are spread.

One might naturally question why we do not simply use the classical estimators after removing the outliers to form robust estimators. The main concern of pursuing such an approach is that detecting outliers can be highly subjective. For the previous example, one investor might disregard the return of -7.16% without hesitation, but another investor might find that this data point provides valuable information since a false report might occur again. Similarly, stock market information from the global financial crisis that began in 2008 might be excluded when constructing a portfolio by someone expecting a market rally, but someone else might necessarily include this period to prepare for future crashes. Furthermore, even when an investor has a reasonable procedure for detecting outliers, the model will inevitably be introduced to new types of errors such as false rejections.

M-Estimators

One well-known type of estimators is *M-estimators*, which are obtained by minimizing a function of the sample data. An *M*-estimator, denoted by $\hat{m}$, is computed by solving a minimization problem:

$$\hat{m} = \arg \min_{m} \sum_{i=1}^{N} \rho(x_i, m)$$

where x_i's are the N samples, and the function $\rho(x_i, m)$ determines the value of the estimator. The notation arg $\min_{m}$ means the set of values of argument m that gives the minimum value of the objective function.

If ρ is differentiable, then we can solve for the estimator by setting it to zero:

$$\sum_{i=1}^{N} \psi(x_i, m) = 0$$

where

$$\psi(x_i, m) = \frac{\partial \rho(x_i, m)}{\partial m}.$$

A special case of M-estimation is *maximum likelihood estimation* (MLE), which finds the parameter θ of a density function f that maximizes the likelihood L,

$$\hat{\theta} = \arg \max_{\theta} L(x_1, \dots, x_N, \theta)$$

where

$$L(x_1, \dots, x_N, \theta) = \prod_{i=1}^{N} f(x_i, \theta).$$

Since the logarithm is a monotonic function, maximizing the log-likelihood is equivalent to maximizing the likelihood, and therefore we can write the problem in the form of M-estimation with $\rho = -\log f$. Hence, the sample mean is also an example of M-estimators, especially when the distribution is assumed to be normal.

L-Estimators

Another type of estimators is *L-estimators*, which are obtained by taking a linear combination of order statistics:

$$l = \sum_{i=1}^{N} c_i x_{(i)}$$

where the constants c_i are usually normalized to sum to one. Each $x_{(i)}$ is the ith order statistic, which is the ith smallest value, so $x_{(1)} \leq x_{(2)} \leq \cdots \leq x_{(N)}$.

Two popular examples of L-estimators are the *trimmed mean* and the *Winsorized mean*. The trimmed mean removes a fraction of the highest and the smallest values from the sample. The Winsorized mean does not completely reject a fraction of the highest and the smallest values, but replaces them with the highest and the smallest values among the remaining samples, respectively. For example, if 10% of the samples from each end were replaced, the Winsorized mean for a sample size of 10 would be the average of the following values:

$$(x_{(2)}, x_{(2)}, x_{(3)}, x_{(4)}, x_{(5)}, x_{(6)}, x_{(7)}, x_{(8)}, x_{(9)}, x_{(9)}).$$

Estimators of Dispersion

Since we have only presented examples on estimators of the center such as the sample median, trimmed mean, and Winsorized mean, we conclude this section on robust statistics with examples for estimators of variability.[5] The standard approach for measuring variability is the sample standard deviation, but it is very sensitive to outliers.

An alternative with decreased sensitivity is the *mean absolute deviation*, which takes the absolute difference without squaring the distance from the mean, and is defined as

$$\frac{1}{N}\sum_{i=1}^{N}|x_i - \overline{x}|.$$

A similar, yet more robust, estimator is the *median absolute deviation*, which is the median value of the differences between a variable and its median,

$$\text{Med}(|x - \text{Med}(x)|)$$

where $\text{Med}(x)$ is the median of x.

Finally, a dispersion estimate that is more robust than the range (the difference between the highest and the lowest values) of a sample data is the *sample interquartile range* (IQR). It is computed as the difference between the 75th and 25th percentiles of the data:

$$\text{IQR} = Q(0.75) - Q(0.25)$$

where $Q(p)$ is the $(100 \times p)^{th}$-percentile.

4.3   SHRINKAGE ESTIMATION

Similar to the robust estimators introduced above, *shrinkage estimators* aim at improving the robustness of portfolios by increasing the robustness of the estimates. As the name suggests, shrinkage estimators shrink unbiased estimators such as the sample mean towards a target that has more structure, thus reducing the variability in its elements.[6] In other words, unbiased estimators are transformed into improved biased estimators. Even though there are shrinkage estimators for both the vector of expected returns and the covariance matrix of stock returns, we begin by briefly discussing estimators for the expected returns.

For a normal distribution, the sample mean, which is unbiased and also the MLE, has the lowest risk for estimating the mean when risk is measured by the sum of squared errors. Similarly, estimating the mean vector of a 2-dimensional multivariate normal distribution by the sample mean has the lowest quadratic loss when the loss function is written as

$$L(\mu, \widehat{\mu}) = (\mu - \widehat{\mu})' \Sigma^{-1} (\mu - \widehat{\mu}),$$

where μ is the true mean, $\widehat{\mu}$ is the estimated value, and Σ is the known covariance matrix. However, for values of N greater than 2, the sample mean is not the best choice for estimating the mean of an N-dimensional multivariate normal variable.[7] In other words, attempting to approximate the mean by their individual averages is not the best estimator, because another method may reduce the overall loss. Shrinkage estimators emerge from this recognition and studies show that a combination with a structured value improves the original estimate.

Shrinkage estimators are often expressed as the following,

$$\widehat{\mu}_S = (1 - w)\widehat{\mu} + w\mu_0\iota$$

where w is the *shrinkage intensity* (or shrinkage constant) and $\mu_0\iota$ is the *shrinkage target*. The shrinkage intensity w determines how close the new estimate is to the sample mean. The value of w is defined to be between 0 and 1, which explains why it is called the *shrinkage* estimator. The estimator can also be written as

$$\widehat{\mu}_S = \widehat{\mu} + w(\mu_0\iota - \widehat{\mu}).$$

Shrinkage estimators can now be interpreted as estimators based on the sample mean with a constant multiplied by the difference between the target and the sample mean added. The study of shrinkage estimators focuses on finding values of shrinkage intensity and target that yield improved portfolio performance.

A well-known shrinkage estimator for the mean is the *James-Stein estimator*, where the shrinkage intensity is set as

$$w_{JS} = \min\left(1, \frac{(N-2)/T}{(\hat{\mu} - \mu_0 \iota)'\Sigma^{-1}(\hat{\mu} - \mu_0 \iota)}\right)$$

where T is the number of observations. The surprising fact, which further shows the superiority of the James-Stein estimator, is that any value of μ_0 will result in an estimator with lower risk than the sample mean.[8]

One of the most common shrinkage estimators for portfolio selection is the model by Jorion who proposes the return of the global minimum-variance (GMV) portfolio as the structured estimate,[9]

$$\mu_0 = \mu_{GMV} = \hat{\mu}'\omega_{GMV} = \hat{\mu}'\frac{\Sigma^{-1}\iota}{\iota'\Sigma^{-1}\iota},$$

and the shrinkage intensity as

$$w_J = \frac{N+2}{N+2+T(\hat{\mu} - \mu_{GMV}\iota)'\Sigma^{-1}(\hat{\mu} - \mu_{GMV}\iota)}.$$

This estimator, which shrinks the sample mean towards the return of the GMV portfolio, is known to result in more robust portfolio weights and also improved out-of-sample performance compared to when the sample mean is used as in the classical mean-variance model.

Shrinkage can also be applied to the covariance matrix of returns in a similar fashion by shrinking the sample covariance matrix towards a more structured matrix.[10] An estimate of the covariance matrix with more structure is important because the sample covariance matrix requires a lot of data to be accurately measured, and it may be unlikely for investors to gather years of returns data, if not tens of years.

The shrinkage estimator for the covariance matrix is expressed as

$$\hat{\Sigma}_S = (1 - w)S + w\Sigma_0$$

where S is the sample covariance matrix and Σ_0 is the shrinkage target. One of the earliest models uses the single-index covariance matrix from the one-factor model as the shrinkage target based on the consensus that the market index is the primary factor driving the movement of the stock market. The intuition for this model is that while the single-index covariance matrix assumes a single factor and the sample covariance matrix assumes N factors, the optimum should lie somewhere in between these two extremes. An alternative is to shrink the sample covariance towards the constant-correlation matrix that has identical pairwise correlations.

Even with these simple structured matrices, the shrinkage estimators for the covariance matrix of stock returns show superior performance than when using the sample covariance matrix.

4.4 MONTE CARLO SIMULATION

The two previous methods for improving robustness focused on improving the inputs that are used in portfolio selection models. An alternative approach is to add additional steps using the outcomes of the model to make it more robust as shown in Exhibit 4.2. An estimator finds one value to represent a random parameter from many data points, but we can instead compute the optimal outcome for each data point and then find one representative solution. The latter approach describes the main idea of simulation.

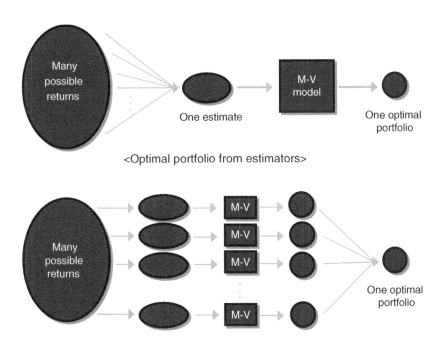

Exhibit 4.2 Comparison between portfolio selection from estimators and simulations

Portfolio Resampling

Monte Carlo simulation (also simply known as the Monte Carlo method) repeatedly solves the given problem using random samples typically from the known probability distribution for the inputs. The random sampling simulates how the inputs may be observed in reality. Once the simulation is performed many times, the results are aggregated to find the optimal solution. This framework using simulation can be applied to portfolio selection as follows:

Step 1: Sample a mean vector and covariance matrix of returns
Step 2: Compute the mean-variance efficient frontier using the sampled values
Step 3: Repeat Steps 1 and 2 many times
Step 4: Average the portfolio weights obtained from the above steps

This technique, known as *portfolio resampling*, was introduced to resolve the sensitivity of the mean-variance model and increase the out-of-sample performance by more realistically modeling the uncertainty in investment information.[11] In portfolio resampling, there is no disagreement that the classical mean-variance efficient frontier represents the efficient portfolios for a given sample. Therefore, the mean-variance efficient frontier is computed for each sample. The many frontiers from the simulation are combined by averaging portfolios with the same level of risk aversion. For example, an investor who is highly risk-averse will always hold the minimum variance portfolio (at the lower-left end of the efficient frontier). On the other hand, an extremely risk-seeking or risk-indifferent investor will always hold the maximum return portfolio (at the upper-right end of the efficient frontier). Hence, the minimum variance portfolios and the maximum return portfolios constructed from the samples can each be averaged to find the two ends of the resampled efficient frontier. For computing the points between the minimum variance and maximum return portfolios, each efficient frontier from a sampled input is equally divided into M points. The mth point of each efficient frontier is considered to be the optimal portfolio for investors with the same level of risk-aversion. So the mth point on the curve of the resampled efficient frontier is calculated by

$$\omega_{resampled,m} = \frac{1}{T}\sum_{i=1}^{T}\omega_{i,m}$$

where $\omega_{i,m}$ is the optimal portfolio of the mth point on the mean-variance efficient frontier for the ith sample among a total of T samples. The resampled efficient frontier will be completed once the weights $\omega_{resampled,m}$ are computed for $m = 1, \dots, M$.

Now we can formalize the portfolio resampling method.

Step 1: Assume that stock returns follow a multivariate distribution $N(\hat{\mu}, \hat{\Sigma})$, and draw S random samples. Use these S samples to estimate a new expected return vector, $\hat{\mu}_i$, and covariance matrix, $\hat{\Sigma}_i$. The values $\hat{\mu}_i$ and $\hat{\Sigma}_i$ are used for a single simulation.

Step 2: Use $\hat{\mu}_i$ and $\hat{\Sigma}_i$ to find the minimum variance and maximum return portfolios. Then use the level of risk to partition efficient frontiers. Since $\sigma_{i,min-var} < \sigma_{i,max-ret}$, we find M equally spaced points in the interval $[\sigma_{i,min-var}, \sigma_{i,max-ret}]$. For the equally partitioned standard deviations, $\sigma_{i,1}, \sigma_{i,2}, \dots, \sigma_{i,M}$, we find the corresponding efficient portfolio with maximum return, $\omega_{i,1}, \omega_{i,2}, \dots, \omega_{i,M}$.[12] These M portfolios will represent the efficient frontier for $\hat{\mu}_i$ and $\hat{\Sigma}_i$.

Step 3: Repeat Steps 1 and 2 a total of T times to compute T sets of efficient portfolios.

Step 4: For every $m = 1, \dots, M$, average the T efficient portfolios, $\omega_{1,m}, \omega_{2,m}, \dots, \omega_{T,m}$. These M resampled portfolio weights are used to represent the resampled efficient frontier.

We can immediately notice that if we plot the efficient frontier from the resampled portfolio weights using the original values $\hat{\mu}$ and $\hat{\Sigma}$ for computing portfolio risk and return, the resampled efficient frontier will always lie below the original efficient frontier. This is because even though the portfolios $\omega_{i,1}, \omega_{i,2}, \dots, \omega_{i,M}$ are efficient for the given sample $\hat{\mu}_i$ and $\hat{\Sigma}_i$, they are not guaranteed to be efficient relative to the original values $\hat{\mu}$ and $\hat{\Sigma}$. Resampled portfolios, which are average weights of inefficient portfolios, can only be inefficient when compared against the original efficient portfolio. However, investors should not be turned off by this because poor in-sample performance does not directly reflect its out-of-sample performance.[13] In fact, since portfolio resampling models uncertainty by randomly sampling stock returns, it is known to perform better out-of-sample.

Despite its robustness, portfolio resampling also has its shortcomings, mostly arising from the fact that the optimal portfolio weights are the result of averaged allocations. First of all, it is very likely that all stocks selected from the candidate stocks will have non-zero weights. If a stock is given a non-zero weight in any one of the simulations, the resampled portfolio will invest at least a very small amount in that stock. Similarly, when additional constraints are imposed when constructing portfolios, the resampled portfolio will be distant from the constrained portfolio. Again, this is due to the average step, and some portfolios will have weights that are not binding to the constraints.

There also may be cases when the resampled portfolio does not satisfy all the constraints even though this is not the case prior to aggregation. These averaged allocations can especially be a problem for actual trading because, for example, investing in all candidate stocks is unrealistic due to transaction costs. We finally note the computational burden of the model. If the efficient frontier is partitioned into M points and the simulation is repeated for a total of T times, the mean-variance optimization problem has to be solved $M \times T$ times. Even if we assume to know the exact risk appetite of the investor, the mean-variance optimal portfolio needs to be solved T times, and this can easily become a big problem especially for large portfolios.

4.5   CONSTRAINING PORTFOLIO WEIGHTS

Robust approaches introduced so far increase robustness by either performing additional steps prior to solving the optimization problem or after finding optimal mean-variance portfolios, instead of modifying the mean-variance framework. Even though these models that do not improve the mean-variance problem directly may seem attractive due to their simplicity, the robustness of the problem can be achieved by adding only a few constraints on portfolio weights. One of the most common approaches is to include additional constraints to set upper and lower bounds on individual weights. Most restrictions on portfolio weights can be expressed as linear equalities or linear inequalities, so the computation of the portfolio optimization problem remains trivial. The mean-variance problem with bounds on portfolio weights can be written with linear equalities such as:

$$\min_{\omega} \lambda \omega' \Sigma \omega - \omega' \mu$$

$$s.t. \quad \omega' \iota = 1$$

$$\omega_{i,l} \leq \omega_i \leq \omega_{i,u} \, , \text{ for } i = 1, \ldots, N$$

where $\omega_{i,l} \in \mathbb{R}$ and $\omega_{i,u} \in \mathbb{R}$ are lower and upper bounds on the allocation for stock i, respectively. By enforcing restrictions on allocated weights, investors can control the variability of portfolio weights and hence reduce their sensitivity to input estimates.[14]

In Exhibit 4.3, we show weights of portfolios that invest in five stocks traded in the U.S. stock market: Apple Inc. (AAPL), Bank of America Corporation (BAC), Ford Motor Company (F), Pfizer Inc. (PFE), and AT&T Inc. (T).[15] Along with the mean-variance portfolio with weights that sum to one, portfolios with no short-selling constraints and portfolios with upper and lower bounds are shown. Portfolios are rebalanced yearly from 2001

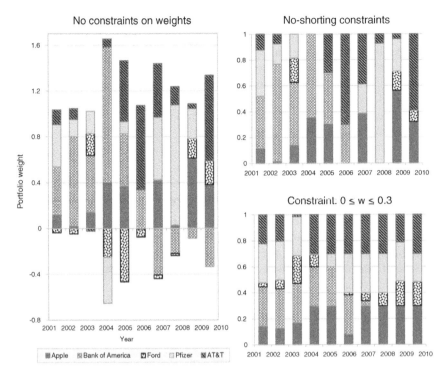

Exhibit 4.3 Weights of mean-variance portfolios with various conditions on weights

to 2010, and only the composition is shown.[16] As clearly shown by the two graphs on the right in Exhibit 4.3, portfolios with additional constraints on weights show allocations that are more stable over time. It should be noted that the stability of weights do not directly reflect robust portfolio performance. However, considering portfolio turnover, the portfolios with extra bounds will be favored due to their robust weights. Turnover is especially important when maintaining a portfolio over multiple periods. The mean-variance model with no additional constraints in our example shows that it would have been ideal for an investor to take a long position in Pfizer in 2003, then a short position in Pfizer in 2004, followed by a long position in 2005. Executing these trades will incur transaction costs that will reduce the overall performance of the portfolio.

The reasoning behind setting upper and lower bounds on portfolio weights to reduce the sensitivity of mean-variance portfolios can be also understood by what some refer to as the *estimation-error maximizing* property of the model. The mean-variance model overweights stocks with high expected returns, small variances, and negative correlations with other stocks. Similarly, the method underweights stocks with low expected returns, high variances, and positive correlations with other stocks.[17] Hence, the stocks that are either overallocated or underallocated are most likely the stocks with estimation error (i.e., it is unlikely to have a stock with high expected return, low variance, and negative correlation with other stocks), and setting bounds on portfolio weights will prevent these *error-contaminated* allocations.

4.6   BAYESIAN APPROACH

Bayesian statistics acknowledge that probability distributions are subject to modification. In the context of stock returns, the true expected returns are unknown to investors, but an investor's belief in the probability distribution of returns may be improved after the investor collects additional information on stock returns. In the Bayesian framework, one begins with a *prior distribution*, which reflects one's belief prior to observing any data. Once some data are examined, one's prior knowledge can be improved using this additional information to compute the *posterior distribution*. This new probability distribution is reached by using *Bayes' rule* for updating the belief.

Black-Litterman Model

The Bayesian framework has also been applied to portfolio selection, and the most studied method is the *Black-Litterman model*.[18] The model is extremely helpful for portfolio managers because it allows them to add their subjective views on market outlook; the observation data used for the Bayesian update step is this market prediction. But, moreover, the Black-Litterman model resolves the main issues associated with the classical mean-variance model. The nontrivial step for portfolio managers when forming mean-variance portfolios is to estimate the expected return of all assets. Most portfolio managers, or more specifically security analysts, have expertise in a specific industry or sector. Therefore, they may have an accurate view of a portion of the market on which they focus, but they are unlikely to have confidence about all market sectors. Black and Litterman directly model this situation, where the optimal portfolio is an equilibrium state of the market (Bayesian prior) unless investors provide predictions on returns, which may only include as many stocks as the portfolio managers feel confident about (Bayesian observation). Black and Litterman explain that:

> ... *our model does not assume that the world is always CAPM [capital asset pricing model] equilibrium, but rather that when expected*

*returns move away from the equilibrium values, imbalances in mar-
kets will tend to push them back. We thus think it is reasonable to
assume that expected returns are not likely to deviate too far from
equilibrium values.*[19]

They extend their argument to state that investors can generate additional returns by combining their subjective views with information from
the equilibrium state of the market.

Equilibrium Model

We begin describing the implementation of the Black-Litterman model where
the equilibrium state is based on the capital asset pricing model (CAPM).[20]
From CAPM, the expected excess return of stock i can be expressed as

$$E(r_i) - r_f = \beta_i(E(r_M) - r_f)$$

where r_i, r_f, and r_M are the returns of stock i, the risk-free asset, and the
market, respectively. The value of β_i, which is the beta of stock i, is defined
as the covariance between the returns of stock i and the market over the
variance of market returns. Furthermore, let $\omega_M = (\omega_{M,1}, \ldots, \omega_{M,N})'$ be the
market capitalization (i.e., weights that form the market return) in a market
with N stocks. Then the expected excess returns of stock i written as Π_i
becomes

$$
\begin{aligned}
\Pi_i &= E(r_i) - r_f \\
&= \beta_i(E(r_M) - r_f) \\
&= \frac{\text{cov}(r_i, r_M)}{\sigma_M^2}(E(r_M) - r_f) \\
&= \frac{E(r_M) - r_f}{\sigma_M^2}\text{cov}\left(r_i, \sum_{j=1}^{N}\omega_{M,j}r_j\right) \\
&= \frac{E(r_M) - r_f}{\sigma_M^2}\sum_{j=1}^{N}\text{cov}(r_i, r_j)\omega_{M,j}
\end{aligned}
$$

where the market return is $r_M = \sum_{j=1}^{N}\omega_{M,j}r_j$ by the definition of ω_M, and σ_M^2
is the variance of market return. The excess return can be further simpli-
fied as

$$\Pi_i = \delta\sum_{j=1}^{N}\text{cov}(r_i, r_j)\omega_{M,j}$$

where $\delta = \frac{E(r_M) - r_f}{\sigma_M^2}$ is the risk premium of the market over its variance. Furthermore, the expected excess returns when written in matrix-form is

$$\Pi = \delta \Sigma \omega_M$$

where $\Pi \in \mathbb{R}^N$, $\Sigma \in \mathbb{R}^{N \times N}$ are given by

$$\Pi = \begin{bmatrix} \Pi_1 \\ \vdots \\ \Pi_N \end{bmatrix}, \ \Sigma = \begin{bmatrix} \text{cov}(r_1, r_1) & \cdots & \text{cov}(r_1, r_N) \\ \vdots & \ddots & \vdots \\ \text{cov}(r_N, r_1) & \cdots & \text{cov}(r_N, r_N) \end{bmatrix}.$$

The equilibrium return can also be determined from reverse optimization. A mean-variance investor will find a portfolio that maximizes the following utility,

$$U(\omega) = \mu' \omega - \frac{\lambda}{2} \omega' \Sigma \omega.$$

By taking the derivative with respect to ω, we find that the optimal portfolio ω_p should satisfy

$$\mu = \lambda \Sigma \omega_p.$$

Based on the CAPM, all mean-variance investors will hold the market portfolio as their risky investment. Thus, by replacing the optimal portfolio with the market portfolio, we find the implied equilibrium return of the market:

$$\Pi = \lambda \Sigma \omega_M$$

where λ is the average risk tolerance of the world. The two approaches allow one to find the equilibrium returns if the market capitalization weights and the covariance matrix are known.

As noted earlier by Black and Litterman, the market is expected to be in the equilibrium state on average but may deviate from it depending on market conditions. The deviation can be expressed as noise $\varepsilon_\Pi \in \mathbb{R}^N$ with its mean at zero resulting in $\mu = \Pi + \varepsilon_\Pi$. Therefore, the prior distribution on the expected return is

$$\mu \sim N(\Pi, \tau \Sigma),$$

where the value of τ represents the confidence of the estimated expected excess return. In other words, it reflects the investor's belief in CAPM; small values of τ show that the investor has high confidence. In addition, the scaling factor τ is normally set to values not greater than one because the uncertainty in expected returns is assumed to not exceed the variability of stock returns.

Views of Investors

The Black-Litterman model combines market equilibrium with investors' views. Since the equilibrium model was discussed, we now demonstrate how an investor can express his or her prediction of the market. An investor may have two types of views: an absolute view and a relative view of the market. For example, a portfolio manager in favor of company A's stock may be certain that the stock will have a return of 9% in the next year, which is an absolute view since a concrete return value is predicted. In contrast, for two other stocks, say B and C, the portfolio manager may only feel confident that stock B will outperform C by 5% without knowing the exact returns. This second outlook is a relative view and it is more common because portfolio managers often use models that only rank stocks without predicting detailed performance. The flexibility of the Black-Litterman model allows investors to incorporate their absolute and relative views into the model.

There are two components for representing absolute and relative views. Let us assume that an investor has K views, which can contain any number of absolute and relative views. The first component is a vector $q \in \mathbb{R}^K$ that states the predicted returns (either absolute or relative) for each view. The second component is a matrix $P \in \mathbb{R}^{K \times N}$ that indicates how each stock is involved in each view (again, each row represents a single view). Therefore, if stock i is irrelevant to the kth view, the entry for (k, i) of matrix P will be zero.

If we revisit the above example with stocks A, B, and C and two subjective views on these stocks, the first component becomes $q = (0.09, 0.05)'$. Furthermore, if we assume that the investment universe contains only the three stocks, the first row of P is $(1, 0, 0)$ since the first view states that stock A will have a return of 9%. Similarly, the second row is given by $(0, 1, -1)$ because the second view predicts stock B to outperform stock C. Together, this view can be written as

$$\begin{bmatrix} 0.09 \\ 0.05 \end{bmatrix} = \begin{bmatrix} 1 & 0 & 0 \\ 0 & 1 & -1 \end{bmatrix} \begin{bmatrix} \mu_A \\ \mu_B \\ \mu_C \end{bmatrix}.$$

We let the weights for the relative view sum to zero for simplicity, but other choices may be used. To incorporate the uncertainty that investors may have in their views, deviation is expressed by $\varepsilon_q \in \mathbb{R}^K$ and the expression for the views becomes:

$$q = P\mu + \varepsilon_q.$$

The covariance matrix of $\varepsilon_q \sim N(0, \Omega)$ is assumed to be a diagonal matrix because the errors in the views are most likely independent of each other. Smaller values in the diagonal of $\Omega \in \mathbb{R}^{K \times K}$ indicate higher confidence for the view, and this allows the investor to express a different level of confidence for each view.

Combining the Equilibrium State with Investors' Views

There is more than one way to combine the portfolio in equilibrium with the subjective views of investors, which results in the Black-Litterman model.[21] Using any of these approaches, the expected return from the model turns out to be

$$\hat{\mu}_{BL} = [(\tau\Sigma)^{-1} + P'\Omega^{-1}P]^{-1}[(\tau\Sigma)^{-1}\Pi + P'\Omega^{-1}q].$$

In other words, the Black-Litterman model finds that the posterior distribution of the expected returns is the following normal distribution:

$$N([(\tau\Sigma)^{-1} + P'\Omega^{-1}P]^{-1}[(\tau\Sigma)^{-1}\Pi + P'\Omega^{-1}q], \ [(\tau\Sigma)^{-1} + P'\Omega^{-1}P]^{-1}).$$

This information, especially the newly calculated expected return, can be used to find the optimal portfolio of the classical mean-variance optimization problem.

We can immediately notice that when an investor has no view (q and Ω are both zero), the expected return from the model is simply Π and the investor winds up holding the market portfolio defined by CAPM. However, when an investor has views, the K views are mapped to the N candidate stocks and this increases the robustness of the model because it has the effect of spreading out the estimation error over all stocks.

4.7 STOCHASTIC PROGRAMMING

Mathematical programming, or optimization, problems introduced in previous chapters were assumed to be expressed with known parameters except for decision variables. However, it is very unlikely for an optimization problem to be completely deterministic, and therefore *stochastic programming* allows optimization with uncertain data. For example, a stochastic linear program is a linear programming problem for which some of the parameters are not known with certainty when solving the problem. In real-world situations, uncertainty in inputs is often inevitable, and randomness may arise from uncontrollable demands in inventory management modeling or from unpredictable stock returns in financial planning.

Stochastic data can affect the problem in several different ways. The uncertain parameter may only be observed after the optimization stage, in which case the decision maker likely finds a conservative solution to prepare for all possible outcomes. On the other hand, it may be that the uncertainty is partially observed before decision making takes place. However, for most portfolio selection problems, some decisions are made before the uncertain stock returns are realized while other decisions are made after some observations. Investors initially allocate their wealth without any realized returns, but rebalance their portfolios after acquiring actual returns during the previous rebalancing period. Therefore, we focus on these types of problems and introduce stochastic programming with recourse.[22]

The *two-stage stochastic linear program with recourse* is written as:

$$\min \ c'x + E[Q(x, \omega)]$$

$$s.t. \ \ Ax = b$$

$$x \geq 0$$

where x is the first-stage decision and c, b, and A are known values as in deterministic linear programs. The second-stage problem $Q(x, \omega)$ for a given realization $\omega \in \Omega$ can be expressed as:

$$\min_{y} \ q(\omega)'y(\omega)$$

$$s.t. \ \ T(\omega)x + W(\omega)y(\omega) = h(\omega)$$

$$y(\omega) \geq 0$$

where the random variables $q(\omega)$, $T(\omega)$, $W(\omega)$, and $h(\omega)$ become known for a realized ω, while $y(\omega)$ is not a function of ω but indicates that y may have unique optimal values for different values of ω. Therefore, the objective function of the two-stage stochastic linear program minimizes the expectation of $Q(x, \omega)$ taken over all realizations of ω. If the random vector ω is considered to follow a discrete and finite distribution, S scenarios can be used to represent the set Ω containing all possible values of ω, and the expectation can be computed by:

$$E[Q(x, \omega)] = \sum_{s=1}^{S} \pi_s Q(x, \omega_s)$$

where π_s represents the probability of realizing scenario s and $\sum_{s=1}^{S} \pi_s = 1$.

The uncertainty in the portfolio selection problem can be modeled as a *multistage stochastic program*.[23] The multistage model can replicate how a portfolio is rebalanced over multiple periods $t = 1, \ldots, T$, where $t = 0$ is the initial investment. It is similar to the two-stage model; the first decision is made prior to any realizations ($t = 0$), but subsequent decisions are made after some observations. Rebalancing takes place at each time period, but the investor cannot add or take out cash once invested. The objective of the problem is to invest initial wealth of W_0 in such a way so as to maximize the utility of wealth W_T at the final time period T. Suppose there are N candidate stocks, and their random returns during time period t are denoted by $r_t = (r_{1,t}, \ldots, r_{N,t})$. Furthermore, assume that there are S possible scenarios of stock returns during the entire investment period, each scenario s with probability π_s and $\sum_{s=1}^{S} \pi_s = 1$. Then the portfolio selection problem can be described as:

$$\max \sum_{s=1}^{S} (\text{probability of scenario } s) \cdot (\text{utility of } W_T \text{ for } s)$$

s.t. (total allocation to N stocks at $t = 0$) $= W_0,$ for each scenario s

     (total allocation to N stocks at $t = T$) $= W_T,$ for each scenario s

     (allocation in stock i at t) $= [1 + (\text{stock } i \text{ return at } t)]$

         $\times$ (allocation in stock i after rebalancing at period $t - 1$),

         for each scenario s, each time period t, and each stock i

     (allocation in stock i at t for scenario s)

         $=$ (allocation in stock i at t for scenario s'),

         for scenarios s and s' with identical past up to time t, $t = 1, \ldots, T$

     All allocations, amounts sold and bought are non-negative.

The problem can be properly formulated as the following while also considering transaction costs. Now, suppose there are $N+1$ candidate stocks with the first element representing cash and their random returns during time period t written as $r_t = (r_{0,t}, r_{1,t}, \ldots, r_{N,t})$. A concave utility function $u(W)$ is used, and vectors w, y, and z represent the amount invested, sold, and bought for each stock, respectively. Transaction costs for selling and buying are c_{sell} and c_{buy}, and superscripts denote which scenario the realized values and decisions are based on.

$$\max \sum_{s=1}^{S} \pi_s \cdot u(W_T^s)$$

$$\text{s.t.} \sum_{i=1}^{N} w_{i,0}^s = W_0, \; s = 1, \ldots, S$$

$$\sum_{i=1}^{N} w_{i,T}^{s} = W_{T}^{s}, \ s = 1, \dots, S$$

$$w_{i,t}^{s} = \left(1 + r_{i,t}^{s}\right)\left(w_{i,t-1}^{s} - y_{i,t-1}^{s} + z_{i,t-1}^{s}\right),$$

$$s = 1, \dots, S, \quad t = 1, \dots, T, \quad i = 1, \dots, N$$

$$w_{0,t}^{s} = \left(1 + r_{0,t}^{s}\right)\left(w_{0,t-1}^{s} + \sum_{i=1}^{N}\left(1 - c_{sell}\right)y_{i,t-1}^{s} - \sum_{i=1}^{N}(1 + c_{buy})z_{i,t-1}^{s}\right),$$

$$s = 1, \dots, S, \quad t = 1, \dots, T$$

$$w_{i,t}^{s}, y_{i,t}^{s}, z_{i,t}^{s} \geq 0, \quad s = 1, \dots, S, \quad t = 1, \dots, T, \quad i = 0, \dots, N$$

$$w_{i,t}^{s} = w_{i,t}^{s'}, \text{ for scenarios } s \text{ and } s' \text{ with identical past up to time } t,$$

$$t = 1, \dots, T, \quad i = 0, \dots, N.$$

The last constraint imposes non-anticipativity to make sure that all scenarios with the same past up to a certain time period have the same decision at that time. Even though this formulation only incorporates transaction costs, it can be modified to allow short-selling and also include bounds on the holdings, amount sold, and amount bought for each stock.

One major assumption in solving the above stochastic portfolio optimization problem is that the S scenarios of stock returns, along with their probability of occurrence, have to be known. Although it may not always be the case, random stock returns are typically reduced to a set of scenarios for modeling their stochastic outcomes. One of the simplest methods for generating scenarios is to use historical stock returns data, where one approach is to randomly select historical dates and use returns on those dates as scenarios. Another method that is easily implementable is to assume the distribution of stock returns and create samples from that distribution. Techniques to construct a distribution that matches the real moments and vector autoregressive models are also used to form scenarios. In addition to how the scenarios are produced, how many scenarios should be used is also important because the number of decision variables and constraints is decided by the number of scenarios, and a large number of scenarios can easily make the problem computationally intractable.

4.8 ADDITIONAL APPROACHES

The *equal-weighted portfolio* (also often referred to as the 1/N portfolio) can be considered as a robust version of the mean-variance portfolio. The sensitivity of the mean-variance portfolio arises from the expected return vector and the covariance matrix of returns, but the equal-weighted portfolio is constructed without using these two inputs that are subject to estimation error. Although it is not highly recommended as a strategic choice for portfolio optimization, it is known to perform well out-of-sample relative to its simplicity in allocating investments.[24] In a similar context, but not as extreme, is the GMV portfolio (or simply the minimum-variance portfolio). Whereas the equal-weighted portfolio disregards both inputs of the mean-variance model, the GMV portfolio only uses the covariance matrix for finding the optimal portfolio. Utilizing the covariance matrix of returns is a better choice than the expected returns, not only because it forms portfolios with low risk, but also because the expected return of stocks is known to have a much larger effect on estimation error.[25]

Another more reasonable approach is not to eliminate the use of the estimated values but to expect the true value to be within an uncertainty set. Therefore, values around the estimation can be considered as possible candidates when constructing the optimal portfolio. To take one step further, by finding the single best portfolio for all possible candidates of the inputs within the defined uncertainty set, the portfolio will become more robust to unforeseen market conditions by reducing the worst lost. What we have just discussed is the basic idea of *robust optimization*. In robust optimization, uncertainty sets of the random inputs are defined and the optimal decision is made by finding the best solution in the worst case (hence, also known as worst-case optimization). The robust optimization framework can be easily applied to portfolio selection, and robust portfolio optimization is one of the main topics of this book, which we will discuss in detail in the following chapters.

KEY POINTS

- Robustness defines models that produce stable outcomes even when changes in model assumptions occur.
- The distinction between aversion to risk and aversion to uncertainty must be made because rational decision makers are averse to uncertainty but the standard mean-variance model only incorporates investors' aversion to risk.
- The simplest approach for constructing robust portfolios is to increase the robustness of the estimates without modifying the mean-variance model. Robust statistics improve estimators so that they are less affected by outliers in the estimated data.
- Robust estimators of the center that are not sensitive to extreme outliers are M-estimators, which include maximum likelihood estimators, and

L-estimators, which include trimmed mean and Winsorized mean. Moreover, mean absolute deviation, median absolute deviation, and sample interquartile range are robust estimators of dispersion.

■ Shrinkage estimators can also be used to increase the robustness of the inputs of the mean-variance model. Shrinkage estimators shrink unbiased estimators towards biased estimators with more structure to increase stability.

■ Monte Carlo simulation models random inputs by random samples, and a robust solution can be found by aggregating all outputs from the samples. Portfolio selection can be solved this way by aggregating optimal portfolios from randomly sampled inputs, known as portfolio resampling.

■ Constraining portfolio weights is a simple way to increase stability by controlling the variability of the optimal portfolio weights. Bounds on portfolio weights can be easily represented as linear constraints in the mean-variance framework.

■ The Black-Litterman model improves portfolio robustness by using a Bayesian approach. The market equilibrium defined by CAPM is updated using subjective views of investors, which can either be absolute or relative views.

■ The stochastic nature of parameters can be reflected in mathematical programs through stochastic programming. Scenarios with their corresponding probabilities of occurrences are often used to present discrete possibilities for finding the optimal solution under the stochastic environment.

■ Removing either one or both of the mean-variance model inputs can be considered as a robust approach by eliminating the source of estimation error. But an alternative is to use the estimates but assume the true values to be close to the estimates. Robust optimization uses this idea to find the best solution for all possible input values within an uncertainty set often defined as points near an estimate.

NOTES

1. This distinction, which had sparked a long discussion on uncertainty in decision theory, was first made in Frank H. Knight, *Risk, Uncertainty and Profit* (Boston, MA: Houghton Mifflin, 1921).
2. The two examples of selecting balls from one or two urns included here demonstrate the Ellsberg paradox, taken from Daniel Ellsberg, "Risk, Ambiguity, and the Savage Axioms," *Quarterly Journal of Economics* 75 (1961), pp. 643–669.
3. For a more detailed discussion of robust statistics, see Peter J. Huber, *Robust Statistics* (New York: John Wiley & Sons, 1981) and Ricardo A. Maronna,

R. Douglas Martin, and Victor J. Yohai, *Robust Statistics: Theory and Methods* (Hoboken, NJ: John Wiley & Sons, 2006).

4. Decline in stock prices due to inaccurate expectations are often regained during subsequent trading days, but we postulate one large decline to demonstrate the sensitivity of the sample mean.

5. Mean-absolute deviation portfolio optimization models are surveyed in Hiroshi Konno and Tomoyuki Koshizuka, "Mean-Absolute Deviation Model," *IIE Transactions* 37, 10 (2005), pp. 893–900, and the performance of various robust estimates of the covariance matrix is discussed in Victor DeMiguel and Francisco J. Nogales, "Portfolio Selection with Robust Estimation," *Operations Research* 57, 3 (2009), pp. 560–577.

6. An empirical Bayesian interpretation is possible where the prior is the shrinkage target with structure and the sample information is treated as the observation for updating the model. We discuss Bayesian methods in section 4.6.

7. This rather unintuitive observation is known as the Stein's paradox, and the basic ideas are effectively explained by Bradley Efron and Carl Morris, "Stein's Paradox in Statistics," *Scientific American* 236 (1977), pp. 119–127.

8. The James-Stein shrinkage estimator applicable to portfolio selection presented here is derived from Philippe Jorion, "Bayes-Stein Estimation for Portfolio Analysis," *Journal of Financial and Quantitative Analysis* 21, 3 (1986), pp. 279–292.

9. Solving the GMV problem is covered in Chapter 6.

10. Shrinkage estimators of the covariance matrix are discussed in Olivier Ledoit and Michael Wolf, "Improved Estimation Of The Covariance Matrix of Stock Returns With an Application to Portfolio Selection," *Journal of Empirical Finance* 10, 5 (2003), pp. 603–621; and Olivier Ledoit and Michael Wolf, "Honey, I Shrunk the Sample Covariance Matrix," *Journal of Portfolio Management* 30, 4 (2004), pp. 110–119.

11. Portfolio resampling is introduced in Richard Michaud, *Efficient Asset Management: A Practical Guide to Stock Portfolio Optimization* (New York: Oxford University Press, 1998); and Richard Michaud and Robert Michaud, "Estimation Error and Portfolio Optimization: A Resampling Solution," *Journal of Investment Management* 6, 1 (2008), pp. 8–28.

12. Additional constraints such as no short-selling constraints or bounds on portfolio weights can be imposed to meet investment requirements.

13. *In-sample data* refers to training data that are used for computing the optimal portfolio, while *out-of-sample data* refers to data not included in the estimation. Thus, in-sample performance does not accurately reflect outcome from unforeseen data.

14. Imposing limits on weights is a common practice in managing portfolios to avoid large exposures, and non-negativity constraints are frequently used to comply with restrictions on short-selling.

15. Daily returns for the five stocks from 2001 to 2010 used in this illustration were obtained from Yahoo! Finance (http://finance.yahoo.com).

16. In this example, we set the risk coefficient that gives annualized portfolio volatilities below 30% each year except in 2008 when the market experienced high volatility due to the financial crisis.

17. The error maximizing behavior is discussed in Richard O. Michaud, "The Markowitz Optimization Enigma: Is 'Optimized' Optimal?" *Financial Analyst Journal* 45 (1989), pp. 31–42; and improved portfolio performance from constraining weights is presented in Peter A. Frost and James E. Savarino, "For Better Performance: Constrain Portfolio Weights," *Journal of Portfolio Management* 15, 1 (1988), pp. 29–34.

18. The Black-Litterman model is introduced in Fischer Black and Robert Litterman, "Asset Allocation: Combining Investor Views with Market Equilibrium," *Goldman, Sachs & Co., Fixed Income Research* (1990); and Fischer Black and Robert Litterman, "Global Portfolio Optimization," *Financial Analysts Journal* 48 (1992), pp. 28–43.

19. Black and Litterman, "Global Portfolio Optimization," p. 29.

20. The details of the Black-Litterman model are explained in Svetlozar T. Rachev, John S. J. Hsu, Biliana S. Bagasheva, and Frank J. Fabozzi, *Bayesian Methods in Finance* (Hoboken, NJ: John Wiley & Sons, 2008), pp. 141–161.

21. Calculation using the traditional Bayes' theorem is explained in Stephen Satchell and Alan Scowcroft, "A Demystification of the Black-Litterman Model: Managing Quantitative and Traditional Portfolio Construction," *Journal of Asset Management* 1, 2 (2000), pp. 138–150; and the generalized least squares estimator is described in Frank J. Fabozzi, Peter N. Kolm, Dessislava A. Pachamanova, and Sergio M. Focardi, *Robust Portfolio Optimization and Management* (Hoboken, NJ: John Wiley & Sons, 2007), pp. 229–253.

22. The main ideas and techniques of stochastic programming are thoroughly introduced in John R. Birge and François Louveaux, *Introduction to Stochastic Programming* (New York: Springer, 1997).

23. We previously have focused on single-period models in this book, but introduce a multiperiod setting because stochastic programming is mostly used for multistage problems. The multistage stochastic model for portfolio selection is further explained in Fabozzi, Kolm, Pachamanova, and Focardi, *Robust Portfolio Optimization and Management*, pp. 294–297.

24. The out-of-sample performance of the equal-weighted portfolio is analyzed in Victor DeMiguel, Lorenzo Garlappi, and Raman Uppal, "Optimal Versus Naïve Diversification: How Inefficient Is the 1/N Portfolio Strategy?" *Review of Financial Studies* 22, 5 (2009), pp. 1915–1953.

25. Vijay Kumar Chopra and William T. Ziemba, "The Effect of Errors in Means, Variances, and Covariances on Optimal Portfolio Choice," *Journal of Portfolio Management* 19, 2 (1993), pp. 6–11.

CHAPTER **5**

Robust Optimization

Robust models that are used for portfolio selection were discussed in the previous chapter. We now introduce robust optimization, which is the focus of the remaining chapters.

Our objectives in this chapter are to

- Explain how uncertainty-averse decisions are a result of thinking about worst-case scenarios
- Provide a brief introduction to convex optimization
- Summarize the different types of optimization problems
- Explain robust counterparts of uncertain mathematical programs
- Illustrate various uncertainty sets used by robust models
- Demonstrate how to construct robust counterparts of linear programs
- Introduce interior point methods for solving robust problems

5.1 WORST-CASE DECISION MAKING

At the beginning of the previous chapter, two examples that involve selecting balls from urns were mentioned to show how rational decision making can result from aversion to uncertainty. Comparing the worst possible outcome of each situation allows us to understand the decision-making process of an uncertainty-averse individual.[1]

Let us revisit one of the examples, in which there are two urns A and B with 100 balls in each of them. The decision maker knows that there are exactly 50 red and 50 green balls in urn B, but no additional information except that there is a mix of red and green balls in urn A. If the decision maker prefers urn B to A when receiving an award if one ball drawn from the selected urn is red, it shows that the decision maker believes there are less than 50 red balls in urn A. However, the decision maker does not prefer urn A to B when an award is received if a green ball is drawn from the selected urn. For the first case of receiving an award for a red ball, even though the worst case for urn B is that there are 50 red balls, the worst case for urn A is that there are zero red balls. Hence, urn B is favored to urn A. Similarly, for the second case of anticipating a green ball, the worst case for urn B is having 50 green balls. The worst case for urn A is again having zero green balls because of the uncertainty with urn A, which is why urn B is again chosen over urn A. The situation can be diagrammed as follows:

	Number of balls in the worst case	
	Red	Green
Urn A	0	0
Urn B	50	50

As summarized earlier, the worst case for urn A is that there are zero red balls and zero green balls, when concentrating only on the number of red and green balls, respectively. Hence, urn B is always preferred to urn A.

In this example, the optimal choice for an uncertainty-averse decision-maker was made by observing the worst state. In the same manner, optimizing the worst case to minimize risk in an uncertain situation can be applied to portfolio selection. Since future stock returns are not known with certainty, the best portfolio for the worst possible return can be selected to reduce future losses in case the actual return turns out to be as low as the predicted worst value. The details of the formulation, such as ways to decide the set of possible future returns, are of course very important for this approach, and we will illustrate these details in the following sections.

5.2 CONVEX OPTIMIZATION

Before we derive the robust versions of the portfolio selection problem, we will briefly review mathematical programming and a subset of the problems categorized as convex optimization.[2]

Mathematical programming or simply *optimization* problems involve finding the optimal objective value (the minimum in the below formulation) that satisfies given constraints of the problem and are generally written as:

$$\min_{x} f(x)$$

$$\text{s.t.} \ \ g_i(x) \leq 0 \text{ for } i = 1, \ldots, m \quad (5.1)$$

$$h_j(x) = 0 \text{ for } j = 1, \ldots, p$$

where

$x \in \mathbb{R}^n$ is the optimization variable (or decision variable)

$f(x)$ is the objective function

$g_i(x) \le 0$ is an inequality constraint

$h_j(x) = 0$ is an equality constraint

(all functions f, g, and h are $\mathbb{R}^n \to \mathbb{R}$).

Without any inequality and equality constraints, the problem is referred to as an *unconstrained* optimization problem. The goal of an optimization problem is often to find the optimal value of x, but there may be no such x satisfying all the constraints, in which case the problem is said to be *infeasible*. Furthermore, if the problem is *feasible* (i.e., there exists a set of values of x that satisfies all constraints) but the objective value asymptotically reaches negative infinity (for a minimization problem), the problem becomes *unbounded*.

Even though the standard form of an optimization problem is mostly written as in (5.1), some transformations of the objective or constraint functions can result in equivalent problems. For example, the minimization problem can be easily switched to a maximization problem with an objective function of $-f(x)$. Moreover, inequality constraints can be replaced by equality constraints by introducing slack variables $s \in \mathbb{R}^n$,

$$\min_{x,s} f(x)$$

$$\text{s.t.} \ \ g_i(x) + s_i = 0 \text{ for } i = 1, \ldots, m$$

$$s_i \ge 0 \text{ for } i = 1, \ldots, m$$

$$h_j(x) = 0 \text{ for } j = 1, \ldots, p.$$

In special cases, inequality or equality constraints can even be eliminated.

Based on the objective and constraint functions, optimization problems can be classified into a set of well-known problems such as linear programming, nonlinear programming, and many more. The main advantage of classifying a given problem is that it allows us to use known algorithms for solving different types of optimization problems. If a given problem has all the characteristics of a linear program, then we immediately know that the problem can be efficiently solved using the simplex method (which we will discuss later in this chapter).

One of the special types of optimization problems is *convex optimization*, which includes problems such as linear programming and special cases of quadratic programming, where the objective and constraints are convex functions. A function $f : \mathbb{R}^n \to \mathbb{R}$ is convex if the following holds for all x and y in the domain of f for $0 \le \theta \le 1$,

$$f(\theta x + (1 - \theta)y) \le \theta f(x) + (1 - \theta)f(y).$$

Therefore, in standard form, a convex optimization problem is written as

$$\min_x f(x)$$

$$\text{s.t. } g_i(x) \le 0 \text{ for } i = 1, \dots, m$$

$$a_j'x = b_j \text{ for } j = 1, \dots, p$$

where $f(x)$ and $g_i(x)$ are convex functions, and the equality constraints are linear for $a_j \in \mathbb{R}^n$, $b_j \in \mathbb{R}$.

Convex optimization problems are especially important because any local optimum is also guaranteed to be globally optimal. A locally optimal solution is a point that is optimal among its neighboring points, so a better solution may exist. Therefore, if an algorithm only finds local optimums, all locally optimal points have to be computed to find the globally optimal point among those. Nonetheless, if a solver finds an optimal point for a convex problem, we can stop the search because we know there are no points better than that one. What makes convex optimization even more valuable is that there are efficient algorithms for finding optimal solutions. Because of these advantages, identifying convex problems or transforming the original problem into convex formulations is commonly an effective step for solving optimization problems.

Duality

The concept of duality is important for solving convex optimization problems.[3] We begin by describing the Lagrangian function. The *Lagrangian* is a modified objective function expressed as a weighted sum of the original objective and the constraint functions. The Lagrangian of the mathematical program given by (5.1) is

$$L(x, \lambda, \gamma) = f(x) + \sum_{i=1}^{m} \lambda_i g_i(x) + \sum_{j=1}^{p} \gamma_j h_j(x)$$

with additional variables $\lambda \in \mathbb{R}^m$ and $\gamma \in \mathbb{R}^p$, which are known as Lagrange multipliers.

The *dual function* is defined as the minimum value (in more mathematical terms, it actually finds the *infimum*) of the Lagrangian over x within its domain,

$$g(\lambda, \gamma) = \min_x L(x, \lambda, \gamma).$$

It can be shown that the dual function is a concave function even when the original problem (5.1) is not convex. More importantly, for any $\lambda \geq 0$ and γ, the dual function gives a lower bound on the optimal value p^* of (5.1),

$$g(\lambda, \gamma) \leq p^*.$$

The Lagrange *dual problem* is the optimization problem that finds the best lower bound,

$$\max_{\lambda, \gamma} g(\lambda, \gamma)$$

$$\text{s.t.} \quad \lambda \geq 0,$$

and the optimal pair (λ^*, γ^*) is called dual optimal. When discussing dual problems, the original problem is referred to as the *primal problem*. The significance of the dual problem comes from the fact that it is a convex optimization problem because it maximizes a concave function (i.e., it minimizes a convex function). Again, this holds regardless of the convexity of the primal problem.

Two properties that outline the strength of the dual problem are weak duality and strong duality. *Weak duality* states that the optimal value d^* of the dual problem is a lower bound of p^*,

$$d^* \leq p^*.$$

The difference $p^* - d^*$ is known as the duality gap. Moreover, *strong duality* explains that the duality gap is zero (i.e., $d^* = p^*$) if the primal problem is a convex problem with some minor conditions (Slater's condition). Hence, duality is especially important for solving convex optimization problems because solving the dual problem yields the same optimal value in most cases.

Linear Programming

We now introduce several types of convex optimization problems essential for solving portfolio optimization problems and their robust counterparts. One of the simplest mathematical programming problems is a linear program where the objective function and constraints are linear.[4] Because linear functions are convex, linear programs are a subset of convex optimization problems. In standard form, a linear programming problem with a decision variable, $x \in \mathbb{R}^n$ (also called the equality form) is written as:

$$\min_{x} c'x$$

$$\text{s.t.} \ \ Ax = b$$

$$x \geq 0$$

where $c \in \mathbb{R}^n$ is a cost vector that defines the linear cost function, each row of $A \in \mathbb{R}^{m \times n}$ and $b \in \mathbb{R}^m$ represents an equality constraint, and the non-negativity constraint is a component-wise inequality. The standard form expressed with only equality and non-negativity constraints is not restrictive because inequality constraints can be transformed into standard form as discussed earlier.

Selecting a portfolio that maximizes expected return with constraints on portfolio weights can be solved as a linear programming problem. Even though the model most likely results in a very risky portfolio, it demonstrates the simplicity of linear programs. A maximum return problem where weights invested in any individual stock is restricted to be between $\omega_l \in \mathbb{R}^N$ and $\omega_h \in \mathbb{R}^N$ can be expressed as

$$\max_{\omega} \mu'\omega$$

$$\text{s.t.} \ \ \omega_l \leq \omega \leq \omega_h$$

where $\omega \in \mathbb{R}^N$ is the portfolio weight, and $\mu \in \mathbb{R}^N$ is the expected returns of N stocks.

Solving a linear programming problem is relatively simpler than other optimization problems because the feasible set defined by linear constraints turns out to be a polyhedron. Furthermore, if the feasible set has at least one corner point, the optimal solution of the problem will be one of the vertices of the polyhedron. Since the positive orthant can be proven to contain corner points, a linear program in standard form has an optimal solution at a corner of its feasible set due to the non-negativity constraints. The most widely known algorithm based on these characteristics of linear programs is the *simplex method*. The simplex method searches through the vertices of the feasible set along the edges of the polyhedron to find the optimal solution. The selection of vertices is based on a direction that reduces cost so that the optimal point can be efficiently found. The algorithm stops and claims the vertex to be the optimal solution when there is no cost-reducing direction.

In MATLAB, linear programming problems are solved by the *linprog* function, and the function details are summarized in Box 5.1.[5]

Quadratic Programming

Quadratic programming is one of the most important optimization problems in portfolio selection because the classical mean-variance model can be

---

Box 5.1 MATLAB FUNCTION FOR SOLVING LINEAR PROGRAMMING

Function: *linprog*

Syntax:
```
x = linprog(f, A, b)
x = linprog(f, A, b, Aeq, beq)
x = linprog(f, A, b, Aeq, beq, lb, ub)
x = linprog(f, A, b, Aeq, beq, lb, ub, x0)
x = linprog(f, A, b, Aeq, beq, lb, ub, x0,
       options)
```

Details: Solve the following linear programming problem:

$$\min_x f'x$$

$$\text{s.t. } A \cdot x \leq b$$

$$Aeq \cdot x = beq$$

$$lb \leq x \leq ub.$$

Suppose x is a vector of length n ($x \in \mathbb{R}^n$), then

$$f \in \mathbb{R}^n, A \in \mathbb{R}^{m \times n}, b \in \mathbb{R}^m, Aeq \in \mathbb{R}^{k \times n},$$

$$beq \in \mathbb{R}^k, lb \in \mathbb{R}^n, ub \in \mathbb{R}^n$$

where m is the number of inequality constraints, and k is the number of equality constraints.

The initial point for x can be set by $x_0 \in \mathbb{R}^n$ and additional options including the algorithm for solving the problem can be set using the final argument *options*.

Note that only f, A, and b are the minimum required arguments for *linprog*.

expressed as a quadratic program. Quadratic programming problems have a quadratic objective function and linear constraints and are written in standard form as:

$$\min_{x} \frac{1}{2}x'Qx + c'x$$

$$\text{s.t. } Ax = b \tag{5.2}$$

$$x \geq 0$$

where all notations are the same as in the standard form of linear programs except for the additional quadratic term with a matrix $Q \in \mathbb{R}^{n \times n}$. Since quadratic programs also have linear constraints, the feasible set is also a polyhedron. Therefore, quadratic programming can be interpreted as minimizing a quadratic function over a polyhedron.

Unlike linear programming, not all quadratic programming problems are convex. The second-order condition of convexity states that a twice-differential function f is convex if and only if $\nabla^2 f(x) \geq 0$. If we let $f(x)$ be the objective function of a quadratic program in standard form,

$$f(x) = \frac{1}{2}x'Qx + c'x,$$

it follows that

$$\nabla f(x) = Qx + c \text{ and } \nabla^2 f(x) = Q.$$

It is clear that a quadratic program given by (5.2) is convex if the matrix Q is either positive semidefinite or positive definite.[6] It also shows the reason for putting $1/2$ in the objective.

In portfolio optimization, the matrix Q in the quadratic term commonly represents the covariance matrix of stock returns. An optimal portfolio is certain to be globally optimal for these portfolio selection problems because the covariance matrix is always positive semidefinite. For a vector of random returns $r \in \mathbb{R}^N$ of N stocks, the covariance matrix of returns is

$$\Sigma = E(r - E(r))(r - E(r))'$$

and therefore

$$x'\Sigma x = E(x'(r - E(r))(r - E(r))'x) \geq 0$$

for any $x \in \mathbb{R}^N$.

One of the formulations of the Markowitz mean-variance model described in Chapter 2 is finding a minimum-risk portfolio for a given level of expected return, which is a quadratic program,

$$\min_{\omega} \frac{1}{2}\omega' \Sigma \omega$$

$$\text{s.t.} \ \ \mu'\omega = r_t$$

$$\omega' \iota = 1$$

where $r_t \in \mathbb{R}$ is the target level of portfolio return. The optimal portfolio is found by applying the first-order optimality condition to the Lagrangian function,[7]

$$L(\omega, \lambda, \gamma) = \frac{1}{2}\omega' \Sigma \omega - \lambda(\mu'\omega - r_t) - \gamma(\omega'\iota - 1)$$

where λ and γ are Lagrange multipliers. The solution can be found by solving the following equations,

$$\frac{\partial L}{\partial \omega} = \Sigma \omega - \lambda\mu - \gamma\iota = 0$$

$$\frac{\partial L}{\partial \lambda} = \mu'\omega - r_t = 0$$

$$\frac{\partial L}{\partial \gamma} = \omega'\iota - 1 = 0$$

because there is the same number of equations and unknowns. This is a special case of quadratic programming with only equality constraints in which case the problem becomes linear as shown. Solving a quadratic programming problem in general is more complex than this, but there are many iterative algorithms that have been developed. We introduce interior-point methods later in this chapter, which is used to solve convex optimization problems including convex quadratic programs.

In MATLAB, quadratic programming problems are solved by the *quadprog* function, and the function details are summarized in Box 5.2.[8]

Conic Programming

Linear programming and quadratic programming problems are the simplest formulations that appear first in most discussions of mathematical programming. But formulations that are much more useful in many applications are

---

Box 5.2 MATLAB FUNCTION FOR SOLVING QUADRATIC PROGRAMMING

Function: *quadprog*

Syntax:
```
x = quadprog(H, f)
x = quadprog(H, f, A, b)
x = quadprog(H, f, A, b, Aeq, beq)
x = quadprog(H, f, A, b, Aeq, beq, lb, ub)
x = quadprog(H, f, A, b, Aeq, beq, lb, ub, x0)
x = quadprog(H, f, A, b, Aeq, beq, lb, ub, x0,
       options)
```

Details: Solve the following quadratic programming problem:

$$\min_{x} \frac{1}{2} x'Hx + f'x$$

$$\text{s.t. } A \cdot x \leq b$$

$$Aeq \cdot x = beq$$

$$lb \leq x \leq ub.$$

Suppose x is a vector of length n ($x \in \mathbb{R}^n$), then

$$H \in \mathbb{R}^{n \times n}, f \in \mathbb{R}^n, A \in \mathbb{R}^{m \times n}, b \in \mathbb{R}^m,$$

$$Aeq \in \mathbb{R}^{k \times n}, beq \in \mathbb{R}^k, lb \in \mathbb{R}^n, ub \in \mathbb{R}^n$$

where m is the number of inequality constraints and k is the number of equality constraints.

The initial point for x can be set by $x_0 \in \mathbb{R}^n$ and additional options including the algorithm for solving the problem can be set using the final argument *options*.

Note that only H and f are the minimum required arguments for *quadprog*.

---

conic programs, which are written in standard form as

$$\min_{x} c'x$$

$$\text{s.t. } Ax = b$$

$$x \in K$$

where K is a closed pointed convex cone with a non-empty interior (a cone is pointed if it contains no lines).[9] Conic optimization problems are convex because they optimize a linear objective function over a convex set. Furthermore, similarities with linear programming in standard form can be immediately noticed. The decision variable $x \in \mathbb{R}^n$ in conic programming is no longer constrained to have non-negative elements but needs to be contained in the cone K. However, when K is defined to be the non-negative orthant (i.e., $K = \mathbb{R}^n_+$), the conic programming becomes a linear programming problem because all elements of x have to be non-negative to be in the non-negative orthant. Optimization problems in conic form can also be expressed as

$$\min_x c'x$$

$$\text{s.t. } Ax = b$$

$$A_i x - b_i \in K_i \text{ for } i = 1, \dots, m$$

where each K_i is a pointed convex cone that is closed with a non-empty interior.[10]

The strength of conic programming comes from the fact that most convex optimization problems can be expressed as conic optimization by appropriately defining the cone that forms the feasible set. Three of the most studied cones for formulating conic optimization problems are the non-negative orthant, second-order cones, and semidefinite matrices. We have already explained how the non-negative orthant leads to linear programming. We now discuss the other two formulations, which in fact appear most often in robust portfolio optimization and can be efficiently solved as convex problems.

Second-Order Cone Programming

Second-order cones (also referred to as Lorentz cones) of dimension k are defined as

$$C_k = \left\{ \begin{bmatrix} u \\ t \end{bmatrix} \middle| u \in \mathbb{R}^{k-1}, t \in \mathbb{R}, \|u\|_2 \leq t \right\} \quad (5.3)$$

where $\|u\|_2$ is the Euclidean norm, $\|u\|_2 = \sqrt{u'u}$. In other words, a vector $x = (x_1, x_2, \dots, x_n)' \in \mathbb{R}^n$ must satisfy

$$\sqrt{\sum_{i=1}^{n-1} x_i^2} \leq x_n$$

to be contained in a set of second-order cones. Second-order cones are also referred to as ice cream cones because of their shape.

Conic programming problems formed using second-order cones are known as second-order cone programming and are written as

$$\min_{x} c'x$$

$$\text{s.t. } Ax = b \qquad\qquad (5.4)$$

$$\|A_i x + b_i\| \le c_i' x + d_i \text{ for } i = 1, \dots, m$$

where $A_i \in \mathbb{R}^{(m_i-1) \times n}$, $b_i \in \mathbb{R}^{(m_i-1)}$, $c_i \in \mathbb{R}^n$, and $d_i \in \mathbb{R}$.[11] The inequality constraint is equivalent to

$$\begin{bmatrix} A_i \\ c_i' \end{bmatrix} x + \begin{bmatrix} b_i \\ d_i \end{bmatrix} \in C_{m_i}$$

which illustrates how the formulation is classified as a conic problem with second-order cones.

In portfolio optimization, an example of second-order cone programming is the formulation with loss risk constraints where stock returns are assumed to follow a multivariate normal (Gaussian) distribution with mean μ and covariance Σ, and therefore the returns of a portfolio with weight ω follow a normal distribution with mean $\mu'\omega$ and covariance $\omega'\Sigma\omega$.[12] The loss risk constraint is defined to limit the probability of portfolio return r_p below a threshold α and denoted as

$$\Pr(r_p \le \alpha) \le \beta$$

where β sets the maximum probability. The loss risk constraint can be drawn as shown, where the curve represents the normally distributed portfolio return graphically shown in Exhibit 5.1. Then the probability of loss less

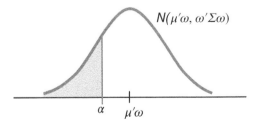

Exhibit 5.1 Probability of loss for a normal distribution

than α can be calculated using the cumulative distribution function Φ of the standard normal distribution (standard normal distribution has a mean of 0 and a variance of 1) by standardizing the original value,

$$\Pr(r_p \leq \alpha) = \Phi\left(\frac{\alpha - \mu'\omega}{\sqrt{\omega'\Sigma\omega}}\right),$$

which leads to this derivation:

$$\Pr(r_p \leq \alpha) = \Phi\left(\frac{\alpha - \mu'\omega}{\sqrt{\omega'\Sigma\omega}}\right) \leq \beta$$

$$\frac{\alpha - \mu'\omega}{\sqrt{\omega'\Sigma\omega}} \leq \Phi^{-1}(\beta),$$

and the constraint can be written in the form of a second-order cone constraint as

$$\Phi^{-1}(\beta)\|\Sigma^{1/2}\omega\|_2 \geq -\mu'\omega + \alpha.$$

Hence, the optimization problem for finding the portfolio with non-negative weights that has maximum expected return while controlling the probability of loss beyond a threshold value becomes a second-order cone program when $\beta \leq 1/2$ (and thus $\Phi^{-1}(\beta) \leq 0$),

$$\max_{x} \mu'\omega$$
$$\text{s.t.} \quad \Phi^{-1}(\beta)\|\Sigma^{1/2}\omega\|_2 \geq -\mu'\omega + \alpha$$
$$\omega'\iota = 1$$
$$x \geq 0.$$

Second-order cone constraints can also represent many of the constraints introduced earlier in this chapter. The second-order cone program given in (5.4) becomes a linear program when $A_i = 0$. More simply, the second-order cone constraint when defined in one-dimension (i.e., $m_i = 0$) reduces to a linear inequality constraint,

$$0 \leq c_i'x + d_i \text{ for } i = 1, \dots, m.$$

Furthermore, a convex quadratic constraint is achieved by setting $c_i = 0$ since the second-order cone constraint becomes

$$\|A_i x + b_i\|_2^2 \leq d_i^2 \text{ for } i = 1, \dots, m$$

when $d_i \geq 0$. From this transformation, quadratic programs written as (5.2) with convex objective functions can be reformulated as second-order cone programs,

$$\min_x t$$

$$\text{s.t.} \quad \left\| \frac{1}{\sqrt{2}} Q^{1/2} x + \frac{\sqrt{2}}{2} Q^{-1/2} c \right\|_2 \leq t$$

$$Ax = b$$

$$x \geq 0$$

when matrix Q is symmetric and positive definite. Even though there may be discrepancies in the optimal objective value because taking the square of the second-order constraint is

$$\frac{1}{2} x' Q x + c' x + \frac{1}{2} c' Q^{-1} c \leq t^2,$$

it will nevertheless find the same optimal x as the original formulation (5.2). By using similar conversions, quadratic constrained quadratic programs (i.e., quadratic programs with additional quadratic constraints) can be expressed as second-order cone programs. Moreover, second-order cone programming is important because many semidefinite programming problems, which we discuss next, can be formulated as second-order cone programs that are solved more efficiently.

Semidefinite Programming

Semidefinite programming is the most inclusive formulation among the three types of conic optimization programs introduced in this chapter.[13] Semidefinite programs, which include a constraint defined using positive semidefinite matrices, are and written as

$$\min_x c' x$$

$$\text{s.t.} \quad Ax = b \qquad\qquad (5.5)$$

$$F_0 + x_1 F_1 + \cdots + x_n F_n \geq 0$$

for symmetric matrices $F_0, \ldots, F_n \in S^m$. Therefore, the inequality constraint is an affine combination of symmetric matrices, and it is also known as linear matrix inequalities (LMIs). An LMI defined as

$$F(x) = F_0 + x_1 F_1 + \cdots + x_n F_n$$

is a function mapping $x \in \mathbb{R}^n$ to $F(x) \in S^m$, and the constraint $F(x) \geq 0$ is convex, which makes semidefinite programming a convex problem.

Semidefinite programs can also be formulated using matrices,

$$\min_x C \bullet X$$

$$\text{s.t.} \quad A_i \bullet X = b_i , \quad i = 1, \ldots, m$$

$$X \geq 0$$

where C and A_i are symmetric matrices in S^n, and $C \bullet X$ is the sum of component-wise multiplication, $C \bullet X = \sum_{i,j=1}^{n} C_{i,j} X_{i,j}$. Considering matrix $X \in \mathbb{R}^{n \times n}$ as a vector x with length n^2 will allow seeing the similarity with previous formulations where the objective function was an inner product of two vectors. Furthermore, the equation is comparable to linear programming; the variable x in the real vector space is substituted with X in the space of symmetric n-by-n matrices and restricting x to have non-negative elements is replaced with the matrix X having non-negative eigenvalues (from the definition of positive semidefinite matrices). It follows that linear programming is a special case of semidefinite programming when X is a diagonal matrix because the eigenvalues of a diagonal matrix are its diagonal elements.

Second-order cone programming can also be casted as semidefinite programming. Consider a matrix $X \in S^n$ that is partitioned into submatrices A, B, and C,

$$X = \begin{bmatrix} A & B \\ B' & C \end{bmatrix}.$$

From the theory of Schur complements, it holds for $A \succ 0$ that $X \geq 0$ if and only if

$$C - B'A^{-1}B \geq 0.$$

Thus, the inequality that must be satisfied in the definition of second-order cones as shown in (5.3) is equivalent to

$$\|u\|_2 \leq t \iff \begin{bmatrix} tI & u \\ u' & t \end{bmatrix} \geq 0$$

where $u \in \mathbb{R}^{k-1}, t \in \mathbb{R}$, and $I \in \mathbb{R}^{(k-1) \times (k-1)}$ is the identity matrix. If elements of u are all non-zero, then $t > 0$ and therefore $tI \succ 0$. This is enough to confirm that

$$t - u'(tI)^{-1}u = t - \frac{1}{t}u'u \geq 0$$

which finally leads to $u'u \leq t^2$ and $\sqrt{u'u} \leq t$. By applying this conversion to the second-order cone programming as shown in (5.4), we arrive at

$$\min_x c'x$$

$$\text{s.t. } Ax = b$$

$$\begin{bmatrix} (c_i^T x + d_i)I & A_i x + b_i \\ (A_i x + b_i)' & c_i^T x + d_i \end{bmatrix} \geq 0 \text{ for } i = 1, \dots, m$$

where $I \in \mathbb{R}^{(m_i-1) \times (m_i-1)}$.

As another example that appears often, consider the following convex quadratic constraint,

$$x'Q'Qx + q'x + r \leq 0.$$

We can form a positive semidefinite matrix that sets the same restrictions as the quadratic constraint,

$$\begin{bmatrix} I & Qx \\ (Qx)' & -(q'x + r) \end{bmatrix} \geq 0.$$

This helps convert quadratically constrained quadratic programs to semidefinite forms. As shown earlier, Schur complements are useful for recognizing mathematical programs that can be reformulated as semidefinite programs. Nevertheless, since it is easier to solve special cases, it will be advantageous to write a given problem as a linear program or a second-order cone program if possible.

5.3 ROBUST COUNTERPARTS

We finally arrive at explaining robust optimization. As mentioned in previous chapters, uncertainty in the inputs when solving problems in the real world is unavoidable in most cases. The use of uncertain data naturally also arises in solving mathematical programs.

When forming the below mathematical programming problem with only inequality constraints,

$$\min_x f_0(x)$$
$$\text{s.t. } f_i(x) \leq 0 \text{ for } i = 1, \dots, m \tag{5.6}$$

we may realize that the functions $f_i(x)$ contain an uncertain component. In that case, we want to find the optimal solution among all possible situations that satisfy the constraints. Thus, the optimization problem can be rewritten as

$$\min_{x} f_0(x)$$

$$\text{s.t. } g_i(x, u) \leq 0 \text{ for all } u \in \mathcal{U}, \ i = 1, \ldots, m$$

(5.7)

where $g_i(x, u)$ is the uncertain version of $f_i(x)$ with the uncertainty set $\mathcal{U} \subseteq \mathbb{R}^n$. The problem (5.7) is called the *robust counterpart* of an uncertain mathematical program given in (5.6). It is important to first note that the robust counterpart of an uncertain problem is a constraint-wise construction. Instead of considering the entire problem at once, we only need to replace each constraint with its robust counterpart,

$$\min_{x} f_0(x)$$

$$\text{s.t. } g_i(x, u_i) \leq 0 \text{ for all } u_i \in \mathcal{U}_i, \ i = 1, \ldots, m$$

where $g_i(x, u_i)$ is the uncertain version of $f_i(x)$ with the uncertainty set $\mathcal{U}_i \subseteq \mathbb{R}^n$ for the uncertain parameter $u_i \in \mathbb{R}^n$. If uncertainty occurs in the objective function, we can introduce a new variable to transfer the uncertainty away from the objective as

$$\min_{x,t} t$$

$$\text{s.t. } g_0(x, u_0) \leq t \text{ for all } u_0 \in \mathcal{U}_0$$

$$g_i(x, u_i) \leq 0, \text{ for all } u_i \in \mathcal{U}_i, \ i = 1, \ldots, m$$

where $g_0(x, u_0)$ is $f_0(x)$ expressed also as a function of uncertain data $u_0 \in \mathbb{R}^n$.

The above robust counterpart can be formulated as a problem with infinitely many constraints. In other words, hard constraints with uncertain parameters can be expressed by adding a constraint for each realization from the uncertainty set. However, this likely results in adding an infinite number of constraints which will likely make the problem intractable. Thus, in robust optimization, the worst case approach is imposed; only the worst situation within the uncertainty set is observed for finding the optimal solution. We illustrate this approach with a portfolio selection problem with uncertain expected stock returns.

Consider the following quadratic programming problem for constructing a minimum risk portfolio with its expected return above a target value $r_t \in \mathbb{R}$,

$$\min_{\omega} \frac{1}{2} \omega' \Sigma \omega$$

$$\text{s.t. } \mu' \omega \geq r_t$$

$$\omega' \iota = 1.$$

If the expected return of stocks $\mu \in \mathbb{R}^N$ is uncertain but known to exist within a set $\mathcal{U}_\mu$, the problem can be written as

$$\min_\omega \frac{1}{2}\omega' \Sigma \omega$$

$$\text{s.t. } \mu'\omega \geq r_t \text{ for all } \mu \in \mathcal{U}_\mu$$

$$\omega' \iota = 1.$$

We can immediately notice that the constraint $\mu'\omega \geq r_t$ will be satisfied for all $\mu \in \mathcal{U}_\mu$ if the minimum possible value of the expected portfolio return is greater than or equal to r_t. Therefore, we can guarantee that

$$\mu'\omega \geq r_t \text{ for all } \mu \in \mathcal{U}_\mu$$

if the constraint holds in the worst case

$$\min_{\mu \in \mathcal{U}_\mu} \mu'\omega \geq r_t.$$

Robust optimization is also known as worst-case optimization for the obvious reasons we have explained here. However, the best solution in the worst case is not always easily computed. The tractability of robust optimization problems is directly affected by how the uncertainty set is defined. We next demonstrate, using uncertainty sets that often appear in the literature, how robust counterparts can be formulated as one of the convex programs categorized in section 5.2.

Uncertainty Sets

Probably the most important component of a robust optimization problem is the uncertainty set because it represents how the uncertainty is modeled. Uncertainty sets are also what distinguishes robust optimization from other methods because many of the alternative approaches directly assume probability distributions instead of defining a set of possible values. Much focus is given to choosing the uncertainty set because it directly affects the tractability of the robust problem. Here, we introduce uncertainty sets that have been widely studied in literature. The uncertain component is represented by a vector $u \in \mathbb{R}^n$.

The simplest form of uncertainty is the *scenario uncertainty set*, defined by

$$\{u^{(1)}, \ldots, u^{(s)}\}$$

where $u^{(1)}, \ldots, u^{(s)} \in \mathbb{R}^n$ are vectors representing s scenarios. Because it can be shown that the robust formulation is unaffected by taking the convex hull of the uncertainty set, the following can also be used:

$$Conv\{u^{(1)}, \ldots, u^{(s)}\}$$

where *Conv* denotes the convex hull of a set. The scenario uncertainty set is one of the most intuitive approaches because the scenarios can be chosen from previously observed data (e.g., historically collected data) or estimated values. Despite its intuitive appeal, a major drawback is that most problems require a large number of scenarios for a realistic illustration of uncertainty, often becoming computationally impossible to solve.

An alternative to including individual scenarios is to set an interval for the possible values. The *interval uncertainty set* is defined using component-wise bounds,

$$\{u \mid |u_i - \hat{u}_i| \leq \delta_i \text{ for } i = 1, \ldots, n\}$$

where $\hat{u}_i$ is a nominal value and $\delta_i \geq 0$ sets the limit of deviation from $\hat{u}_i$. In simpler cases, the uncertainty can be written as

$$\{u \mid \|u - \hat{u}\|_\infty \leq \delta\}$$

where $\|u\|_\infty = \max(|u_1|, \ldots, |u_n|)$ and $\delta \geq 0$. Similar to scenario uncertainty sets, the intervals can be chosen from observed data or estimated bounds. Confidence intervals can also be used for setting boundaries if the probability distribution of u is assumed. The interval uncertainty is also known as *box uncertainty* because the shape of the set defined by intervals resembles a box.

Geometries other than a box are also used for expressing uncertainty. The *ball uncertainty set* is defined as

$$\{u \mid \|u - \hat{u}\|_2 \leq r\}$$

where the nominal value $\hat{u} \in \mathbb{R}^n$ is the center of the ball and $r \geq 0$ is the radius, and it can also be written as

$$\{\hat{u} + rv \mid \|v\|_2 \leq 1\}$$

for $v \in \mathbb{R}^n$. Similarly, the *ellipsoid uncertainty set* is formulated as

$$\{u \mid \|P^{-1}(u - \hat{u})\|_2 \leq \delta\} \text{ or } \{\hat{u} + Pv \mid \|v\|_2 \leq \delta\}$$

for a non-singular matrix $P \in \mathbb{R}^{n \times n}$. Ellipsoids are also expressed as

$$\{u \mid (u - \hat{u})'Q^{-1}(u - \hat{u}) \leq \delta^2\}$$

where $Q \in \mathbb{R}^{n \times n}$ is a symmetric positive definite matrix. The ball and ellipsoid uncertainty sets are relatively less conservative than the interval uncertainty set because the box contains extreme corner cases.

The *budgeted uncertainty set* is expressed as

$$\{ u \mid \|u - \widehat{u}\|_\infty \leq \delta, \ \|u - \widehat{u}\|_1 \leq \gamma \}$$

where $\|u_1\| = \sum_{i=1}^{n} |u_i|$, and it is called the budgeted uncertainty because the value of γ controls the given budget of uncertainty. Therefore, this uncertainty set models deviations in individual elements as well as the total deviation. An alternative is the *cardinality constrained uncertainty set*, which restricts the number of elements that are uncertain rather than limiting the total amount of deviation.

As we have shown here, there are many ways to define uncertainty sets when forming robust optimization problems. We have only introduced the basic models, but there are more complex approaches such as using general norms. Although there are no restrictions on forming uncertainty sets, it is critical to select one that results in a tractable robust formulation. Hence, geometries such as a box and an ellipsoid are often used for this reason. Before we present examples for constructing robust counterparts from several uncertainty sets, we summarize which uncertainty sets lead to efficiently solvable problems.

Exhibit 5.2 compiles publications on formulating robust optimization problems that focus on generic theorems on tractability.[14] Even though it does not contain an exhaustive list (e.g., trivial scenario uncertainty is excluded, as well as more complex structures), it certainly shows that robust counterparts result in more complex mathematical programs than the original uncertain problems for most uncertainty sets. For the more expressive formulations such as semidefinite programs, approximation methods are used for building tractable problems, which basically approximate the robust feasible region with a more conservative one.

Robust Linear Programming

Among many geometries, box and ellipsoidal uncertainty sets appear the most often in the academic literature because they often lead to formulations that can be efficiently solved. We demonstrate forming robust linear programs from these two uncertainty sets.

Consider the following uncertain linear program with inequality constraints:

$$\min_{x} c'x$$

$$\text{s.t. } a_i'x \leq b_i \text{ for all } a_i \in \mathcal{U}_i, \ i = 1, \ldots, m$$

$$x_i \geq 0 \text{ for } i = 1, \ldots, n$$

Exhibit 5.2   Uncertainty Sets That Form Tractable Robust Counterparts

	Uncertain Problem	Uncertainty Set	Robust Counterpart
(1)	LP	Interval, Linear Inequalities, Budgeted, Cardinality Constrained	LP
(2)	LP	Ellipsoid, Conic Quadratic Inequalities	SOCP
(3)	LP	Linear Matrix Inequalities	SDP
(4)	QCQP, SOCP	Ellipsoid	SDP
(5)	SDP	Approximate Approaches (e.g., with intervals or balls)	SDP

Publication references for each robust transformation
(1) Aharon Ben-Tal and Arkadi Nemirovski, "Robust Optimization—Methodology and Applications," *Mathematical Programming* 92, 3 (2002), pp. 453–480; Dimitris Bertsimas and Melvyn Sim, "The Price of Robustness," *Operations Research* 52, 1 (2004), pp. 35–53; Dimitris Bertsimas, Dessislava Pachamanova, and Melvyn Sim, "Robust Linear Optimization under General Norms," *Operations Research Letters* 32 (2004), pp. 510–516; and Dimitris Bertsimas, David B. Brown, and Constantine Caramanis, "Theory and Applications of Robust Optimization," *SIAM Review* 53, 3 (2011), pp. 464–501.
(2) Aharon Ben-Tal and Arkadi Nemirovski, "Robust Convex Optimization," *Mathematics of Operations Research* 23, 4 (1998), pp. 769–805; Aharon Ben-Tal and Arkadi Nemirovski, "Robust Solutions of Uncertain Linear Programs," *Operations Research Letters* 25 (1999), pp. 1–13; Ben-Tal and Nemirovski, "Robust Optimization—Methodology and Applications"; and Bertsimas, Brown, and Caramanis, "Theory and Applications of Robust Optimization."
(3) Ben-Tal and Nemirovski, "Robust Optimization—Methodology and Applications."
(4) Ben-Tal and Nemirovski, "Robust Convex Optimization"; and Bertsimas, Brown, and Caramanis, "Theory and Applications of Robust Optimization."
(5) Laurent El Ghaoui, Francois Oustry, and Hervé Lebret, "Robust Solutions to Uncertain Semidefinite Programs," *SIAM Journal on Optimization* 9, 1 (1998), pp. 33–52; and Ben-Tal and Nemirovski, "Robust Optimization— Methodology and Applications."

where $c \in \mathbb{R}^n$, $b_i \in \mathbb{R}$ are known, but uncertainty arises from $a_i \in \mathbb{R}^n$. Recall that robust formulations are constraint-wise constructions. Let us first express a_i with a box uncertainty set, which is defined by bounds such as

$$a_{0i} - \delta_i \leq a_i \leq a_{0i} + \delta_i \text{ for } i = 1, \dots, m$$

where $a_{0i} \in \mathbb{R}^n$ is a nominal value, often an estimated value of a_i, and $\delta_i \in \mathbb{R}^n$ with non-negative values limits the deviation from the nominal value. Thus, the size of the box uncertainty set can be controlled by δ_i, and the solution becomes more robust as the value of δ_i increases since the problem considers a larger set of values. For this uncertainty set, the worst case is clearly its upper bound due to the non-negativity constraint,

$$\max_{a_i \in \mathcal{U}_i} a_i' x = (a_{0i} + \delta_i)' x,$$

and the robust counterpart of the original problem remains a linear program,

$$\min_x c'x$$

$$\text{s.t. } (a_{0i} + \delta_i)'x \le b_i \text{ for } i = 1, \ldots, m$$

$$x_i \ge 0 \text{ for } i = 1, \ldots, n.$$

The same problem can also be formulated by structuring the uncertainty set $\mathcal{U}_i$ as an ellipsoid,

$$\mathcal{U}_i = \{a_{0i} + P_i v \mid \|v\|_2 \le 1\}$$

where v is a vector in $\mathbb{R}^n$, $P_i \in \mathbb{R}^{n \times n}$ is a non-singular matrix, and $a_{0i} \in \mathbb{R}^n$ is again a nominal value. If $P_i = 0$, then a_i is considered to be known with certainty. The worst case within this ellipsoid can be derived as

$$\max\{a_i'x \mid a_i \in \mathcal{U}_i\}$$

$$= \max\{(a_{0i} + P_i v)'x \mid \|v\|_2 \le 1\}$$

$$= a_{0i}'x + \max\{v'P_i'x \mid \|v\|_2 \le 1\}$$

$$= a_{0i}'x + \|P_i'x\|_2.$$

The last inequality holds from the Cauchy-Schwarz inequality,

$$|v'P_i'x| \le \|v\|_2 \|P_i'x\|_2.$$

Then, the robust formulation with an ellipsoidal uncertainty set becomes

$$\min_x c'x$$

$$\text{s.t. } a_{0i}'x + \|P_i'x\|_2 \le b_i \text{ for } i = 1, \ldots, m$$

which is a second-order cone program; therefore, efficient algorithms exist for solving the problem. As presented here, an optimization problem with uncertain components can be formulated in more than one way depending on the geometry of the uncertainty set. Furthermore, the resulting robust problem may vary greatly, which emphasizes the importance of structuring uncertainty sets that lead to computationally tractable forms.

Portfolio selection problems that are generally expressed as quadratic programs are special cases where robust counterparts become convex conic programs, even with relatively simple uncertainty sets. We discuss these models in detail in the next chapter.

5.4   INTERIOR POINT METHODS

Before exploring applications in portfolio optimization, we explain how to solve robust optimization problems. Since robust counterparts can be formulated as conic programming problems such as second-order cone programming or semidefinite programming, algorithms for finding optimal solutions to conic programs can be used for computing robust solutions. In practice, robust problems will almost always be solved using optimization software packages such as MATLAB, but we will illustrate the basic ideas because solvers included in software packages are also based on these algorithms.

Unconstrained optimization problems and problems with only equality constraints can be easily solved from iterative methods that search for a feasible descent direction in each step to find a sequence of solutions that eventually leads to the optimal point (i.e., an iterative algorithm begins with a starting point x_0 and makes improvements each step). A classic example is Newton's method, which replaces the objective function with its second-order Taylor approximation to solve a quadratic problem instead for finding the best descent direction. The same techniques cannot be directly applied to inequality constrained problems because the descent directions are likely no longer feasible for the additional inequality constraints.[15]

For inequality constrained optimization problems, the basic idea is to replace the inequality constraints with additional terms in the objective function that force the problem to have similar feasible regions. Consider a problem written as in (5.8), where the feasible set X is defined by equality and inequality constraints:

$$\min_x f(x)$$
$$\text{s.t.} \ \ x \in X. \tag{5.8}$$

We can reformulate the problem by replacing the constraint with a penalty term in the objective function,

$$\min_x \ f(x) + c\, P(x)$$

where $c > 0$ and $P(x) > 0$, unless when $x \in X$, in which case $P(x) = 0$. The new objective function penalizes the objective value when $x \notin X$ while penalizing less as x moves closer to the boundary of the set X. Whereas this formulation allows values of x outside the original feasible set X and forces x to move closer to the feasible region, an alternative would be to only allow values of x inside the original feasible set X and make sure it does not leave the feasible region. This latter method is an example of *interior point methods* known as the *barrier method*. If we define a barrier function $B(x)$ that is continuous, and $B(x) \to \infty$ as x approaches the boundary of X, then the minimization problem (5.8) can be written as:

$$\min_{x} f(x) + \frac{1}{t} B(x)$$

$$\text{s.t.} \quad x \in \text{int } X$$

where $t > 0$ and int X denotes the interior of X.

We now further illustrate how barrier functions can help solve constrained problems by looking at convex optimization problems in standard form:

$$\min_{x} f(x)$$

$$\text{s.t.} \quad g_i(x) \le 0 \text{ for } i = 1, \dots, m$$

$$Ax = b.$$

One of the most utilized approaches is the logarithmic barrier function (or simply the log barrier function):

$$\phi(x) = -\sum_{i=1}^{m} \log(-g_i(x)).$$

The domain of the logarithmic barrier function is the set of values of x that strictly satisfy the inequalities of the standard form, $g_i(x) < 0$. Moreover, $\phi(x) \to \infty$ as $g_i(x)$ approaches zero from the left. Therefore, the original problem can be approximated by

$$\min_{x} f(x) + \frac{1}{t} \left(-\sum_{i=1}^{m} \log\left(-g_i(x)\right) \right) \qquad (5.9)$$

$$\text{s.t.} \quad Ax = b$$

where $t > 0$. Note that the problem is still convex because the objective function is a convex function (which can be easily checked using the second-order condition of convexity). By increasing the value of t, the new formulation will better approximate the original feasible region; but, at a cost because it will be difficult to solve using quadratic approximations, as in Newton's method when the logarithmic barrier function is too close to the boundary of the feasible region.

Since we now formulated the problem shown in (5.9) with only linear constraints, it seems we should be able to find the optimal solution by properly setting the parameter t. Unfortunately, directly solving a problem formulated as (5.9) does not work well in practice. However, it is found that an iterative approach efficiently finds the optimal solution. In this method, the optimal value of x found at each iteration is used as the starting point for the following iteration, and the value of t is also increased after each iteration. The sequence of points x_t for each t is known as the central path, which eventually leads to the optimal solution as t is increased. In other words, x moves in the direction of the optimal solution while the approximation of the barrier function improves every iteration. At each iteration, algorithms such as Newton's method can be used to find the optimal value of x_t. The stopping criterion of the barrier method can be set to $m/t < \varepsilon$ for a tolerance level of ε because duality shows that x_t can only be m/t-suboptimal. This also indicates that the optimal solution will be reached by increasing the value of t.

We have learned that most robust optimization problems are formulated as conic optimizations, so the inequality constraints will be expressed in terms of cones. The barrier method can be applied to conic problems by introducing a generalized logarithm for proper cones. A function $\psi(x)$ is a generalized logarithm for a proper cone K if $\psi(x)$ is concave, closed, twice continuously differentiable, and $\nabla^2\psi(x) \prec 0$ for $x \in \text{int } K$ with its domain as the interior of K; and there exists $\theta > 0$ such that for all $x \in K$ and $s > 0$,

$$\psi(sx) = \psi(x) + \theta \log(s).$$

Based on this definition, the non-negativity constraint on x can be expressed by the following generalized logarithm:

$$\psi(x) = \sum_{i=1}^{n} \log(x_i).$$

Furthermore, a generalized logarithm for the second-order cone, expressed as

$$\left\{ x \in \mathbb{R}^n \;\middle|\; \sqrt{\sum_{i=1}^{n-1} x_i^2} \leq x_n \right\}$$

becomes

$$\psi(x) = \log\left(x_n^2 - \sum_{i=1}^{n-1} x_i^2 \right),$$

and the logarithmic barrier function for the second-order cone programming problem given by (5.4) is

$$\phi(x) = -\sum_{i=1}^{m} \log((c_i'x + d_i)^2 - \|A_ix + b_i\|_2^2).$$

Similarly, a generalized logarithm for a positive semidefinite cone X can be defined as

$$\psi(X) = \log(\det X),$$

and the corresponding barrier function for the semidefinite programming problem (5.5) is

$$\phi(x) = -\log(\det(F_0 + x_1F_1 + \cdots + x_nF_n)).$$

With these barrier functions for cones, we can find the optimal solution of robust problems formulated as second-order cone programming or semidefinite programming by iteratively solving the following problem for tracing the central path of x,

$$\min_{x} f(x) + \frac{1}{t}\phi(x)$$
$$\text{s.t. } Ax = b$$

where the parameter value of t is increased each iteration, and the optimal point for a given t is computed using the optimal x from the previous iteration as the starting point.

Another method for computing robust solutions is the *primal-dual interior point method*, which is actually known to have better performance for problems in second-order cones and semidefinite cones compared to barrier methods. Barrier methods trace the central path for the primal variable by optimizing for x_t while increasing the value of t. Primal-dual interior point methods, on the other hand, find the primal and dual central paths together, which is where the advantage in performance comes from.

Finally, we illustrate how the interior-point method can be used for solving optimization problems in MATLAB. The *fmincon* function explained in Box 5.3 is a method for solving constrained nonlinear programming problems. Thus, the convex optimization problems mentioned in this chapter can be solved using the *fmincon* function, and the optimization algorithm is set to interior-point method by default.[16]

Box 5.3 MATLAB FUNCTION FOR SOLVING CONSTRAINED NONLINEAR PROGRAMMING

Function: *fmincon*

Syntax: x = fmincon(fun, x0, A, b)

            x = fmincon(fun, x0, A, b, Aeq, beq)

            x = fmincon(fun, x0, A, b, Aeq, beq, lb, ub)

Details: Solve the following constrained nonlinear programming problem

$$\min_x f(x)$$

$$\text{s.t. } A \cdot x \leq b$$

$$Aeq \cdot x = beq$$

$$lb \leq x \leq ub.$$

Suppose x is a vector of length n ($x \in \mathbb{R}^n$), then

$$A \in \mathbb{R}^{m \times n}, \; b \in \mathbb{R}^m, \; Aeq \in \mathbb{R}^{k \times n}, \; beq \in \mathbb{R}^k,$$

$$lb \in \mathbb{R}^n, \; ub \in \mathbb{R}^n$$

where m is the number of inequality constraints, and k is the number of equality constraints.

The first input *fun* is the function to be minimized, which accepts the vector $x \in \mathbb{R}^n$ and returns a scalar, and the algorithms starts at $x_0 \in \mathbb{R}^n$ for finding the optimal solution.

Additional arguments of the *fmincon* function include setting the algorithm and further options for the chosen algorithm.

KEY POINTS

■ The optimal choice for an uncertainty-averse decision maker can be explained by observing the worst case.

■ Mathematical programs with convex objective and constraint functions are known as convex optimization.

- Convex optimization is important because a local optimum of a convex problem is guaranteed to be globally optimal as well.
- Dual problems are valuable for convex optimization because strong duality argues that a convex problem and its dual have the same optimal value under minor conditions.
- Linear programming is the simplest form of convex optimization where the objective and constraints are linear functions, and it is efficiently solved because the feasible set is a polyhedron.
- The classical mean-variance model for portfolio selection is written as a quadratic program, and it is convex because the covariance matrix of stock returns is positive semidefinite.
- Most convex optimization problems can be expressed as conic programming, and the two formulations that often arise in portfolio selection are second-order cone programming and semidefinite programming.
- Formulations that incorporate uncertainty sets are called robust counterparts of the original uncertain problems, and they solve the problem by optimizing the worst case.
- Structuring the uncertainty set is extremely important in robust optimization because it determines how the robust counterpart is formulated and also its tractability, and the most applied uncertainty sets include scenarios, intervals, balls, and ellipsoids.
- Interior point methods are adopted for solving equality and inequality constrained optimization problems. Logarithmic barrier functions are frequently used to eliminate inequality constraints, and the solution of the resulting problem is found through iterative methods.

NOTES

1. Minimizing the maximum risk is discussed among others in Abraham Wald, "Statistical Decision Functions Which Minimize the Maximum Risk," *Annals of Mathematics* 46, 2 (1945), pp. 265–280; and the Ellsberg example is explained as maximizing the minimum utility in Itzhak Gilboa and David Schmeidler, "Maxmin Expected Utility with Non-unique Prior," *Journal of Mathematical Economics* 18 (1989), pp. 141–153.
2. The theory and application of convex optimization, including the optimization problems introduced in this chapter, are comprehensively discussed in Stephen Boyd and Lieven Vandenberghe, *Convex Optimization* (Cambridge University Press, 2004).
3. This section on duality can be regarded as a summary of the key points whereas a thoroughly description is included in Boyd and Vandenberghe, *Convex Optimization*, pp. 215–271.
4. An introduction to linear programming along with examples and algorithms, is included in Dimitris Bertsimas and John N. Tsitsiklis, *Introduction to Linear*

Optimization (Belmont, MA: Athena Scientific, 1997); and David G. Luenberger and Yinyu Ye, *Linear and Nonlinear Programming* (New York: Springer, 2008).

5. The full detail of the *linprog* function can be found in http://www.mathworks.com/help/optim/ug/linprog.html and setting options are explained in http://www.mathworks.com/help/optim/ug/optimoptions.html

6. A real symmetric matrix Q is positive semidefinite if $x'Qx \geq 0$ for all $x \in \mathbb{R}^n$ and positive definite if $x'Qx > 0$ for all $x \in \mathbb{R}^n$ where $x \neq 0$.

7. The first-order optimality condition states that if a convex function f is differential and $\nabla f(x) = 0$ for a given x in the domain of f, then x is the optimal solution.

8. The full detail of the *quadprog* function can be found in http://www.mathworks.com/help/optim/ug/quadprog.html

9. Conic programming is explained in much more detail in Arkadi Nemirovski, "Advances in Convex Optimization: Conic Programming," *Proceedings of the International Congress of Mathematicians: Madrid, August 22-30, 2006* (2006), pp. 413–444.

10. The constraint of the form $Ax - b \in K$ is more often written as $Ax - b \succeq_K 0$ or $Ax \succeq_K b$ with inequality constraints, but we will skip the discussion of generalized inequalities.

11. The basic theory of second-order cone programming along with its applications and algorithms are covered in Miguel S. Lobo, Lieven Vandenberghe, Stephen Boyd, and Hervé Lebret, "Applications of Second-Order Cone Programming," *Linear Algebra and its Applications* 284, 1 (1998), pp. 193-228; and Farid Alizadeh and Donald Goldfarb, "Second-Order Cone Programming," *Mathematical Programming* 95, 1 (2003), pp. 3–51.

12. Portfolio optimization with loss risk constraints appears in Boyd and Vandenberghe, *Convex Optimization*, pp. 158–159. In some cases, the loss risk constraint is written as $\Pr(-r_p \geq \alpha_{loss}) \leq \beta$ where α_{loss} is the threshold in the amount of portfolio loss.

13. A survey on the theory and application of semidefinite programming is given in Lieven Vandenberghe and Stephen Boyd, "Semidefinite Programming," *SIAM Review* 38, 1 (1996), pp. 49–95.

14. The ideas from the publications listed in Exhibit 5.2 along with approximation methods are thoroughly presented by Aharon Ben-Tal, Laurent El Ghaoui, and Arkadi Nemirovski, *Robust Optimization* (Princeton University Press, 2009).

15. Algorithms for unconstrained and equality constrained as well as inequality constrained problems are thoroughly explained in Boyd and Vandenberghe, *Convex Optimization*, pp. 457–630. Solving constrained problems is also covered in Luenberger and Ye, *Linear and Nonlinear Programming*, pp. 359–505. These two books also describe the primal-dual interior point method mentioned at the end of this section.

16. Examples using the *fmincon* function are included in the next chapter where we implement robust optimization formulations in MATLAB. Details about the *fmincon* function can be found in http://www.mathworks.com/help/optim/ug/fmincon.html

CHAPTER 6

Robust Portfolio Construction

In this chapter, the construction of mean-variance and robust portfolios using optimization tools is explained. For robust portfolios, robust optimization formulations with an uncertainty set on the expected returns are covered. The use of optimization tools is important because when the number of candidate stocks is large, even the construction of mean-variance portfolios is difficult to formulate without these tools.

Our objectives in this chapter are to:

- Solve the classical mean-variance problem using MATLAB
- Formulate robust counterparts as min-max problems with box and ellipsoidal uncertainty sets for the expected return of stocks
- Explain how to construct box and ellipsoidal uncertainty sets
- Demonstrate how to reformulate robust problems in min-max form into minimization convex optimization problems
- Solve robust portfolio optimization problems using MATLAB
- Demonstrate the use of a MATLAB-based modeling system (CVX) for solving convex problems

6.1 SOME PRELIMINARIES

At this point in the book, the mean-variance model, its shortcomings, and methods to improve the classical model including a general idea of robust portfolio optimization have been explained. We now advance one step further and explain how robust portfolios can be computed using optimization tools. As shown in the previous chapter, most robust formulations cannot be solved in closed form and therefore require utilizing solvers in software tools. By the end of this chapter, the reader will be able to build robust portfolios using stock return data. We will continue to use MATLAB as our choice of tool and also describe solving portfolio problems using CVX, a MATLAB-based modeling system for convex optimization.[1] To familiarize ourselves with these tools, we will begin by tackling the classical mean-variance problem. We finally note that MATLAB contains Financial Toolbox, which includes many classes and functions for constructing

Markowitz mean-variance portfolios. However, we demonstrate the use of generic optimization functions even for mean-variance portfolios because robust counterparts are not solved by the Financial Toolbox.

6.2   MEAN-VARIANCE PORTFOLIOS

In contrast to most robust optimization formulations, the optimal portfolio for the Markowitz problem can be also expressed analytically. However, optimization tools are essential when there are a large number of candidate stocks and especially when plotting the efficient frontier for viewing a set of efficient portfolios.

The Markowitz model expressed as a trade-off between risk and return is written as

$$\min_{\omega} \ \omega' \Sigma \omega - \lambda \mu' \omega$$
$$\text{s.t.} \ \ \omega' \iota = 1 \tag{6.1}$$

where

$\mu \in \mathbb{R}^N$ is the expected returns

$\Sigma \in \mathbb{R}^{N \times N}$ is the covariance matrix

$\omega \in \mathbb{R}^N$ is the portfolio weights

$\iota \in \mathbb{R}^N$ is a vector of ones

$N \in \mathbb{N}$ is the number of stocks

$\lambda \in \mathbb{R}$ is the risk-seeking coefficient.

In many cases, λ is attached to the risk term, where it becomes a coefficient representing risk aversion. The main reason we attach the risk coefficient to the return term is that by setting the value of λ to zero, the problem (6.1) finds the global minimum-variance (GMV) portfolio. Recall from Chapter 5 that this is a convex quadratic problem. The exact solution of the optimal portfolio can be found mathematically using the following steps.

Form the Lagrangian of (6.1):

$$L(\omega, \gamma) = \omega' \Sigma \omega - \lambda \mu' \omega - \gamma(\omega' \iota - 1).$$

Take the derivative of the Lagrangian with respect to ω and γ:

$$\frac{\partial L}{\partial \omega} = 2\Sigma \omega - \lambda \mu - \gamma \iota$$

$$\frac{\partial L}{\partial \gamma} = \omega' \iota - 1.$$

Set these equations to zero and solve for the optimal portfolio ω^*:

$$2\Sigma\omega - \lambda\mu - \gamma\iota = 0 \tag{6.2}$$

$$\omega'\iota - 1 = 0. \tag{6.3}$$

From (6.2), we get

$$\omega^* = \frac{1}{2}\Sigma^{-1}(\lambda\mu + \gamma\iota)$$

and by plugging this into (6.3),

$$\lambda\iota'\Sigma^{-1}\mu + \gamma\iota'\Sigma^{-1}\iota = 2$$

$$\gamma = \frac{2 - \lambda\iota'\Sigma^{-1}\mu}{\iota'\Sigma^{-1}\iota}.$$

Then the optimal portfolio becomes

$$\omega^* = \frac{\lambda}{2}\Sigma^{-1}\mu + \frac{1 - \frac{\lambda}{2}\iota'\Sigma^{-1}\mu}{\iota'\Sigma^{-1}\iota}\Sigma^{-1}\iota. \tag{6.4}$$

It now becomes more obvious that solving this without a computer tool can become extremely challenging.

Since an equation for the optimal portfolio is given by (6.4), one approach is to use MATLAB to solve (6.1) by using (6.4) without having to consider solvers for mathematical programs. A function that directly solves the equation given by (6.4) is presented in Box 6.1. For multiplications involving the inverse of matrices, MATLAB advises using $A\backslash b$ for computing $A^{-1}b$ and b'/A for $b'A^{-1}$, when $A \in \mathbb{R}^{n\times n}$ and $b \in \mathbb{R}^n$, to enhance computational speed and accuracy.

A more conventional way for solving this problem in MATLAB is to use the function *quadprog*, which is included in the package for solving quadratic programming problems. Exploiting the inherent functions becomes increasingly important when the optimal portfolio cannot be expressed in closed form. The problem given by (6.1) is solved as shown in Box 6.2 by properly setting the arguments for the *quadprog* function.

Additional constraints on portfolio weights can be easily added to the function. For example, the body of the function can be modified as shown in Box 6.3 if an investor needs to restrict short-selling and also desires to limit allocating more than 50% of wealth in any single stock.

Another approach for solving more general optimization problems in MATLAB is to use the function *fmincon*. This function requires the user to provide the objective function that is minimized, and quadratic programs

Box 6.1 FUNCTION THAT SOLVES THE MEAN-VARIANCE PROBLEM USING ITS CLOSED-FORM SOLUTION

```
% ===============================================================
% portfolioclosedform.m
%
% Find the optimal mean-variance portfolio using its closed-form
% solution
%
% Input:
%   returns: matrix of stock returns (each column represents
%            a single stock)
%   lambda: value of the risk-seeking coefficient
% Output:
%   optPortfolio: optimal mean-variance portfolio (a column
%                 vector)
% ===============================================================
function optPortfolio = portfolioclosedform( returns, lambda )

    mu = mean(returns)';
    sigma = cov(returns);

    n = length(mu);
    oneVector = ones(n,1);

    optPortfolio = ((lambda/2) * (sigma \ mu)) ...
        + ((1 - (lambda/2) * (oneVector'/sigma) * mu) ...
        / ((oneVector'/sigma) * oneVector)) ...
        * (sigma \ oneVector);
end
```

can be formulated by giving a convex quadratic objective function. The portfolio problem given by (6.1) becomes what is shown in Box 6.4 where the objective function is defined as a nested function. In Box 6.4, we specify *fmincon* to use the interior-point method. Even though they are skipped in these examples, additional optimization options should be used for increasing accuracy and performance.

Finally, another extremely helpful tool for solving convex programs is CVX, which is implemented in MATLAB. The strengths of CVX include its efficient solvers and its very intuitive syntax. Readers familiar with MATLAB will be able to easily pick up using CVX. The Markowitz problem we have been considering is simply written in CVX, as shown in Box 6.5. The coding style of CVX is clearly more straightforward when compared to inherent

Box 6.2 FUNCTION THAT SOLVES THE MEAN-VARIANCE PROBLEM USING *QUADPROG*

```
% ================================================================
% portfolioquadprog.m
%
% Find the optimal mean-variance portfolio using "quadprog"
%
% Input:
%   returns: matrix of stock returns (each column represents
%            a single stock)
%   lambda: value of the risk-seeking coefficient
% Output:
%   optPortfolio: optimal mean-variance portfolio (a column
%                 vector)
% ================================================================
function optPortfolio =  portfolioquadprog( returns, lambda )

    mu = mean(returns)';
    sigma = cov(returns);

    n = length(mu);
    Aeq = ones(1,n);
    beq = 1;

    optPortfolio = quadprog(2 * sigma, -lambda * mu', [], [], ...
       Aeq, beq);
end
```

Box 6.3 SETTING UPPER AND LOWER BOUNDS ON PORTFOLIO WEIGHTS USING *QUADPROG*

```
n = length(mu);
Aeq = ones(1,n);
beq = 1;
lb = zeros(n,1);       % Lower bound of portfolio weight
ub = 0.5 * ones(n,1);  % Upper bound of portfolio weight

optPortfolio = quadprog(2 * sigma, -lambda * mu', [], [], ...
   Aeq, beq, lb, ub);
```

Box 6.4 FUNCTION THAT SOLVES THE MEAN-VARIANCE PROBLEM USING *FMINCON*

```
% =================================================================
% portfoliofmincon.m
%
% Find the optimal mean-variance portfolio using "fmincon"
%
% Input:
%    returns: matrix of stock returns (each column represents
%             a single stock)
%    lambda: value of the risk-seeking coefficient
% Output:
%    optPortfolio: optimal mean-variance portfolio (a column
%                  vector)
% =================================================================
function optPortfolio = portfoliofmincon( returns, lambda )

    mu = mean(returns)';
    sigma = cov(returns);

    n = length(mu);
    Aeq = ones(1,n);
    beq = 1;

    % Nested function which is used as the objective function
    function objValue = objfunction(x)
        objValue = x' * sigma * x - lambda * mu' * x;
    end

    % Use the equal-weighted portfolio as the starting point
    x0 = ones(n,1) / n;

    % Set the algorithm to interior-point method
    options = optimset('Algorithm', 'interior-point');

    optPortfolio = fmincon(@objfunction, x0, [], [], Aeq, beq,...
        [], [], [], options);
end
```

functions of MATLAB. Similar to using *quadprog* and *fmincon*, advanced solver settings can be used to control the precision of CVX.

Another important portfolio problem is to find the portfolio with the maximum Sharpe ratio, which is the expected excess return per unit of risk over the risk-free rate. The problem of constructing the portfolio with

Box 6.5 FUNCTION THAT SOLVES THE MEAN-VARIANCE PROBLEM USING CVX

```
% ================================================================
% portfoliocvx.m
%
% Find the optimal mean-variance portfolio using CVX
%
% Input:
%   returns: matrix of stock returns (each column represents
%            a single stock)
%   lambda: value of the risk-seeking coefficient
% Output:
%   optPortfolio: optimal mean-variance portfolio (a column
%                 vector)
% ================================================================
function optPortfolio =  portfoliocvx( returns, lambda )

    mu = mean(returns)';
    sigma = cov(returns);

    n = length(mu);

    % Use CVX for solving the mean-variance problem
    cvx_begin
        variable w(n)
        minimize ( w' * sigma * w - lambda * mu' * w )
        subject to
            ones(1,n) * w == 1
    cvx_end

    optPortfolio = w;
end
```

maximum Sharpe ratio is

$$\max_{\omega} \frac{\mu'\omega - r_f}{\sqrt{\omega'\Sigma\omega}}$$
$$\text{s.t. } \omega'\iota = 1$$

where r_f is the risk-free rate. This problem can also be written as

$$\max_{\omega} \frac{(\mu - r_f\iota)'\omega}{\sqrt{\omega'\Sigma\omega}}$$
$$\text{s.t. } \omega'\iota = 1,$$

which clearly shows the use of expected excess return (the excess return can also be represented by $\mu - r_f$ where $r_f \in \mathbb{R}^N$).

The portfolio with the maximum Sharpe ratio is the portfolio on the efficient frontier that has the maximum slope when connected with the risk-free rate. Graphically, it is the portfolio at the upper-left point of the efficient frontier. Thus, drawing the efficient frontier is one method for finding the portfolio with the maximum Sharpe ratio. The portfolios on the efficient frontier are found by plotting the optimal portfolios of (6.5) for various levels of expected portfolio return r_p,

$$\min_{\omega} \omega' \Sigma \omega$$

$$\text{s.t.} \quad \mu'\omega = r_p \qquad\qquad (6.5)$$

$$\omega'\iota = 1.$$

Box 6.6 FUNCTION THAT PLOTS THE EFFICIENT FRONTIER AND FINDS THAT PORTFOLIO WITH MAXIMUM SHARPE RATIO

```
% ================================================================
% maxsharperatio.m
%
% Plot the efficient frontier and find the portfolio with
% maximum Sharpe ratio (no-shorting constraints are imposed)
%
% Input:
%    returns: matrix of stock returns (each column represents
%             a single stock)
%    riskFreeRates: risk-free rate represented as a vector
%             (same number of rows as the matrix 'returns')
%    numPortfolios: number of efficient portfolios to plot
%             between the minimum-variance
%             portfolio and the max-return portfolio
% Output:
%    optPortfolio: optimal mean-variance portfolio (a column
%             vector)
% ================================================================
function optPortfolio = maxsharperatio( returns, ...
    riskFreeRates, numPortfolios )

    DAYS_IN_YEAR = 252;
```

```
n = size(returns,2);
% Expected  excess return
mu = mean(returns - riskFreeRates*ones(1,n))';
sigma = cov(returns);

Aeq = ones(1,n);
beq = 1;
lb = zeros(n,1);

% Find the GMV portfolio and its expected return
gmv = quadprog(sigma, [], [], [], Aeq, beq, lb, []);
gmvReturn = mu' * gmv;

% Portfolio results will be saved here
portfolios = zeros(n, numPortfolios);

% Compute the optimal portfolio for various levels of return
returnLevels = linspace(gmvReturn, max(mu), numPortfolios);
for iPortfolio = 1:numPortfolios
    Aeq = [ones(1,n); mu'];
    beq = [1; returnLevels(iPortfolio)];
    optPortfolio = quadprog(sigma, [], [], [], Aeq, beq, ...
                   lb, []);

    % Save the optimal portfolio for this iteration
    portfolios(:,iPortfolio) = optPortfolio;
end

% Compute portfolio expected return and standard deviation
portfolioReturns = mu' * portfolios;
portfolioVols = diag(sqrt(portfolios' * sigma *portfolios))';

% Plot the annualized values
plot(sqrt(DAYS_IN_YEAR) * portfolioVols, ...
    DAYS_IN_YEAR * portfolioReturns, '*-');

% Find the portfolio with maximum Sharpe ratio
[~,maxIndex] = max(portfolioReturns ./ portfolioVols);
optPortfolio = portfolios(:,maxIndex);
end
```

In Box 6.6, we present a MATLAB function that finds portfolios on the efficient frontier with no-shorting constraints, plots the resulting efficient frontier, and selects the portfolio with maximum Sharpe ratio based on the efficient portfolios. Plotting more points on the efficient frontier will provide a more accurate portfolio with maximum Sharpe ratio.

6.3 CONSTRUCTING ROBUST PORTFOLIOS

In Chapter 5, it was shown that one way to find a robust optimal solution is to find the optimal solution that satisfies the constraints for all realizations of the uncertainty set. But this is unrealistic when the uncertainty set contains infinitely many values. We also discussed an alternative approach that optimizes the worst case because if a solution satisfies a constraint for its worst case, it will surely meet the constraint for other cases. For the portfolio problem with uncertain expected return of stocks given by (6.1), the robust counterpart is written as

$$\min_{\omega} \max_{\mu \in \mathcal{U}_{\mu}} \; \omega' \Sigma \omega - \lambda \mu' \omega$$
$$\text{s.t. } \omega' \iota = 1 \tag{6.5}$$

where $\mathcal{U}_{\mu}$ is the uncertainty set for μ.

We summarize solving these types of robust problems using optimization tools into the following three steps:

1. Formulate a robust optimization problem by defining an uncertainty set.
2. Reformulate the robust counterpart into standard convex optimization form.
3. Use optimization tools to solve the reformulated robust problem.

When defining an uncertainty set in the first step, there may be extra parameters that control the variability or the size of the set. Deciding on how to compute these parameters should be completed in the first step as well. Since most optimization tools do not directly solve complex min-max problems as shown in (6.5), we must reformulate the problem as a standard convex program.[2]

In this chapter, we discuss robust formulations that only consider uncertainty in the expected returns of stocks. One reason we begin with uncertainty sets for the expected returns is because the expected return vector contains fewer values to estimate than the covariance matrix, and the robust formulations for the uncertain expected returns normally result in simpler optimization problems. But more importantly, estimation errors in expected returns are much more important for portfolios to achieve robust performance.[3]

6.4   ROBUST PORTFOLIOS WITH BOX UNCERTAINTY

Step 1. Formulate the Robust Problem by Defining the Box Uncertainty Set

The box or interval uncertainty set for the expected return is defined as

$$\{\mu \mid |\mu_i - \widehat{\mu}_i| \leq \delta_i \text{ for } i = 1,\ldots,N\} \tag{6.6}$$

where $\widehat{\mu} \in \mathbb{R}^N$ is an estimate for the expected return, and the range of the interval is decided by the values of $\delta \in \mathbb{R}^N$. Hence, the robust formulation can be initially written as

$$\min_{\omega} \max_{\mu \in \{\mu \mid |\mu_i - \widehat{\mu}_i| \leq \delta_i \text{ for } i=1,\ldots,N\}} \omega' \Sigma \omega - \lambda \mu' \omega$$
$$\text{s.t. } \omega' \iota = 1. \tag{6.7}$$

Since each element of δ controls the expected return of a single stock, its value should be computed individually for each stock. There are many ways for deciding the value of δ, and there is no one dominant method that one should always follow. A simple method is to choose the variability δ_i from the estimate $\widehat{\mu}_i$ by finding the historical maximum distance of return from $\widehat{\mu}_i$ for stock i. More commonly, the distribution of returns for a stock from historical returns is modeled, and the confidence interval of the mean decides the interval for the expected return. For example, if the stock returns are assumed to follow a normal distribution or through the central limit theorem by assuming independent and identically distributed samples, the confidence interval for the mean is computed by

$$\left(\widehat{\mu} - \frac{z_{\alpha/2}\sigma}{\sqrt{T}}, \ \widehat{\mu} + \frac{z_{\alpha/2}\sigma}{\sqrt{T}} \right)$$

where T is the sample size, and $z_{\alpha/2}$ is the standard normal critical point for representing $1 - \alpha$ confidence level. Of course, both approaches do not necessarily require data for historical returns; information from simulation can be used, or confident investors can follow their estimations for defining the intervals. Finally, the estimated expected return $\widehat{\mu}$ is also determined with much freedom. The most common approach is to use the arithmetic mean of returns, which also coincides with the use of confidence intervals of the mean for setting the value of δ.

Step 2. Reformulate the Robust Counterpart with Box Uncertainty

As mentioned earlier, even though we have constructed a robust formulation with box uncertainty set as shown in equation (6.7), the min-max formulation is not suitable for many optimization solvers. Let us look into the worst case of a single stock because the box uncertainty set is a stock-wise construction. For stock i, the range of possible returns based on the uncertainty set of equation (6.6) is

$$\hat{\mu}_i - \delta_i \leq \mu_i \leq \hat{\mu}_i + \delta_i.$$

If weight ω_i is allocated to stock i, then the worst return from this investment becomes

$$\begin{cases} \left(\hat{\mu}_i - \delta_i\right)\omega_i & \text{if } \omega_i > 0 \\ 0 & \text{if } \omega_i = 0 \\ (\hat{\mu}_i + \delta_i)\omega_i & \text{if } \omega_i < 0. \end{cases}$$

If stock i is given positive weight, the worst return is realized when stock i has the lowest possible return. On the other hand, if negative weight (short-selling) is given to stock i, the worst performance is obtained when the stock has the highest possible return within the set. The previous three cases are equivalent to the following:

$$\begin{cases} \hat{\mu}_i\omega_i - \delta_i\omega_i \text{ if } \omega_i > 0 \\ \hat{\mu}_i\omega_i + \delta_i\omega_i \text{ otherwise;} \end{cases}$$

and the expression for the worst return can be further summarized as

$$\hat{\mu}_i\omega_i - \delta_i|\omega_i|.$$

Therefore, the robust counterpart from the first step given by equation (6.7) is reformulated as

$$\min_{\omega} \omega'\Sigma\omega - \lambda(\hat{\mu}'\omega - \delta'|\omega|)$$
$$\text{s.t. } \omega'\iota = 1. \tag{6.8}$$

So far, we have transformed the min-max problem into a minimization problem. But some functions in optimization tools may limit the use of absolute values in the objective function. Therefore, the explicit use of absolute values needs to be further revised. By introducing a new variable $\psi \in \mathbb{R}^N$, the problem given by (6.8) becomes

$$\min_{\omega,\psi} \omega' \Sigma \omega - \lambda(\hat{\mu}'\omega - \delta'\psi)$$

$$\text{s.t.} \quad \omega'\iota = 1$$

$$\psi \geq \omega, \ \psi \geq -\omega.$$

Dividing the weight vector ω into its positive component $\omega_+ \in \mathbb{R}^N$ and negative component $\omega_- \in \mathbb{R}^N$, where both vectors are represented as non-negative values, results in another formulation:

$$\min_{\omega,\omega_+,\omega_-} \omega' \Sigma \omega - \lambda(\hat{\mu}'\omega - \delta'(\omega_+ + \omega_-))$$

$$\text{s.t.} \quad \omega'\iota = 1 \tag{6.9}$$

$$\omega = \omega_+ - \omega_-$$

$$\omega_+ \geq 0, \ \omega_- \geq 0.$$

The problem formulated as (6.9) may seem more complex because it contains three variables. Nonetheless, it can be expressed as a problem with a single variable of length $2N$ and proper transformation matrices.

- Instead of ω, introduce $x \in \mathbb{R}^{2N}$ where the first N elements represent the positive components of ω, and the second N elements represent the negative components of ω (hence, all values of x are non-negative).
- Define two transformation matrices $T \in \mathbb{R}^{N \times 2N}$ and $T_{abs} \in \mathbb{R}^{N \times 2N}$

$$T = \begin{bmatrix} 1 & & 0 & -1 & & 0 \\ & \ddots & & & \ddots & \\ 0 & & 1 & 0 & & -1 \end{bmatrix} = \begin{bmatrix} I & -I \end{bmatrix}$$

$$T_{abs} = \begin{bmatrix} 1 & & 0 & 1 & & 0 \\ & \ddots & & & \ddots & \\ 0 & & 1 & 0 & & 1 \end{bmatrix} = \begin{bmatrix} I & I \end{bmatrix}.$$

- Weight vectors ω and $|\omega|$ are expressed using T and T_{abs} as

$$\omega = Tx \text{ and } |\omega| = T_{abs}x.$$

Since portfolio weight ω and its absolute value can be expressed in terms of x, it becomes obvious that the objective function of the problem given by

(6.9) is the same as

$$x'T'\Sigma Tx - \lambda(\mu'Tx - \delta'T_{abs}x),$$

and the complete robust counterpart is written as

$$\min_x x'T'\Sigma Tx - \lambda(\hat{\mu}'T - \delta'T_{abs})x$$

$$\text{s.t. } x'T'\iota = 1 \qquad\qquad (6.10)$$

$$x \geq 0$$

where the optimal portfolio is computed by $\omega^* = Tx^*$ for the optimal solution x^* of (6.10). This revised objective function has the exact same format as the original mean-variance portfolio problem. For $\Sigma_T = T'\Sigma T$ and $\hat{\mu}_T = \hat{\mu}'T - \delta'T_{abs}$, we get

$$x'T'\Sigma Tx - \lambda(\hat{\mu}'Tx - \delta'T_{abs}x) = x'\Sigma_T x - \lambda\mu_T'x,$$

which clearly demonstrates how the robust version can be solved similarly to the original quadratic program with revised input values. We exploit this fact when writing MATLAB functions to solve the robust problem with box uncertainty set on expected returns.

Step 3. Use Optimization Tools to Solve the Box Uncertainty Problem

The robust portfolio optimization problem as written in (6.10) is a quadratic program. Thus, the problem is first programmed by using the *quadprog* function in MATLAB (see Box 6.7). In the functions presented in Box 6.7, the value of δ is calculated from the confidence interval of the mean of a normal distribution. Even though, conventionally, the critical point for a two-sided interval with $1 - \alpha$ confidence level is written as $z_{\alpha/2}$, we will represent the confidence level by α and the corresponding critical point as $z_{(1-\alpha)/2}$. The critical points are calculated from the *norminv* function.

The use of *quadprog* is almost identical to solving the classical mean-variance portfolio problem with only minor changes to its inputs; the arguments of the function are modified using the transformation matrices, and a lower bound of zero is set because the new variable x of the reformulated robust problem has only non-negative values.

Similarly, the code for calling the *fmincon* function is comparable to the case for the classical Markowitz problem with adjustments in the arguments and the nested function as demonstrated in Box 6.8.

Box 6.7 FUNCTION THAT SOLVES THE ROBUST PROBLEM WITH A BOX UNCERTAINTY SET USING *QUADPROG*

```
% ==================================================================
% robustboxquadprog.m
%
% Find the optimal robust portfolio with box uncertainty using
% "quadprog"
%
% Input:
%   returns: matrix of stock returns (each column represents
%            a single stock)
%   lambda: value of the risk-seeking coefficient
%   alpha: confidence level of the uncertainty set
% Output:
%   optPortfolio: optimal mean-variance portfolio (a column
%                 vector)
% ==================================================================
function optPortfolio = robustboxquadprog( returns, lambda, ...
  alpha )

    [nDays,n] = size(returns);
    mu = mean(returns)';
    sigma = cov(returns);

    % Compute delta (use confidence interval of mean for
    % normal distribution)
    z = norminv(1 - (1 - alpha) / 2, 0, 1);
    delta = z * sqrt(var(returns))' / sqrt(nDays);

    identity = eye(n);
    transform = [identity, -identity];
    transformAbs = [identity, identity];
    muTransformed = (mu' * transform - (delta' * transformAbs))';
    Aeq = [ones(1, n), - ones(1, n)];
    beq = 1;
    lb = zeros(2 * n, 1);

    x = quadprog(2 * transform' * sigma * transform, ...
        -lambda * muTransformed, [], [], Aeq, beq, lb, []);
    optPortfolio = transform * x;
end
```

Box 6.8 FUNCTION THAT SOLVES THE ROBUST PROBLEM WITH A BOX UNCERTAINTY SET USING *FMINCON*

```
% ================================================================
% robustboxfmincon.m
%
% Find the optimal robust portfolio with box uncertainty using
% "fmincon"
%
% Input:
%   returns: matrix of stock returns (each column represents
%            a single stock)
%   lambda: value of the risk-seeking coefficient
%   alpha: confidence level of the uncertainty set
% Output:
%   optPortfolio: optimal mean-variance portfolio (a column
%                 vector)
% ================================================================
function optPortfolio =  robustboxfmincon( returns, lambda, ...
  alpha )

    [nDays,n] = size(returns);
    mu = mean(returns)';
    sigma = cov(returns);

    % Compute delta (use confidence interval of mean for
    % normal distribution)
    z = norminv(1 - (1 - alpha) / 2, 0, 1);
    delta = z * sqrt(var(returns))' / sqrt(nDays);

    identity = eye(n);
    transform = [identity, -identity];
    transformAbs = [identity, identity];
    muTransformed = (mu' * transform - (delta' * transformAbs));
    Aeq = [ones(1, n), - ones(1, n)];
    beq = 1;
    lb = zeros(2 * n, 1);

    % Nested function which is used as the objective function
    function objValue = objfunction(x)
        objValue = x' * transform' * sigma * transform * x ...
            - lambda * muTransformed * x;
    end

    % Use the equal-weighted portfolio as the starting point
    x0 = [ones(n,1) / n; zeros(n,1)];
```

```
      % Set the algorithm to interior-point method
      options = optimset('Algorithm', 'interior-point');

      x = fmincon(@objfunction, x0, [], [], Aeq, beq, lb, [], [], ...
         options);
      optPortfolio = transform * x;
   end
```

The expressiveness of CVX is further demonstrated when solving the robust problem given by (6.8) because imposing absolute values in the objective function is directly handled without any issues in CVX, as shown in Box 6.9. Consequently, the code itself is not too much different from the CVX code for building the optimal classical mean-variance portfolio.

6.5 ROBUST PORTFOLIOS WITH ELLIPSOIDAL UNCERTAINTY

Step 1. Formulate the Robust Problem by Defining the Ellipsoidal Uncertainty Set

The robust portfolio optimization problem with an ellipsoidal uncertainty set on expected returns is more complex than the case for a box uncertainty set in many ways. As shown next, the ellipsoidal set is a combined uncertainty rather than a stock-wise construction of uncertainty, as in the box definition:

$$\{\mu \mid (\mu - \widehat{\mu})' \Sigma_\mu^{-1} (\mu - \widehat{\mu}) \leq \delta^2\} \tag{6.11}$$

where $\Sigma_\mu \in \mathbb{R}^{N \times N}$ is the covariance matrix of estimation errors, and $\delta \in \mathbb{R}$ controls the size of the ellipsoid. The min-max problem with this uncertainty is given by

$$\min_{\omega} \quad \max_{\mu \in \{\mu \mid (\mu - \widehat{\mu})' \Sigma_\mu^{-1} (\mu - \widehat{\mu}) \leq \delta^2\}} \quad \omega' \Sigma \omega - \lambda \mu' \omega \tag{6.12}$$

$$\text{s.t. } \omega' \iota = 1.$$

For the robust optimization problem with box uncertainty set, δ in (6.8) is a vector because the size of the uncertainty set is controlled individually for each stock. But δ in (6.11) is a single value that controls the combined deviation. Nonetheless, similar to the box uncertainty set, it is possible to fix the value of δ for the ellipsoid constraint if stock returns are assumed to be normally distributed. With the assumption that μ follows a multivariate

Box 6.9 FUNCTION THAT SOLVES THE ROBUST PROBLEM WITH A BOX UNCERTAINTY SET USING CVX

```
% ===============================================================
% robustboxcvx.m
%
% Find the optimal robust portfolio with box uncertainty using
% CVX
%
% Input:
%   returns: matrix of stock returns (each column represents
%            a single stock)
%   lambda: value of the risk-seeking coefficient
%   alpha: confidence level of the uncertainty set
% Output:
%   optPortfolio: optimal mean-variance portfolio (a column
%                 vector)
% ===============================================================
function optPortfolio = robustboxcvx( returns, lambda, alpha )

    [nDays,n] = size(returns);
    mu = mean(returns)';
    sigma = cov(returns);

    % Compute delta (use confidence interval of mean for
    % normal distribution)
    z = norminv(1 - (1 - alpha) / 2, 0, 1);
    delta = z * sqrt(var(returns))' / sqrt(nDays);

    % Use CVX for solving the robust problem
    cvx_begin
        variables x(n)
        minimize ( x' * sigma * x - lambda * (mu' * x ...
        - delta' * abs(x)) )
        subject to
            ones(1,n) * x == 1
    cvx_end

    optPortfolio = x;
end
```

normal distribution, $(\mu - \hat{\mu})' \Sigma_\mu^{-1} (\mu - \hat{\mu})$ is estimated as a chi-squared distribution with N degrees of freedom. Consequently, the value of δ^2 becomes the $(100 \times \alpha)^{th}$ percentile of the chi-squared distribution with N degrees of freedom for a confidence level of α. For this approach, the most reasonable estimator $\hat{\mu}$ is the arithmetic mean of the sample stock returns.

Another parameter of the ellipsoidal uncertainty set that is as important as δ is the estimation error covariance matrix of expected returns denoted as Σ_μ. The symmetric positive semidefinite matrix Σ_μ in equation (6.11) is the component that distinguishes ellipsoidal uncertainty sets from simpler ball uncertainty sets, and it also determines the shape of the ellipsoid. There are several methods for constructing the covariance matrix of estimation errors by analyzing a sample of stock returns. The simplest approach is to assume that stock return samples are independent and identically distributed. In this case, the estimation error matrix of the mean is $\frac{1}{T}\Sigma$, where Σ is the covariance matrix of stock returns, and T is the sample size. In other words, the estimation error variance of a stock and the estimation error covariance between stocks decrease as more samples are observed. Unfortunately, this approach is accurate only when stock returns follow a stationary process. Moreover, accurately estimating the covariance matrix Σ is itself not an easy task. However, we find that this is a good starting point because even this simple structure for the estimation error covariance matrix creates portfolios with more robust performance than classical mean-variance portfolios, as we show in Chapter 10.

Suppose the sample data contain estimates of expected return $\mu^t \in \mathbb{R}^N$ and realized return $r^t \in \mathbb{R}^N$ for periods t from 1 to T. The error for period t can be represented as $\varepsilon^t = \mu^t - r^t$, and the error for stock i is the ith component, ε_i^t. Consider the sampling distribution of the mean using these samples for stock i. The standard error of the mean is the standard deviation of the sampling distribution of the mean. If estimation error is normally distributed or by applying the central limit theorem, the standard deviation of the sampling distribution is

$$\sigma_i = \frac{\sigma_i}{\sqrt{T}}$$

where σ_i is the standard deviation of errors for stock i. Since σ_i is an unknown value, it can be replaced by the sample standard deviation,

$$s_i = \sqrt{\frac{1}{T-1}\sum_{t=1}^{T}\left(\varepsilon_i^t - \bar{\varepsilon}_i\right)^2}$$

where

$$\bar{\varepsilon} = \frac{1}{T}\sum_{t=1}^{T}\varepsilon_i^t.$$

Thus, the variance of the sampling distribution is

$$\hat{\sigma}_i^2 = \frac{\Sigma_{t=1}^{T}(\varepsilon_i^t - \bar{\varepsilon}_i)^2}{T(T-1)}, \qquad (6.13)$$

which can be used as the variance of estimation errors for the expected return of stock i. As it is the case for estimating any covariance matrix, accurately measuring the covariances of estimation errors is much more difficult than for the variances and requires a larger dataset. Therefore, it is sometimes advised to approximate Σ_μ as a diagonal matrix with only estimation error variances calculated as shown in (6.13).[4]

When computing the expected stock return and covariance of stock returns, one strategy is to use factor models because stock movements can be expressed from factor returns, and there are usually fewer factors than stocks. We can use the same approach for the estimation error covariance matrix as well. In addition to fundamental factors, the grouping of stocks that characterize stock movements such as industries or sectors is also a sufficient choice. Consider that we have a list of industry constituents in addition to the sample data with estimates of expected return μ^t and realized return r^t for periods t from 1 to T, and each stock falls under exactly one industry. Then, the variance of estimation errors for industry k in period t is found similarly to the formula given by (6.13),

$$\hat{\sigma}_{k,t}^2 = \frac{\Sigma_{\{i|\text{stock } i \text{ in industry } k\}}\left(\varepsilon_i^t - \bar{\varepsilon}_k^t\right)^2}{n_k(n_k - 1)}$$

where n_k is the number of stocks contained in industry k and

$$\bar{\varepsilon}_k^t = \frac{1}{n_k}\sum_{\{i|\text{stock } i \text{ in industry } k\}}\varepsilon_i^t.$$

These give us the sample mean and variance of errors for industry k in each period. Suppose errors for industry k are independent between different periods. Then the sample mean for the entire period is

$$\bar{\varepsilon}_k = \frac{1}{T}\sum_{t=1}^{T}\bar{\varepsilon}_k^t,$$

and the variance of the sample mean is

$$\hat{\sigma}_k^2 = \text{Var}(\bar{\varepsilon}_k) = \frac{1}{T^2} \sum_{t=1}^{T} \text{Var}(\bar{\varepsilon}_k^t) = \frac{\sum_{t=1}^{T} \hat{\sigma}_{k,t}^2}{T^2}.$$

The industry-level estimation error covariances can directly replace the stock-level estimation error variances. As mentioned earlier, including only the industry-level variances without the covariances is a sufficient option for defining the ellipsoid.

Another approach for measuring estimation error covariances is to use a factor model directly. If expected stock returns are estimated from a linear regression, which is the case when using linear factor models, the estimation error covariance matrix can be obtained from regression errors. We will demonstrate the approach for a single stock and then generalize to the case with N stocks. Suppose the return of a stock is expressed by a multivariate linear regression model,

$$r = \beta_0 + \beta_1 f_1 + \cdots + \beta_M f_M + \epsilon$$

where β_0 is the intercept for the case with M factors, and the error term follows a normal distribution, $\epsilon \sim N(0, \sigma_\epsilon^2)$. Then T observations on stock and factor returns are written in matrix form as

$$R = F\beta + E$$

$$\begin{bmatrix} r^1 \\ \vdots \\ r^T \end{bmatrix} = \begin{bmatrix} 1 & f_1^1 & f_M^1 \\ \vdots & \vdots & \vdots \\ 1 & f_1^T & f_M^T \end{bmatrix} \cdots \begin{bmatrix} \beta_0 \\ \vdots \\ \beta_M \end{bmatrix} + \begin{bmatrix} \epsilon^1 \\ \vdots \\ \epsilon^T \end{bmatrix}$$

where $R \in \mathbb{R}^{T \times 1}$, $F \in \mathbb{R}^{T \times (M+1)}$, $\beta \in \mathbb{R}^{(M+1) \times 1}$, and $E \in \mathbb{R}^{T \times 1}$. The least-squares estimate (LSE) of β is found by minimizing $(R - F\beta)'(R - F\beta)$. From the LSE of β, which we denote as $\hat{\beta}$, the error can be computed to follow a multivariate normal distribution, $\hat{\beta} - \beta \sim N_{M+1}(0, (F'F)^{-1}\sigma_\epsilon^2)$. Furthermore, for a given value $\bar{f} = [1, \bar{f}_1, \ldots, \bar{f}_M]'$, the mean return can be predicted by $\bar{f}'\hat{\beta}$. From the error in estimating β, the distribution of estimation error in mean return becomes

$$\bar{f}'\hat{\beta} - \bar{f}'\beta \sim N(0, \bar{f}'(F'F)^{-1}\bar{f}\sigma_\epsilon^2).$$

For N candidate stocks, T observations are similarly expressed as

$$R = F\beta + E$$

where $R \in \mathbb{R}^{T \times N}$, $F \in \mathbb{R}^{T \times (M+1)}$, $\beta \in \mathbb{R}^{(M+1) \times N}$, and $E \in \mathbb{R}^{T \times N}$. The errors now follow a multivariate normal distribution $N_N(0, \Sigma_\epsilon)$ for $\Sigma_\epsilon \in \mathbb{R}^{N \times N}$. Then, similar to the single stock case, the covariance matrix of the estimation error in mean return using $\bar{f} \in \mathbb{R}^{(M+1)}$ is

$$\bar{f}'(F'F)^{-1}\bar{f}\Sigma_\epsilon.$$

The estimation error covariance matrix we are looking for is calculated from

$$\bar{f}'(F'F)^{-1}\bar{f}\hat{\Sigma}_\epsilon$$

where $\hat{\Sigma}_\epsilon = \frac{1}{T}(R - F\hat{\beta})'(R - F\hat{\beta})$ is the maximum likelihood estimator of Σ_ϵ.

We have shown how to form an ellipsoidal uncertainty set, including ways to select the parameters that define the ellipsoid. We next explain how to build optimal robust portfolios from the ellipsoidal uncertainty set.

Step 2. Reformulate the Robust Counterpart with Ellipsoidal Uncertainty

As mentioned earlier, the ellipsoidal uncertainty set is a combined representation in the shape of an ellipsoid. Thus, instead of finding the worst case for each stock, the overall worst case must be identified for a robust problem with an ellipsoidal uncertainty set. The value of μ that exhibits the worst case for the problem given by (6.12) is the optimal solution of the following problem for a fixed value of ω,

$$\max_{\mu} \omega' \Sigma \omega - \lambda \mu' \omega$$
$$\text{s.t.} \quad (\mu - \hat{\mu})' \Sigma_\mu^{-1}(\mu - \hat{\mu}) \leq \delta^2. \tag{6.14}$$

In contrast to the original mean-variance problem, the decision variable for this inner problem is μ even though the objective function is identical. The Lagrangian method that solves the classical portfolio problem (6.1) can be applied to find the value of μ that maximizes the objective function.

1. Form the Lagrangian of (6.14):

$$L(\mu, \gamma) = \omega' \Sigma \omega - \lambda \mu' \omega - \gamma((\mu - \hat{\mu})' \Sigma_\mu^{-1}(\mu - \hat{\mu}) - \delta^2).$$

2. Take the derivative of the Lagrangian with respect to μ and γ:

$$\frac{\partial L}{\partial \mu} = -\lambda \omega - 2\gamma \Sigma_\mu^{-1}(\mu - \hat{\mu})$$

$$\frac{\partial L}{\partial \gamma} = (\mu - \hat{\mu})' \Sigma_\mu^{-1}(\mu - \hat{\mu}) - \delta^2.$$

3. Set these equations to zero and solve for the optimal value μ^*:

$$-\lambda\omega - 2\gamma\,\Sigma_\mu^{-1}(\mu^* - \hat{\mu}) = 0 \tag{6.15}$$

$$(\mu^* - \hat{\mu})'\,\Sigma_\mu^{-1}(\mu^* - \hat{\mu}) - \delta^2 = 0. \tag{6.16}$$

Then, from (6.15),

$$\mu^* - \hat{\mu} = -\frac{\lambda}{2\gamma}\,\Sigma_\mu\omega,$$

and plugging this into (6.16) gives

$$\left(-\frac{\lambda}{2\gamma}\,\Sigma_\mu\omega\right)' \Sigma_\mu^{-1} \left(-\frac{\lambda}{2\gamma}\,\Sigma_\mu\omega\right) = \delta^2$$

$$\frac{\lambda^2}{4\gamma^2}\,\omega'\,\Sigma_\mu'\,\Sigma_\mu^{-1}\,\Sigma_\mu\omega = \delta^2$$

$$\frac{\lambda^2}{4\delta^2}\,\omega'\,\Sigma_\mu\omega = \gamma^2$$

$$\gamma = \frac{\lambda}{2\delta}\,\sqrt{\omega'\,\Sigma_\mu\omega}. \tag{6.17}$$

Finally, by substituting (6.17) into (6.15), we arrive at μ^* that represents the worst case,

$$\mu^* = \hat{\mu} - \frac{\delta}{\sqrt{\omega'\,\Sigma_\mu\omega}}\,\Sigma_\mu\omega. \tag{6.18}$$

Since we have an expression for the worst estimate of the expected return within the uncertainty set expressed as (6.11), the robust problem is formulated by replacing μ of the classical problem (6.1) with (6.18):

$$\min_{\omega}\ \omega'\,\Sigma\omega - \lambda\left(\hat{\mu} - \frac{\delta}{\sqrt{\omega'\,\Sigma_\mu\omega}}\,\Sigma_\mu\omega\right)'\omega \tag{6.19}$$

$$\text{s.t. } \omega'\iota = 1,$$

which is more simply written as

$$\min_{\omega}\ \omega'\,\Sigma\omega - \lambda(\hat{\mu}'\omega - \delta\sqrt{\omega'\,\Sigma_\mu\omega}) \tag{6.20}$$

$$\text{s.t. } \omega'\iota = 1.$$

Note that in several calculations, we used the fact that Σ_μ is a symmetric matrix, $\Sigma_\mu = \Sigma'_\mu$. In some cases, (6.20) is also written as

$$\min_{\omega} \omega' \Sigma \omega - \lambda \left(\hat{\mu}' \omega - \delta \left\| \Sigma_\mu^{1/2} \omega \right\|_2 \right)$$

$$\text{s.t. } \omega' \iota = 1. \tag{6.21}$$

Depending on the optimization tool, either (6.20) or (6.21) may be preferred, and we will now demonstrate building MATLAB functions for solving robust counterparts with ellipsoidal uncertainty sets.

Step 3. Use Optimization Tools to Solve the Ellipsoidal Uncertainty Problem

The robust optimization problem with an ellipsoidal uncertainty set cannot be formulated as a quadratic program, and thus it is impossible to utilize the *quadprog* function, unlike the previous two problems. But the function using *fmincon* is coded with minimal changes from the function for solving the classical portfolio problem as shown in Box 6.10. In the examples presented in Boxes 6.10 and 6.11, we approximate the value of δ from the chi-squared distribution with degrees of freedom, as the number of stocks and Σ_μ is estimated as $\frac{1}{T}\Sigma$ where T is the sample size (i.e., the number of observations).

The CVX version also requires minor changes from the earlier functions that use CVX. Between the two robust formulations (6.20) and (6.21) with ellipsoidal uncertainty sets, CVX only accepts the formulation expressed using the Euclidean norm, so we have shown that case in Box 6.11.

6.6   CLOSING REMARKS

In this chapter, we have covered the basics of solving robust portfolio optimization problems. The examples given in MATLAB should serve as general guidelines for constructing robust portfolios. Nonetheless, additional portfolio constraints or parameter options on optimization solvers may be necessary to construct robust portfolios with specific targets. Moreover, the values of λ and δ should also be chosen carefully in order to properly represent the investor's aversion to risk and uncertainty. In Chapter 10, we illustrate further how to form various portfolios using historical data and evaluate the performance of robust portfolios. These demonstrations will provide more details on constructing the optimal robust portfolio.

Box 6.10 FUNCTION THAT SOLVES THE ROBUST PROBLEM WITH AN ELLIPSOIDAL UNCERTAINTY SET USING *FMINCON*

```
% ================================================================
% robustellipsoidfmincon.m
%
% Find the optimal robust portfolio with ellipsoid uncertainty
% using "fmincon"
%
% Input:
%   returns: matrix of stock returns (each column represents
%            a single stock)
%   lambda: value of the risk-seeking coefficient
%   alpha: confidence level of the uncertainty set
% Output:
%   optPortfolio: optimal mean-variance portfolio (a column
%                 vector)
% ================================================================
function optPortfolio = robustellipsoidfmincon( returns, ...
  lambda, alpha )

    [nDays,n] = size(returns);
    mu = mean(returns)';
    sigma = cov(returns);
    sigmaMu = sigma / nDays;


    % Compute delta
    delta = sqrt(chi2inv(alpha,n));

    Aeq = ones(1, n);
    beq = 1;


    % Nested function which is used as the objective function
    function objValue = objfunction(x)
        objValue = x' * sigma * x - lambda * mu' * x ...
            + lambda * delta * sqrt(x' * sigmaMu * x);
    end


    % Use the equal-weighted portfolio as the starting point
    x0 = ones(n,1) / n;


    % Set the algorithm to interior-point method
    options = optimset('Algorithm', 'interior-point');


    optPortfolio = fmincon(@objfunction, x0, [], [], Aeq, beq, ...
        [], [], [], options);
end
```

Box 6.11 FUNCTION THAT SOLVES THE ROBUST PROBLEM WITH AN ELLIPSOIDAL UNCERTAINTY SET USING CVX

```
% =============================================================
% robustellipsoidcvx.m
%
% Find the optimal robust portfolio with ellipsoid uncertainty
% using CVX
%
% Input:
%   returns: matrix of stock returns (each column represents
%            a single stock)
%   lambda: value of the risk-seeking coefficient
%   alpha: confidence level of the uncertainty set
% Output:
%   optPortfolio: optimal mean-variance portfolio (a column
%                 vector)
% =============================================================
function optPortfolio = robustellipsoidcvx( returns, lambda, ...
  alpha )

    [nDays,n] = size(returns);
    mu = mean(returns)';
    sigma = cov(returns);
    sigmaMu = sigma / nDays;
    sqrtSigmaMu = sqrtm(sigmaMu);

    % Compute delta
    delta = sqrt(chi2inv(alpha,n));

    % Use CVX for solving the robust problem
    cvx_begin
        variables x(n)
        minimize ( x' * sigma * x - lambda * mu' * x ...
            + lambda * delta * norm(sqrtSigmaMu * x, 2) )
        subject to
            ones(1,n) * x == 1
    cvx_end

    optPortfolio = x;
end
```

KEY POINTS

- Optimization packages such as MATLAB are essential for solving portfolio problems, especially for solving robust versions of the mean-variance problem.
- The classical mean-variance problem can be expressed as a quadratic programming problem and thus is solved using *quadprog* and *fmincon* functions in MATLAB.
- We describe constructing robust portfolios in three steps: (1) formulate a robust problem by defining an uncertainty set, (2) reformulate the robust problem into standard convex optimization form, and (3) use optimization tools to solve the reformulated problem.
- Uncertainty in expected returns is the most important for achieving portfolio robustness, and we thus introduce robust counterparts where the uncertainty set for expected returns is represented as a box or an ellipsoid.
- Robust portfolio optimization problems with box and ellipsoidal uncertainty sets are solved using MATLAB with minor changes to the code for solving the non-robust classical problem.
- CVX is also a useful tool for solving convex optimization problems, and it often computes optimal robust portfolios with more straightforward syntax.

NOTES

1. For information on CVX, visit "CVX: Matlab Software for Disciplined Convex Programming," available at http://cvxr.com/cvx
2. Reformulating robust portfolio optimization problems into simpler forms is also discussed in Chapter 12 in Frank J. Fabozzi, Peter N. Kolm, Dessislava A. Pachamanova, and Sergio M. Focardi, *Robust Portfolio Optimization and Management* (Hoboken, NJ: John Wiley & Sons, 2007).
3. Errors in means are known to be at least 10 times more important than errors in variances, and errors in variances are about twice as important as errors in covariances. Detailed analyses can be found in Vijay K. Chopra and William T. Ziemba, "The Effect of Errors in Means, Variances, and Covariances on Optimal Portfolio Choice," *Journal of Portfolio Management* 19 (1993), pp. 6–11.
4. Stubbs and Vance argue the effectiveness of omitting the off-diagonal values and also introduce several methods for determining the covariance matrix of estimation errors including the ones we cover in this chapter. See Robert A. Stubbs and Pamela Vance, "Computing Return Estimation Error Matrices for Robust Optimization," *Axioma Research Paper* 1 (2005). A few simpler estimation methods are discussed in Anthony Renshaw, "Real World Case Studies in Portfolio Construction Using Robust Optimization," *Axioma Research Paper* 7 (2008).

CHAPTER 7

Controlling Third and Fourth Moments of Portfolio Returns via Robust Mean-Variance Approach

While the third or higher moments of portfolio returns are important for managing a portfolio, they are often neglected in portfolio construction problems due to the computational difficulties associated with them. In this chapter, we illustrate that robust mean-variance approach can control portfolio skewness and kurtosis without imposing higher moment terms in the optimization problem. More specifically, if the uncertainty sets are properly constructed, robust portfolios based on the worst-case approach within the mean-variance framework favor skewness and penalize kurtosis. This implies that robust portfolios tend to produce positively skewed return distributions with thinner tails than their non-robust counterparts and are thus less likely to be affected by outliers.[1]

7.1 CONTROLLING HIGHER MOMENTS OF PORTFOLIO RETURN

The classical mean-variance model, introduced in Chapter 2, takes the first two moments (the expectation and variance) of a portfolio return as the performance and risk measures and determines the optimal portfolio by solving a quadratic program. However, from the practitioner's perspective, these first two moments do not fully capture the performance of the portfolio, and higher moments provide useful qualitative information. For instance, when the third moment is negative (or equivalently, when the portfolio return is negatively skewed), it is more likely to have an extreme left-tail event than one in the right tail. Therefore, the typical investor prefers more positively skewed return distributions; a more positively skewed portfolio has better Sortino ratio and lower semi-deviation.[2] A similar argument can be applied to the fourth moment. If the fourth moment, or kurtosis, of portfolio returns is low, it tends to have less extreme events, thus is preferred by most investors.

Since the mean-variance approach only considers the first two moments, a revised approach is required to incorporate and control the third and fourth moments when constructing a portfolio. The most straightforward approach would be to modify the objective function by introducing new terms for portfolio skewness and kurtosis. Recall that the traditional mean-variance formulation can be written as

$$\max_{w \in C} \mu'w - \beta w' \Sigma w \tag{7.1}$$

where C is a convex subset of the hyperplane $\{w \in \mathbb{R}^n | \Sigma_i w_i = 1\}$, $\mu \in \mathbb{R}^n$, $\Sigma \in \mathbb{R}^{n \times n}$ are the expected return and covariance matrix, respectively, and $\beta > 0$ is the parameter to reflect investor's risk aversion.[3]

Then, the third central moment of portfolio return $w'r$ is

$$S(w, M_3) := \mathbb{E}(w'r - \mathbb{E}w'r)^3 = w'M_3(w \otimes w)$$

where $M_3 = \mathbb{E}[(r - \mathbb{E}r)(r - \mathbb{E}r)' \otimes (r - \mathbb{E}r)'] \in \mathbb{R}^{n \times n^2}$ is the co-skewness matrix for a random return vector $r \in \mathbb{R}^n$ and $\otimes$ denotes the Kronecker product. Similarly, for a co-kurtosis matrix $M_4 = \mathbb{E}[(r - \mathbb{E}r)(r - \mathbb{E}r)' \otimes (r - \mathbb{E}r)' \otimes (r - \mathbb{E}r)'] \in \mathbb{R}^{n \times n^3}$, its fourth central moment is defined as

$$K(w, M_4) := \mathbb{E}(w'r - \mathbb{E}w'r)^4 = w'M_4(w \otimes w \otimes w).$$

Based on these expressions for the higher moments, the mean-variance formulation given by (7.1) could be modified by adding third and fourth central moments,

$$\max_{w \in C} \mu'w - \beta w' \Sigma w + \gamma S(w, M_3) - \delta K(w, M_4)$$

$$\text{for parameters } \beta, \gamma, \delta \geq 0. \tag{7.2}$$

While the problem written as (7.2) is intuitive, there are two critical issues when solving the optimization problem for finding optimal portfolios. First, the third central moment term $S(w, M_3)$ is a cubic function, resulting in the problem (7.2) being non-convex, which causes a significant increase in computational cost. Second, as the co-skewness matrix M_3 is three-dimensional, the number of parameters is of the order of n^3, which makes it practically impossible to obtain reliable estimators. The same issues apply to the kurtosis term, only with more difficulties.

One of the properties of robust equity portfolios is that, when the uncertainty sets are properly imposed, higher moments are controlled in a way that investors prefer. This allows controlling the higher moments to some degree without facing computational difficulties thanks to the convexity of the robust portfolio problems. The following section provides intuition behind this property.

7.2   WHY ROBUST FORMULATION CONTROLS HIGHER MOMENTS

This section presents an intuitive argument behind why and how robust portfolio optimization controls higher moments of portfolio returns in a desirable fashion.[4] We begin by describing the robust formulation. The robust version of the mean-variance problem given by (7.1) can be expressed as

$$\max_{w \in C} \min_{(\hat{\mu}, \hat{\Sigma}) \in U_{(\hat{\mu}, \hat{\Sigma})}} \hat{\mu}'w - \beta w' \hat{\Sigma} w \qquad (7.3)$$

where $U_{(\hat{\mu}, \hat{\Sigma})}$ is a joint uncertainty set of $\left(\hat{\mu}, \hat{\Sigma} \right)$,

$$U_{(\hat{\mu}, \hat{\Sigma})} = \left\{ \left(\hat{\mu}_1, \hat{\Sigma}_1 \right), \dots, \left(\hat{\mu}_i, \hat{\Sigma}_i \right), \dots, \left(\hat{\mu}_I, \hat{\Sigma}_I \right) \right\},$$

$$\hat{\mu}_i = \frac{1}{J} \sum_j r_{i,j} \text{ and } \hat{\Sigma}_i = \frac{1}{J-1} \sum_j (r_{i,j} - \hat{\mu}_i)(r_{i,j} - \hat{\mu}_i)'$$

are the sample mean and sample covariance matrix for the ith sample set, respectively. Moreover, let $r \in \mathbb{R}^n$ be the random vector representing returns of n risky assets with finite moments up to order four, and let $r_{i,j} \in \mathbb{R}^n$ for $i = 1, \dots, I$, and $j = 1, \dots, J$ be independent and identically distributed samples of r.

The first step toward understanding the higher moment controllability of robust formulation is to identify the specific relationship between the sample mean and the sample variance (or standard deviation) depending on the skewness of the return distribution. More specifically, as the distribution gets more negatively (positively) skewed, the sample mean and sample variance tend to be negatively (positively) correlated.

To illustrate this, let us first introduce skew normal distributions. A random variable X follows a skew normal distribution with a shape parameter α, $X \sim SN(\alpha)$, if its probability density function is $f_X(x|\alpha) = 2\phi(x)\Phi(\alpha x)$ for all $x \in \mathbb{R}$, where $\phi(x)$ and $\Phi(x)$ are the probability density function and the cumulative distribution function of a standard normal random variable, respectively, and $\alpha \in \mathbb{R}$. Furthermore, a skew normal distribution has the following main properties.

- The skewness of the distribution increases as the shape parameter α increases. Especially, when $\alpha = 0$, the distribution becomes standard normal. See Exhibit 7.1.

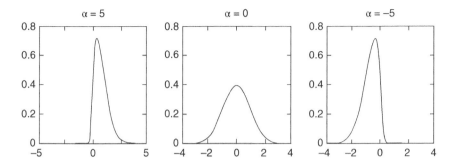

Exhibit 7.1 PDFs for skew normal distribution ($\alpha = 5, 0,$ and -5)

- $E(X) = \sqrt{\frac{2}{\pi}}d$, $Var(X) = 1 - \frac{2d^2}{\pi}$, and $\gamma_1 = \frac{(4-\pi)\mathbb{E}(X)^3}{2\,Var(X)^{\frac{3}{2}}}$, where γ_1 is the skewness factor and $d = \alpha/\sqrt{1+\alpha^2}$.
- The linear transform $Y = m + wX$ is a skew normal random variable, and denoted by $Y \sim SN(m, w^2, \alpha)$.
- $E(Y) = m + wX$, $Var(Y) = w^2\,Var(X)$, and the skewness of Y is γ_1.
- The sum of skew normal random variables is again skew normal. This is a very handy property upon calculating portfolio return when individual security returns are *n*-dimensional skew normal.
- $\gamma_1 \in (-0.995, 0.995)$

Now, let us consider three skew normal random variables X_1, X_2, and X_3. We set their means to 0 and variances to 1. In addition, the skewness factors are chosen so that X_1 is positively skewed, X_2 is symmetric (not skewed), and X_3 is negatively skewed. Next, from each skew normal distribution, we generate 100 samples, obtain sample mean and sample variance from these samples, and repeat this many times. Exhibit 7.2 illustrates the test results. Each point in the figure represents a single pair of sample mean and sample variance of 100 samples. Clearly, as the skewness increases, the correlation between the sample mean and sample standard deviation increases.

Now, let us restate this observation from the perspective of portfolio management. Suppose a portfolio has a return distribution that is negatively skewed. Then, for the period that its realized return is relatively low, its realized volatility is likely to be high, and vice versa. When the portfolio return is positively skewed, the realized volatility tends to increase as realized return increases. This explains why portfolio managers prefer to have portfolios with positively skewed return distributions.

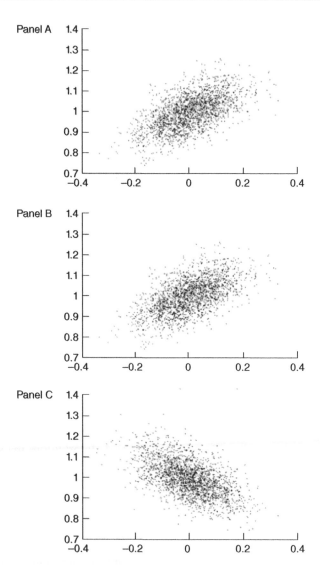

Exhibit 7.2 Sample mean and sample variance from
three skew normal distributions
Panel A. From positively skewed distribution
Panel B. From symmetric distribution
Panel C. From negatively skewed distribution

The main implication is that the risk measured by realized volatility increases when a portfolio performs poorly if the portfolio is negatively skewed. As stated, this justifies the preference of positively skewed portfolios over negatively skewed portfolios from a risk management perspective. Notice that the paths for the realized return and the realized volatility have a "mirror image" if the portfolio is negatively skewed as illustrated in the left panel of Exhibit 7.3. Exhibit 7.4 depicts that "mirror image" behaviors are commonly found in the equity market, as the equity returns are generally negatively skewed.

In fact, one can show that the covariance between sample mean and sample variance is proportionate to the skewness,[5]

$$\mathrm{Cov}[\overline{X}_i, S_i^2] = \frac{\mu_3}{J}.$$

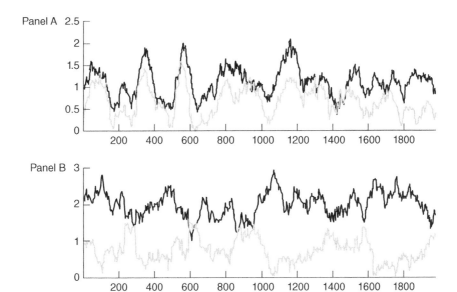

Exhibit 7.3 Sample paths of log-prices (dark lines) and realized volatilities (grey lines) generated from skew normal distributions (Panel A: skewness = 0.995; Panel B: skewness = -0.995)
Panel A. Sample log-price and realized volatility paths from positively skew normal distribution
Panel B. Sample log-price and realized volatility paths from negatively skew normal distribution

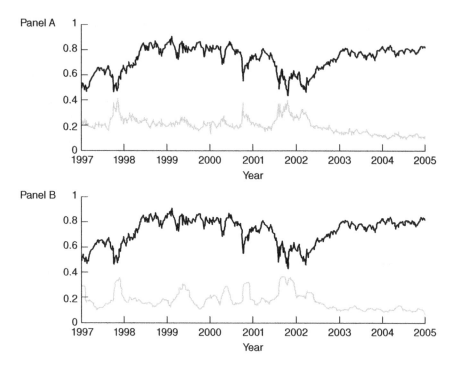

Exhibit 7.4   Dow-Jones Industrial Average Index (DJIA) log-price with implied and realized volatilities from 1997 to 2005
Panel A. Log-price (dark line) and implied volatility (grey line) of DJIA
Panel B. Log-price (dark line) and 60-day realized volatility (grey line) of DJIA

Given these observations, we revisit the problem given by equation (7.3). Intuitively speaking, as a portfolio w becomes more positively skewed, $f_i(w) = \overline{X}_i - \beta S_i^2$ becomes less dispersed. More specifically, since $\mathrm{Cov}[\overline{X}_i, S_i^2] = \mu_3/J$, a sample variance from a more positively skewed portfolio tends to increase as the realized value of the corresponding sample mean increases. Thus, $\overline{X}_i$ and $-\beta S_i^2$ tend to move in opposite directions, causing a "diversification effect" between the two terms. Thus, the worst case solution of problem (7.3) gets better as the portfolio becomes more skewed, ultimately making problem (7.3) more likely to favor portfolios that are more skewed.

Exhibit 7.5 graphically illustrates this reasoning—that is, the value of problem (7.3) is likely to be higher for a positively skewed portfolio (left figure) than for a negatively skewed one (right figure). Thus, it is preferred by the robust approach previously described. While the first two moments

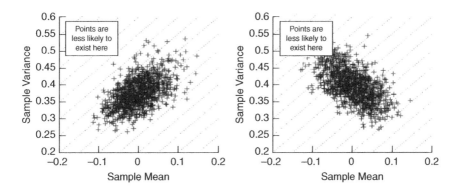

Exhibit 7.5   Sample means and sample variances of skew normal random variables

of the random variables represented by the two figures in Exhibit 7.5 are identical, the left figure is positively skewed, whereas the right figure is negatively skewed. The dotted lines in both figures represent the indifference curves for the objective function of the problem given by (7.3) when the value of β is set to one, which shows that the solution for the inner problem of (7.3) becomes worse as more points appear in the upper-left region. A positively skewed portfolio (left) is less likely to have points in the upper-west region than a negatively skewed portfolio (right) and, therefore, likely to have a higher value.

The same intuition holds for the kurtosis. The worst case solution tends to get worse as the variance of $f_i(w)$ increases, and because $\text{Var}[S_i^2] = \mu_4 - \sigma^4$, a portfolio with a heavy tailed return distribution is penalized by problem (7.3). Findings show that robust portfolios tend to produce return distributions with thinner tails than their nonrobust counterparts and are thus less likely to be affected by outliers. Some empirical results are presented in the following section.

7.3   EMPIRICAL TESTS

Empirically comparing mean-variance optimal portfolios and robust portfolios demonstrates their different attributes as reflected by the higher moments. The outcomes summarized in this section are from portfolios constructed with daily returns of 10 industry portfolios for the years ranging from 1983 to 2012, yielding 7,566 days in total.[6] Exhibit 7.6 provides summary statistics for the 10 industry portfolios along with the U.S. market portfolio.

To find the robust optimal portfolio from the problem given by (7.3), we solve the following equivalent convex quadratically constrained quadratic

Exhibit 7.6 Summary statistics of 10 industry portfolios with market portfolio based on daily returns

Moments	First $(\times 10^{-4})$	Second Central $(\times 10^{-4})$	Third Central $(\times 10^{-7})$	Fourth Central $(\times 10^{-7})$
Market	2.97	1.26	−9.02	3.00
Consumer Nondurables	4.07	0.93	−6.94	2.04
Consumer Durables	2.52	2.24	−11.34	5.67
Manufacturing	3.60	1.34	−13.97	4.05
Oil, Gas, and Coal Extraction and Products	4.21	2.14	−8.10	8.67
Business Equipment	2.96	2.59	−1.91	7.93
Telephone and Television Transmission	3.08	1.62	−2.58	4.02
Wholesale, Retail, and Some Services	3.51	1.40	−6.03	2.75
Healthcare, Medical Equipment, and Drugs	3.61	1.35	−9.36	2.90
Utilities	3.00	0.95	−0.37	2.17
Other	2.86	1.72	−5.82	4.91

program (QCQP) formulation,[7]

$$\max_{w \in C, z} z$$

$$\text{s.t.} \quad z \le \hat{\mu}_i' w - \beta w' \hat{\Sigma}_i w \text{ for } i = 1, \dots, I.$$

The MATLAB code for solving the QCQP formulation using CVX is shown in Box 7.1.

Three sets of empirical tests that confirm the claims in the previous section are summarized. The analyses compare third and fourth moments of mean-variance optimal portfolios and robust portfolios by varying (1) β, the risk aversion parameter, (2) I, the number of pairs of sample means and sample covariance matrices in the uncertainty set, and (3) J, the number of daily returns used to obtain sample mean and sample covariance matrix. The parameters for the base case are set as $\beta = 1$, $I = 100$, and $J = 1000$.

Box 7.1 FUNCTION FOR THE ROBUST PORTFOLIO PROBLEM WRITTEN AS A QCQP

```
% ================================================================
% robustqcqp.m
%
% Solve the QCQP problem in Theorem 7.4 using CVX
%
% Input:
%   muAgg: n-by-I matrix where each column is a sample mean
%   sigmaAgg: a three dimensional (n-by-n-by-I) matrix where
%   each page (n-by-n matrix) is a sample covariance matrix
% Output:
%   w: portfolio weights
% ================================================================
function w = robustqcqp ( muAgg, sigmaAgg )
    % Identify the number of assets and the number of sets
    % of samples
    [n,I] = size(muAgg);

    % Set beta to 1 (can change value as needed)
    beta = 1;

    % Invoke CVX
    cvx_begin

    % Define two variables: z and w
    variables z w(n);
    % Objective for QCQP
    maximize(z);
    % Constraints
    subject to
        % Sum of weights = 1
        ones(1,n) * w == 1;
        % I quadratic constraints
        for i = 1:I
            z <= muAgg(:,i)'*w - beta*quad_form
                (w,sigmaAgg(:,:,i));
        end

    cvx_end
end
```

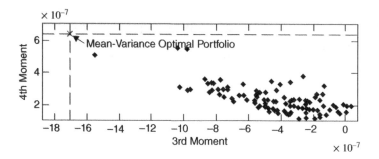

Exhibit 7.7   Test results for base case ($\beta = 1$, $I = 100$, and $J = 1000$)

Exhibit 7.7 illustrates the results for the base case, which contains 100 robust portfolios along with the mean-variance optimal portfolio whose parameters are obtained from the whole sample data. Each dot in Exhibit 7.7 represents the pair of third and fourth central moments for a single robust portfolio estimated over the whole sample period. All of the 100 robust portfolios constructed have higher third central moments and lower fourth central moments, indicating that the robust formulation given by equation (7.3) indeed favors skewness and penalizes kurtosis.

Exhibits 7.8, 7.9, and 7.10 depict the test results when β (Exhibit 7.8), I (Exhibit 7.9), and J (Exhibit 7.10) are varied while other parameters are set as the base case. In each exhibit, Panel A shows the number of cases where robust portfolios dominate mean-variance portfolios in both third and fourth central moments. Panels B and C represent the number of cases where robust portfolios have higher third central moments and lower fourth central moments, respectively. Panel D illustrates the number of cases where robust portfolios are dominated by mean-variance portfolios in both third and fourth central moments. Exhibit 7.8 illustrates that, in most of the cases, the robust portfolios dominate the mean-variance optimal portfolios in both moments (that is, higher third central moment and lower fourth central moment), indicating that our argument is insensitive to the changes in β. Exhibits 7.9 and 7.10 summarize the results when the values of I and J are varied, respectively. These results depict that the robust portfolios are likely to have better third and fourth central moments than the mean-variance portfolios as I and J increase. These findings provide strong evidence that robust portfolios favor skewness and penalize kurtosis, which reflect return distributions that are favored for effectively managing portfolio risk.

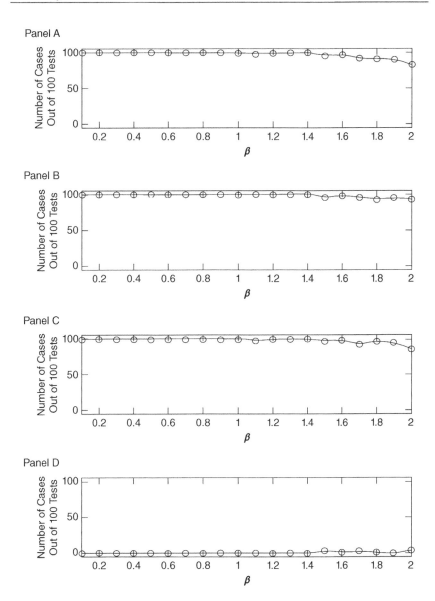

Exhibit 7.8 Test results when β is varied

Panel A. Robust portfolio dominates mean-variance optimal portfolio in both third and fourth central moments.

Panel B. Robust portfolio dominates mean-variance optimal portfolio in third central moment.

Panel C. Robust portfolio dominates mean-variance optimal portfolio in fourth central moment.

Panel D. Robust portfolio is dominated by mean-variance portfolio in both third and fourth central moments.

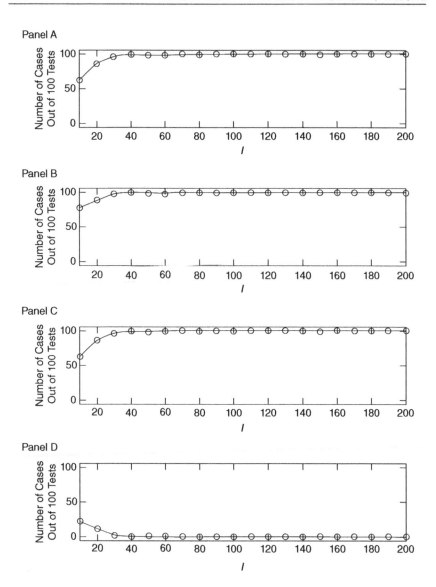

Exhibit 7.9 Test results when *I* is varied

Panel A. Robust portfolio dominates mean-variance optimal portfolio in both third and fourth central moments.

Panel B. Robust portfolio dominates mean-variance optimal portfolio in third central moment.

Panel C. Robust portfolio dominates mean-variance optimal portfolio in fourth central moment.

Panel D. Robust portfolio is dominated by mean-variance portfolio in both third and fourth central moments.

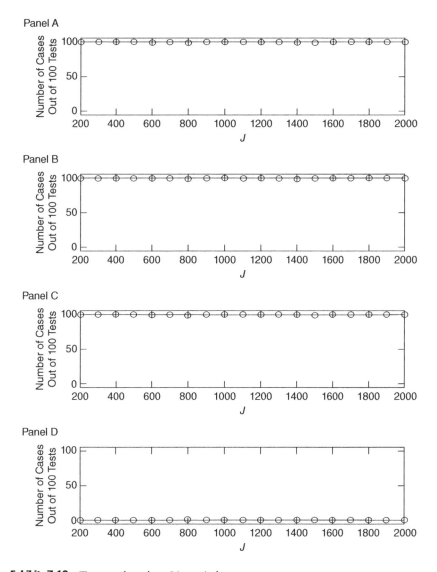

Exhibit 7.10 Test results when *J* is varied

Panel A. Robust portfolio dominates mean-variance optimal portfolio in both third and fourth central moments.

Panel B. Robust portfolio dominates mean-variance optimal portfolio in third central moment.

Panel C. Robust portfolio dominates mean-variance optimal portfolio in fourth central moment.

Panel D. Robust portfolio is dominated by mean-variance portfolio in both third and fourth central moments.

KEY POINTS

- While the mean-variance model uses the first two moments, returns in equity markets are not always fully explained by mean and variance.
- Investors favor a portfolio with positive skewness and lower kurtosis because it shows less extreme returns in the left tail.
- If the uncertainty sets are properly constructed, robust portfolios based on the worst case approach under the mean-variance setting favor skewness and penalize kurtosis.
- A simple economic interpretation is that if a portfolio is negatively skewed, it tends to have higher risk when it performs poorly; consequently, its downside tends to be significant, thus it is penalized by the worst-case approach.
- This observation in robust portfolio formulations allows an investor to control the higher moments to some degree without facing computational difficulties due to the convexity of robust portfolio problems.

NOTES

1. This chapter is based on Woo Chang Kim, Frank J. Fabozzi, Patrick Cheridito, and Charles Fox, "Controlling Portfolio Skewness and Kurtosis without Directly Optimizing Third and Fourth Moments," *Economics Letters* 122 (2014), pp. 154–158. It mostly follows the paper with some modification to enhance readability.
2. Sortino ratio is similar to the Sharpe ratio but uses downside deviation as the measure of risk. For more details, see Frank A. Sortino and Robert van der Meer, "Downside Risk," *Journal of Portfolio Management* 17, 4 (1991), pp. 27–31.
3. Note that the mean-variance formulation in Chapter 6 was expressed as a minimization problem with λ attached to the portfolio return term for representing the willingness to take risk. For example, see the formula given by equation (6.1) in Chapter 6.
4. The mathematical arguments on the ability of robust portfolio formulations to control higher moments are included in section 2 in Kim, Fabozzi, Cheridito, and Fox, "Controlling Portfolio Skewness and Kurtosis without Directly Optimizing Third and Fourth Moments." Their theorems focus on analyzing the problem given by equation (7.3).
5. Lingyun Zhang. "Sample Mean and Sample Variance: Their Covariance and Their (In)Dependence." *The American Statistician* 61, 2 (2007), pp. 159–160.
6. The 10 industry portfolio returns are obtained from the data library of Kenneth R. French, http://mba.tuck.dartmouth.edu/pages/faculty/ken.french/data_library .html
7. The equivalence between the two problems is stated in Theorem 2.4 in Kim, Fabozzi, Cheridito, and Fox, "Controlling Portfolio Skewness and Kurtosis without Directly Optimizing Third and Fourth Moments."

CHAPTER 8

Higher Factor Exposures of Robust Equity Portfolios

Identifying the factors in the equity market that drive returns and understanding the sensitivity of a portfolio to factor movements are extremely important for portfolio construction and risk management. Significant factors explain the major movements in the equity market and thus will affect the performance of equity portfolios. In this chapter, the factor exposure of robust equity portfolios is investigated. If robust optimization has a significant impact on a portfolio's factor exposure, one cannot simply update the original portfolio to its robust counterpart without fully recognizing the new risk exposures. In this chapter, we discuss the central topics related to the factor exposures of robust portfolios, including the following:

- The importance of portfolio factor exposure for managing risk
- Common factors in the equity market
- Theoretical argument that increasing portfolio robustness leads to higher factor exposures
- Empirical findings on the higher factor dependency of robust portfolios compared to classical mean-variance portfolios
- Robust formulations that control factor exposure

8.1   IMPORTANCE OF PORTFOLIO FACTOR EXPOSURE

Factors explain large underlying price movements in the financial market for an asset class. Macroeconomic theory is a good starting point for identifying potential factors such as inflation, interest rates, and unemployment rates. As discussed in Chapter 2, the use of factors significantly reduces the number of estimations required for the mean-variance model because factor-level estimations of mean, variance, and covariance are used for estimating individual stock-level mean, variance, and covariance. Furthermore, from a portfolio manager's perspective, understanding the portfolio's exposure to the major factors is essential for managing overall portfolio risk. For example, if a portfolio has high exposure to short-term interest rates, then a period of anticipated high interest rate volatility will affect the volatility of portfolio returns. Moreover, by obtaining a good forecast of interest rate volatility, a portfolio manager can structure a portfolio to capitalize on the forecast of this factor.

Numerical values representing factor exposures of a portfolio are found from a factor model. A *factor model* is written as[1]

$$r = \alpha + \beta_1 f_1 + \beta_2 f_2 + \cdots + \beta_M f_M + \varepsilon$$

where

r = return of a portfolio or an asset
f_i = return of the ith factor
β_i = sensitivity of the return of the ith factor
M = total number of factors
ε = error term that represents the portion of return not explained by the factor model

The errors, or residuals, of the factor model are assumed to be uncorrelated with the factor returns. The parameters of the model that must be estimated are α's and β's. These parameters can be estimated statistically using regression analysis.[2] Following the common terminology from regression analysis, α is interpreted as the intercept and β's are the coefficients. Once factor returns are observed, the parameters α and β are used to find the return of a portfolio or an asset. Identifying factors in the equity market is discussed in section 8.2.

Suppose our goal is to estimate U.S. large-cap stock returns using a factor model. In this simple example, our portfolio would be a 100% investment in a U.S. large-cap stock index. If we believe that the following major industry categories are the five main factors:[3]

1. *Cnsmr* (Consumer Durables, NonDurables, Wholesale, Retail, and Some Services)
2. *Manuf* (Manufacturing, Energy, and Utilities)
3. *HiTec* (Business Equipment, Telephone and Television Transmission)
4. *Hlth* (Healthcare, Medical Equipment, and Drugs)
5. *Other* (Other—Mines, Constr, BldMt, Trans, Hotels, Bus Serv, Entertainment, Finance)

the factor model becomes

$$r = \alpha + \beta_1 f_1 + \beta_2 f_2 + \beta_3 f_3 + \beta_4 f_4 + \beta_5 f_5 + \varepsilon$$

with only five factors, where β_i is the sensitivity to the ith industry.

The estimated relationship between factor returns and portfolio returns can be found by using a regression on historical returns. The monthly returns for U.S. large-cap stocks and the five industries from 2012 to 2014 are shown in Exhibit 8.1. In MATLAB, the coefficients are found using the *regress* function, as shown in Box 2.3 in Chapter 2. When inserting the returns in Exhibit 8.1 as the inputs, the following values are the resulting outputs:

$$\alpha = 0.000883 \ \beta_3 = 0.271$$

$$\beta_1 = 0.202 \ \beta_4 = 0.0724$$

$$\beta_2 = 0.228 \ \beta_5 = 0.191.$$

From regression analysis, the coefficient of determination or goodness of fit, more commonly known as the R^2 value, indicates the fit of the model by measuring how much of the return variance is explained by the five factors. An R^2 value of one shows that the factor model explains all variability in portfolio returns. For our factor model with five industries, the R^2 value is 0.989, indicating that the five factors are appropriate choices for analyzing the returns of U.S. large-cap stocks. The β values suggest that the portfolio is exposed to all industries at similar levels except for the fourth industry, which represents healthcare industries. Due to the low dependency on healthcare industry, this portfolio is expected to react less to large movements or volatility forecasts in the return to the healthcare industry.

8.2 FUNDAMENTAL FACTOR MODELS IN THE EQUITY MARKET

There are several approaches for identifying the factors of a factor model.[4,5] One of the most straightforward approaches is to use macroeconomic variables for explaining movements in the equity market. Another common approach is to use the fundamental attributes as factors such as firm size, dividend yield, and price–earnings ratio.[6] Because the *fundamental factors* reflect firm-specific characteristics, they are appropriate for analyzing stock behaviors.

The fundamental factors most widely used in academic research are size, book-to-market equity, and the overall market, which are known as the *Fama-French three factors*.[7] The size factor, or the SMB (small minus big) factor, is based on the market capitalization of firms. The book-to-market equity factor, or the HML (high minus low) factor, utilizes the book-equity to market-equity ratio. The market factor is the excess return of the market compared to the risk-free rate. For constructing the returns of these factors,

Exhibit 8.1   Monthly returns of U.S. large-cap stocks and five industries

Date	U.S. Large-cap	Cnsmr	Manuf	HiTec	Hlth	Other
Jan-12	4.87%	3.40%	3.11%	6.89%	3.38%	6.77%
Feb-12	4.24%	3.60%	4.41%	6.31%	1.31%	3.87%
Mar-12	3.30%	4.07%	−0.67%	4.24%	3.95%	4.74%
Apr-12	−0.61%	0.23%	−0.66%	−1.23%	0.63%	−1.66%
May-12	−6.15%	−3.27%	−7.79%	−6.40%	−3.39%	−7.19%
Jun-12	3.87%	2.00%	3.22%	3.82%	6.64%	4.78%
Jul-12	1.12%	1.26%	2.08%	0.48%	1.69%	−0.97%
Aug-12	2.51%	1.84%	1.83%	3.71%	1.04%	2.81%
Sep-12	2.55%	1.72%	2.44%	2.28%	4.74%	3.82%
Oct-12	−1.77%	−0.78%	−0.82%	−5.33%	−1.84%	0.67%
Nov-12	0.63%	2.21%	0.00%	1.46%	1.48%	−0.03%
Dec-12	1.05%	−0.87%	1.81%	0.50%	−0.43%	3.44%
Jan-13	5.31%	5.24%	6.50%	3.04%	8.11%	6.87%
Feb-13	1.35%	1.67%	1.08%	0.97%	1.36%	1.76%
Mar-13	3.63%	4.75%	2.88%	3.34%	6.57%	4.01%
Apr-13	2.00%	3.17%	0.70%	1.51%	2.57%	0.87%
May-13	2.19%	1.12%	1.52%	2.71%	1.86%	5.92%
Jun-13	−1.35%	−0.06%	−1.72%	−1.67%	−1.43%	−1.21%
Jul-13	5.35%	5.15%	5.44%	5.44%	7.84%	5.31%
Aug-13	−2.86%	−3.85%	−2.29%	−0.79%	−3.67%	−3.66%
Sep-13	3.44%	3.72%	3.44%	3.87%	4.04%	3.81%
Oct-13	4.44%	4.53%	4.46%	4.26%	3.73%	3.75%
Nov-13	2.81%	2.67%	1.51%	2.82%	4.48%	4.47%
Dec-13	2.65%	1.12%	2.84%	4.06%	0.72%	3.08%
Jan-14	−3.33%	−6.05%	−4.24%	−1.76%	2.05%	−4.37%
Feb-14	4.65%	4.89%	5.15%	4.63%	6.51%	3.45%
Mar-14	0.71%	0.64%	1.41%	−0.66%	−2.70%	2.28%
Apr-14	0.51%	−0.04%	2.95%	−0.88%	-0.28%	−1.57%
May-14	2.37%	1.71%	1.00%	3.58%	1.85%	1.78%
Jun-14	2.14%	1.53%	3.02%	2.66%	2.74%	2.11%
Jul-14	−1.38%	−3.28%	−4.35%	0.41%	−0.42%	−2.14%
Aug-14	4.00%	5.25%	4.00%	3.42%	5.40%	4.40%
Sep-14	−1.56%	−1.71%	−4.63%	−1.43%	0.12%	−1.04%
Oct-14	2.36%	3.07%	0.74%	1.31%	5.67%	3.31%
Nov-14	2.76%	6.39%	−2.09%	4.00%	2.82%	2.78%
Dec-14	0.70%	0.07%	0.41%	−1.44%	−0.92%	1.06%

Fama and French build six value-weighted portfolios formed on size and book-to-market ratio. The portfolios are characterized as

- small-value
- small-neutral
- small-growth

- big-value
- big-neutral
- big-growth

Here, the division among value, neutral, and growth is attributed to book-to-market ratio because firms with high book-equity compared to market-equity are classified as value stocks, and firms with high market-equity to book-equity ratio are grouped as growth stocks. The returns of the SMB factor are constructed by subtracting the average of the three big portfolios from the average of the three small portfolios. Similarly, the returns of the HML factor are calculated by subtracting the average of the two growth portfolios from the average of the two value portfolios. The market factor returns (excess returns on the market) are found by subtracting the one-month Treasury bill rate from value-weighted return of all stocks in the U.S. market.

According to the Fama-French three-factor model, the expected excess return on a portfolio, r, is explained by the three factors,

$$E(r) - r_f = \beta_M E(r_M - r_f) + \beta_{SMB} E(r_{SMB}) + \beta_{HML} E(r_{HML})$$

where

$$
\begin{aligned}
r_f &= \text{risk-free rate} \\
r_M - r_f &= \text{excess return on the market} \\
r_{SMB} &= \text{return of the SMB factor} \\
r_{HML} &= \text{return of the HML factor.}
\end{aligned}
$$

Similar to our earlier example with five industries, Exhibit 8.2 shows monthly returns of an equally weighted portfolio along with the Fama-French three factors. The equally weighted portfolio invests 50% in Exxon Mobil Corporation (XOM) and 50% in JPMorgan Chase & Co. (JPM), which is rebalanced to equal weights at the beginning of each month. The regression's R^2 value is 0.703. The R^2 value is not as high as the previous example because a U.S. large-cap index is much more diversified than our portfolio with only two companies. Nevertheless, a regression with an R^2 value of 0.703 still provides informative details. The coefficients for the regression are

$$\alpha = -0.00894 \qquad \beta_1 = 1.361 \qquad \beta_2 = 0.0424 \qquad \beta_3 = 1.008.$$

Exhibit 8.2 Monthly returns of a portfolio and the Fama-French three factors

Date	Equally Weighted Portfolio	$r_M - r_f$	SMB	HML
Jan-12	5.90%	5.05%	2.53%	−2.16%
Feb-12	4.52%	4.42%	−1.64%	0.04%
Mar-12	8.73%	3.11%	−0.24%	−0.06%
Apr-12	−3.19%	−0.85%	−0.62%	−0.17%
May-12	−15.58%	−6.19%	−0.12%	0.11%
Jun-12	8.30%	3.89%	0.82%	0.48%
Jul-12	1.55%	0.79%	−2.60%	0.02%
Aug-12	2.16%	2.55%	0.71%	0.55%
Sep-12	6.87%	2.73%	0.49%	1.57%
Oct-12	1.71%	−1.76%	−1.07%	4.14%
Nov-12	−2.07%	0.78%	0.67%	−1.10%
Dec-12	2.62%	1.18%	1.62%	3.25%
Jan-13	5.84%	5.57%	0.47%	1.31%
Feb-13	2.07%	1.29%	−0.39%	0.29%
Mar-13	−1.18%	4.03%	0.83%	−0.06%
Apr-13	1.33%	1.56%	−2.40%	0.41%
May-13	6.87%	2.80%	1.95%	1.32%
Jun-13	−1.72%	−1.20%	1.23%	−0.44%
Jul-13	5.05%	5.65%	1.87%	0.74%
Aug-13	−7.85%	−2.71%	0.29%	−2.46%
Sep-13	0.50%	3.77%	2.85%	−1.59%
Oct-13	2.30%	4.18%	−1.57%	1.30%
Nov-13	8.02%	3.12%	1.34%	−0.33%
Dec-13	5.23%	2.81%	−0.43%	−0.15%
Jan-14	−6.82%	−3.32%	0.84%	−1.86%
Feb-14	3.91%	4.65%	0.32%	−0.48%
Mar-14	4.16%	0.43%	−1.83%	4.67%
Apr-14	−1.18%	−0.19%	−4.19%	1.57%
May-14	−0.96%	2.06%	−1.87%	−0.38%
Jun-14	1.92%	2.61%	2.99%	−0.66%
Jul-14	−0.47%	−2.04%	−4.28%	0.01%
Aug-14	2.15%	4.23%	0.49%	−0.75%
Sep-14	−2.05%	−1.97%	−3.80%	−1.61%
Oct-14	1.95%	2.52%	4.17%	−1.89%
Nov-14	−3.11%	2.54%	−2.14%	−3.42%
Dec-14	3.06%	−0.06%	2.60%	1.52%

Exhibit 8.3 Factors included in the Northfield U.S. Fundamental Equity Risk Model and MSCI Barra U.S. Total Market Equity Models

Northfield Model[a]	MSCI Barra Model[b]
price/earnings ratio	growth
book/price ratio	leverage
dividend yield	earnings
trading activity	quality
12-month relative strength	management quality
market capitalization	dividend yield
earnings variability	earnings yield
growth rate of earnings per share	momentum
revenue/price ratio	liquidity
debt/equity ratio	beta
price volatility	residual volatility
	long-term reversal
	prospect
	size
	mid-capitalization

[a] For a description of how each of these factors is measured, see "Northfield: U.S. Fundamental Equity Risk Model" available at http://www.northinfo.com/documents/8.pdf
[b] For a description of how each of these factors is measured, see MSCI, "Barra US Total Market Equity Models" available at http://www.msci.com/resources/factsheets/MSCI_Barra_USTotalMarket_Equity_Model_Factsheet.pdf

As expected, the value of β for HML is higher than the value for SMB because the two companies are relatively large in size and categorized as value stocks.

Note that we are only illustrating a simple example, and more data points may provide a better relationship between the returns of factors and the portfolio returns. Moreover, in practice, more research effort is devoted to identifying the most relevant factors and the number of factors that drive returns. One notable extension of the three-factor model is the four factor model which includes momentum in addition to the three Fama-French factors.[8]

Commercial vendors have identified even more fundamental factors. Here are a few examples of such models.[9] The Northfield U.S. Fundamental Equity Risk Model has 11 fundamental factors described in Exhibit 8.3; the MSCI Barra U.S. Total Market Equity Model uses the long-term fundamental factors shown in Exhibit 8.3.[10]

8.3   FACTOR DEPENDENCY OF ROBUST PORTFOLIOS: THEORETICAL ARGUMENTS

The factor dependency of robust equity portfolios is analyzed by focusing on the ellipsoid model, where the ellipsoidal uncertainty set formulates the original mean-variance model as below:[11]

$$\min_{\omega} \frac{1}{2}\omega' \Sigma \omega - \lambda \left(\hat{\mu}'\omega - \delta \sqrt{\omega' \Sigma_\mu \omega} \right)$$
$$\text{s.t. } \omega' \iota = 1$$

(8.1)

where

$\mu \in \mathbb{R}^N$ is the estimate of expected returns

$\Sigma \in \mathbb{R}^{N \times N}$ is the covariance matrix

$\Sigma_\mu \in \mathbb{R}^{N \times N}$ is the covariance matrix of estimation errors

$\omega \in \mathbb{R}^N$ is the portfolio weights

$\iota \in \mathbb{R}^N$ is a vector of ones

$N \in \mathbb{N}$ is the number of stocks

$\lambda \in \mathbb{R}$ is the risk-seeking coefficient

$\delta \in \mathbb{R}$ controls the size of the ellipsoid

As the value of δ increases, the optimal portfolio becomes more robust because the formulation given by (8.1) considers a larger ellipsoid and hence more possible outcomes. The theoretical argument on the factor dependency of robust portfolios looks at how the value of δ affects portfolio factor exposure.[12]

The analysis consists of two major parts. The second part includes the analytical derivation of how robustness leads to a portfolio that is highly affected by factor movements. This is the main goal of the analysis. Nevertheless, the first part is as important as the second because it lays the foundation for the analysis. In the first part, the original robust formulation given by (8.1) is converted into a simpler formulation that allows us to analytically investigate the composition of the optimal robust portfolio. Since the robust formulation given by (8.1) is a second-order cone program, it is not a trivial task to reveal properties of robust portfolios generated directly from (8.1). Fortunately, it is possible to find a quadratic program with an extra parameter similar to δ where increasing this extra parameter has the equivalent effect on portfolios as expanding the ellipsoidal uncertainty set of the robust formulation (8.1). Mathematically investigating this quadratic program provides behavioral patterns of robust portfolios. It is found that increasing the value of $a \in \mathbb{R}$ in the formulation,

$$\min_{\omega} \frac{1}{2}\omega' \Sigma \omega - \lambda \hat{\mu}' \omega + \frac{\lambda a}{2}\omega' \Sigma_\mu \omega$$

$$\text{s.t. } \omega' \iota = 1,$$

(8.2)

has the same effect on the optimal portfolio as increasing the value of δ in (8.1), which is identical to increasing portfolio robustness. The comparison between problems (8.1) and (8.2) is shown using the first-order conditions, and the proof is summarized in Box 8.1.[13]

Box 8.1 PROOF OF THE SIMILARITY BETWEEN PROBLEMS (8.1) AND (8.2)

Since the problem given by (8.1) is a convex problem with only equality constraints, the optimal portfolio can be expressed by the first-order conditions where the Lagrangian is

$$L_{(1)}(\omega, \gamma) = \frac{1}{2}\omega' \Sigma \omega - \lambda \omega' \hat{\mu} + \lambda \delta \sqrt{\omega' \Sigma_\mu \omega} + \gamma(\omega' \iota - 1),$$

and its first-order conditions for the optimal solution $(\omega^*_{(1)}, \gamma^*_{(1)})$ are

$$\Sigma \omega^*_{(1)} - \lambda \hat{\mu} + \lambda \delta \frac{\Sigma_\mu \omega^*_{(1)}}{\sqrt{\omega^{*'}_{(1)} \Sigma_\mu \omega^*_{(1)}}} + \gamma^*_{(1)} \iota = 0, \quad \omega^{*'}_{(1)} \iota - 1 = 0. \quad (8.3)$$

Now, let us consider the following problem with inequality constraints,

$$\min_{\omega} \frac{1}{2}\omega' \Sigma \omega - \lambda \hat{\mu}' \omega$$

$$\text{s.t. } \omega^T \iota = 1$$

(8.4)

$$\sqrt{\omega^T \Sigma_\mu \omega} \leq \sqrt{\delta_0},$$

and its Lagrangian function is written as

$$L_{(4)}(\omega, \xi, \gamma) = \frac{1}{2}\omega' \Sigma \omega - \lambda \omega' \hat{\mu} + \xi(\sqrt{\omega' \Sigma_\mu \omega} - \sqrt{\delta_0}) + \gamma (\omega' \iota - 1).$$

(Continued)

The Karush-Kuhn-Tucker (KKT) conditions of (8.4) for the optimal solution $(\omega^*_{(4)}, \xi^*_{(4)}, \gamma^*_{(4)})$ includes:[14]

$$\Sigma\omega^*_{(4)} - \lambda\hat{\mu} + \xi^*_{(4)} \frac{\Sigma_\mu\omega^*_{(4)}}{\sqrt{\omega^{*\prime}_{(4)}\Sigma_\mu\omega^*_{(4)}}} + \gamma^*_{(4)}\iota = 0, \quad \omega^{*\prime}_{(4)}\iota - 1 = 0. \qquad (8.5)$$

The conditions for (8.3) and (8.5) are the same when $\lambda\delta = \xi^*_{(4)}$, $\gamma^*_{(1)} = \gamma^*_{(4)}$, and thus $\omega^*_{(1)} = \omega^*_{(4)}$. The inequality constraint in (8.4) can be modified as below because the estimation error covariance matrix is positive-semidefinite:

$$\min_\omega \frac{1}{2}\omega'\Sigma\omega - \lambda\hat{\mu}'\omega$$

$$\text{s.t. } \omega'\iota = 1 \qquad (8.6)$$

$$\omega^T\Sigma_\mu\omega \le \delta_0,$$

which unquestionably results in a problem that finds the equivalent optimal portfolio as (8.4). Hence, we have so far shown the relevance between (8.1) and (8.6).

We finally compare (8.2) and (8.6) by also writing their optimal conditions. Similar to deriving the KKT conditions earlier, the following should hold for the optimal solution $(\omega^*_{(6)}, \xi^*_{(6)}, \gamma^*_{(6)})$ for (8.6),

$$\Sigma\omega^*_{(6)} - \lambda\hat{\mu} + 2\xi^*_{(6)}\Sigma_\mu\omega^*_{(6)} + \gamma^*_{(6)}\iota = 0, \quad \omega^{*\prime}_{(6)}\iota - 1 = 0. \qquad (8.7)$$

The first-order conditions of problem (8.2) for the optimal solution $(\omega^*_{(2)}, \gamma^*_{(2)})$ are

$$\Sigma\omega^*_{(2)} - \lambda\hat{\mu} + \lambda a\Sigma_\mu\omega^*_{(2)} + \gamma^*_{(2)}\iota = 0, \quad \omega^{*\prime}_{(2)}\iota - 1 = 0. \qquad (8.8)$$

From (8.7) and (8.8), it is shown that problems (8.6) and (8.2) have equivalent solutions $\omega^*_{(6)} = \omega^*_{(2)}$ when $2\xi^*_{(6)} = \lambda a$ and $\gamma^*_{(6)} = \gamma^*_{(2)}$.

In summary, solving the revised formulation given by (8.2) becomes equivalent to solving the original robust problem given by (8.1) with a proper choice of parameters. Therefore, there exists an a in (8.2) that finds the optimal portfolio of (8.1).

The second part of the analysis is implemented in two steps. In the first step, the portfolio that depends the most on factor variance is derived. In the second step, it is shown that the optimal portfolio asymptotically approaches the portfolio from the first step when increasing the level of a. We refer to the portfolio with maximum dependency on factors as the *max-factor portfolio* and denote it by ω_{max}.

For explaining the dependency on factor movements, the following common assumptions on stock returns and factor models are important:

- Covariance matrix of returns Σ is positive-definite.
- Stock returns $r \in \mathbb{R}^N$ are explained by a factor model $r = \alpha + Bf + \varepsilon$ with the returns of M ($\leq N$) factors $f \in \mathbb{R}^M$, where the vector $\alpha \in \mathbb{R}^N$ is the intercept, $B \in \mathbb{R}^{N \times M}$ is the factor loadings, and $\varepsilon \in \mathbb{R}^N$ is the error term.
- Variance of factor returns is denoted by $\Sigma_f \in \mathbb{R}^{M \times M}$.
- Error term, from the factor model, is uncorrelated with stock returns
- Estimation errors of expected returns between stocks are uncorrelated (i.e., the covariance matrix $\Sigma_\varepsilon \in \mathbb{R}^{N \times N}$ is a diagonal matrix).

Furthermore, the following simplified structures on covariance matrices help understand the portfolios before generalizing the findings. First, let the covariance Σ have the same diagonal terms and the same off-diagonal terms where $\rho > 0$, and let Σ_ε also have the same diagonal values:

$$\Sigma = \begin{bmatrix} \sigma^2 & & \rho\sigma^2 \\ & \ddots & \\ \rho\sigma^2 & & \sigma^2 \end{bmatrix} \text{ and } \Sigma_\varepsilon = \begin{bmatrix} \sigma_\varepsilon^2 & & 0 \\ & \ddots & \\ 0 & & \sigma_\varepsilon^2 \end{bmatrix}. \tag{8.9}$$

Second, let the estimation error covariance matrix have a simplified diagonal form given by:

$$\Sigma_\mu = \begin{bmatrix} \sigma_\mu^2 & & 0 \\ & \ddots & \\ 0 & & \sigma_\mu^2 \end{bmatrix}. \tag{8.10}$$

Based on the factor model, the variance of a portfolio can be decomposed as

$$\text{Var}(\omega'r) = \text{Var}(\omega'Bf + \omega'\varepsilon) = \omega'B\Sigma_f B'\omega + \omega'\Sigma_\varepsilon\omega.$$

Since $\omega'B\Sigma_f B'\omega$ is the variance of the portfolio due to the factors, whereas $\omega'\Sigma_\varepsilon\omega$ is the variance attributable to the errors, the portfolio with variance that is the most dependent on f is the solution to the following maximization problem:

$$\max_{\omega} \frac{\omega' B \Sigma_f B' \omega}{\omega' \Sigma_\varepsilon \omega}$$

$$\text{s.t.} \quad \omega' \iota = 1.$$

The optimal portfolio, which is the max-factor portfolio, is found using the properties of eigenvalues and is expressed as

$$\omega_{max} = \frac{1}{\iota' \Sigma_\varepsilon^{-1/2} x_{max}} \Sigma_\varepsilon^{-1/2} x_{max}$$

where x_{max} is the eigenvector corresponding to the largest eigenvalue of the matrix $\Sigma_\varepsilon^{-1/2} B \Sigma_f B' \Sigma_\varepsilon^{-1/2}$. Moreover, this optimal portfolio becomes the equally weighted portfolio when the structures given by (8.9) are assumed.[15] Thus, in the simple case, the portfolio that depends the most on factors is the portfolio that allocates equal amounts to all investable stocks. The findings indicate that the equally weighted portfolio is the one most affected by factor movements due to the assumptions imposed. Nonetheless, the result is intuitive because the equally weighted portfolio is a diversified portfolio that invests in all stocks and thus is representative of various elements in the market.

The final step is to examine the composition of robust portfolios as the robustness is increased. When the simple structures of covariance matrices given by (8.9) and (8.10) are assumed, a matrix $\Sigma_a = \Sigma + a\Sigma_\mu$ for $a \geq 0$ has identical diagonal terms and identical off-diagonal terms, and its inverse Σ_a^{-1} also has the simplified structure

$$\Sigma_a^{-1} = \begin{bmatrix} \alpha_a & & \beta_a \\ & \ddots & \\ \beta_a & & \alpha_a \end{bmatrix}.$$

Furthermore, since Σ and Σ_μ are positive-definite, the two matrices Σ_a and Σ_a^{-1} also are positive-definite. From the definition of Σ_a, the problem given by (8.2) can be reformulated as

$$\min_{\omega} \frac{1}{2} \omega' \Sigma_a \omega - \lambda \hat{\mu}' \omega \qquad (8.11)$$

$$\text{s.t.} \quad \omega' \iota = 1.$$

where λa from (8.2) is represented simply by a in (8.11) since λ is a constant term.

The structure of Σ_a provides an analytic solution to the portfolio problem given by (8.11). The optimal robust portfolio is a combination of two components where the first component is the equally weighted portfolio, and the second component is the weights based on the expected excess returns. Thus, portfolio weights are deviations from the equal weights, and the amount of deviation is based on the expected excess return of each stock. More importantly, the deviation decreases and moves closer to the equally weighted portfolio as portfolio robustness is increased.[16]

The derivations explained here are based on some assumptions that may not apply in equity markets. Some assumptions such as the factor model are more common, but other conditions such as the simple structure of covariance matrices may be more distant from observed market behavior. However, the max-factor portfolio can be constructed with only the common assumptions, and empirical analysis supports how robustness pushes the optimal allocation closer to the max-factor portfolio without the stylized assumptions.

8.4 FACTOR DEPENDENCY OF ROBUST PORTFOLIOS: EMPIRICAL FINDINGS

The objective of the previous section was to examine the composition of robust portfolios analytically, and the intermediate steps required simplifications in order to solve complex portfolio problems. The factor dependency of robust portfolios can also be illustrated empirically with historical stock returns. The advantages of empirical experiments are that they do not require unrealistic assumptions and the results reflect the actual historical market behavior. Empirical findings from regression analysis are presented here where the independent variables are the three Fama-French factors.[17]

The following investment conditions are considered in the experiment. Robust portfolios are constructed from the formulation with an ellipsoidal uncertainty set on the expected return as shown in (8.1). Furthermore, for forming robust portfolios, the analysis chooses 49 industry portfolios, which are portfolios that partition stocks in the U.S. equity market based on their industry classification.[18] In other words, the optimal portfolio is a weight vector of 49 elements representing allocation to 49 industry groups. The adoption of industry portfolios as candidate assets is a more realistic case because it is unlikely that a portfolio manager will consider thousands of stocks as a candidate for building a stock portfolio. The investment horizon in our experiment is from the beginning of 1985 to the end of 2014. During this 30-year period, the optimal allocation is found every three years.[19] The framework for this analysis is summarized in Exhibit 8.4.[20]

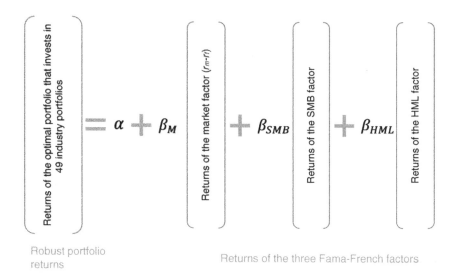

Robust portfolio
returns   Returns of the three Fama-French factors

Exhibit 8.4   Framework of the empirical analysis

The primary comparison is between the R^2 of the classical mean-variance portfolios and the R^2 of the robust portfolios. Exhibit 8.5 shows R^2 values from the regression analysis for both mean-variance and robust portfolios for various values of λ. The different λ values produce multiple efficient portfolios. Hence, six comparisons are included in Exhibit 8.5. For every value of λ, the R^2 value for the robust portfolio is higher than the R^2 value for the mean-variance portfolio, indicating the higher dependency on factors for robust portfolios. Among the six cases, while all the R^2 values for mean-variance portfolios are below 0.6, only two R^2 values are below 0.6 for robust portfolios. This difference is observed regardless of the investment period.

Exhibit 8.5 R^2 values for mean-variance and robust portfolios

λ	Mean-Variance	Robust (90% confidence)
0.01	0.491	0.524
0.02	0.551	0.599
0.04	0.583	0.685
0.06	0.571	0.739
0.08	0.550	0.776
0.1	0.528	0.804

The same framework can be applied to further investigate the relationship between portfolio robustness and factor movements. Instead of analyzing robust and nonrobust (i.e., classical mean-variance) portfolios, we repeated the analysis comparing robust portfolios with distinct levels of robustness. The resulting R^2 values are organized in Exhibit 8.6 where confidence levels between 1% and 99% are observed. Increasing the confidence level expands the uncertainty set, which increases the possible values considered and makes the solution more robust. Hence, as the confidence level increases from 1% to 99%, the robustness of the portfolio will also increase. Similar to the first experiment summarized in Exhibit 8.5, the

Exhibit 8.6 R^2 values for robust portfolios with various confidence levels

Confidence	Value of λ		
	0.01	0.02	0.04
1%	0.510	0.577	0.648
10%	0.514	0.582	0.658
20%	0.516	0.585	0.662
30%	0.517	0.587	0.666
40%	0.518	0.589	0.669
50%	0.519	0.590	0.671
60%	0.520	0.592	0.674
70%	0.521	0.594	0.677
80%	0.523	0.596	0.680
90%	0.524	0.599	0.685
95%	0.526	0.602	0.689
99%	0.529	0.606	0.696

Confidence	Value of λ		
	0.06	0.08	0.1
1%	0.690	0.720	0.742
10%	0.704	0.737	0.763
20%	0.710	0.744	0.771
30%	0.715	0.750	0.776
40%	0.718	0.754	0.781
50%	0.722	0.758	0.785
60%	0.725	0.761	0.789
70%	0.729	0.765	0.793
80%	0.733	0.770	0.798
90%	0.739	0.776	0.804
95%	0.743	0.781	0.809
99%	0.752	0.790	0.818

comparison is repeated for several values of λ to validate any patterns. The pattern in Exhibit 8.6 is very clear: the R^2 value increases with robustness. The values here present stronger evidence than when comparing robust portfolios with mean-variance portfolios.

The pattern is also observed when constructing portfolio from robust optimization formulation with an interval (box) uncertainty set,[21]

$$\min_{\omega} \omega' \Sigma \omega - \lambda(\hat{\mu}'\omega - \delta'|\omega|)$$
$$\text{s.t.} \quad \omega' \iota = 1.$$
(8.12)

Similar to the formulation with an ellipsoidal uncertainty set, increasing the confidence level increases the value of δ in (8.12), which is equivalent to increasing the robustness. Exhibit 8.7 compares the R^2 values for the classical mean-variance portfolios and robust portfolios. The R^2 values for robust portfolios are not as high as the values in Exhibit 8.5 for the ellipsoidal model, but the values are still higher than that for mean-variance portfolios. The R^2 values in Exhibit 8.8 for robust portfolios, as the confidence level is increased from 1% to 99%, are also not as high as the values shown in Exhibit 8.6. Furthermore, the values are not always increasing, as the confidence is increased except for when the value of λ is set to 0.08 and 0.1. Nonetheless, other values of λ also portray an overall increasing pattern, especially as the confidence reaches 90% or more.

The experiment is repeated for a one-year estimation period; even though the same 30-year horizon from 1985 to 2014 is analyzed, the optimal allocation is computed by solving the optimization problem at the beginning of each year. The one-year estimation period is applied to both mean-variance and robust portfolios, and the comparisons are summarized in Exhibit 8.9. While the robust portfolios with box uncertainty sets show lower R^2 values than the ones with ellipsoidal uncertainty sets, they both reveal higher dependencies than the classical mean-variance approach. Furthermore, Exhibits 8.10 and 8.11 observe changes as the robustness

Exhibit 8.7 R^2 values for mean-variance and robust portfolios (box uncertainty)

λ	Mean-Variance	Robust (90% confidence)
0.01	0.491	0.500
0.02	0.551	0.555
0.04	0.583	0.592
0.06	0.571	0.601
0.08	0.550	0.604
0.1	0.528	0.603

Exhibit 8.8 R^2 values for robust portfolios (box uncertainty) with various confidence levels

Confidence	Value of λ		
	0.01	0.02	0.04
1%	0.490	0.549	0.582
10%	0.494	0.552	0.586
20%	0.494	0.550	0.589
30%	0.493	0.549	0.587
40%	0.491	0.549	0.585
50%	0.491	0.548	0.584
60%	0.493	0.547	0.584
70%	0.495	0.548	0.585
80%	0.497	0.549	0.587
90%	0.499	0.555	0.592
95%	0.506	0.560	0.598
99%	0.512	0.572	0.616

Confidence	Value of λ		
	0.06	0.08	0.1
1%	0.572	0.552	0.529
10%	0.583	0.569	0.552
20%	0.589	0.580	0.566
30%	0.590	0.580	0.566
40%	0.587	0.580	0.566
50%	0.588	0.580	0.567
60%	0.589	0.581	0.569
70%	0.589	0.582	0.574
80%	0.591	0.589	0.586
90%	0.601	0.604	0.603
95%	0.613	0.618	0.614
99%	0.634	0.634	0.623

Exhibit 8.9 R^2 values for mean-variance and robust portfolios (1-year estimation period)

λ	Mean-Variance	Robust Ellipsoid (90% confidence)	Robust Box (90% confidence)
0.01	0.408	0.523	0.479
0.02	0.422	0.615	0.547
0.04	0.374	0.711	0.594
0.06	0.326	0.762	0.608
0.08	0.289	0.794	0.610
0.1	0.261	0.816	0.609

Exhibit 8.10 R^2 values for robust portfolios (ellipsoid uncertainty) with various confidence levels for a 1-year estimation period

Confidence	Value of λ			
	0.01	0.02	0.06	0.1
1%	0.489	0.565	0.682	0.724
10%	0.499	0.580	0.710	0.759
20%	0.503	0.586	0.720	0.772
30%	0.506	0.590	0.727	0.780
40%	0.508	0.594	0.733	0.786
50%	0.511	0.598	0.738	0.792
60%	0.513	0.601	0.743	0.797
70%	0.515	0.605	0.748	0.802
80%	0.519	0.609	0.754	0.808
90%	0.523	0.615	0.762	0.816
95%	0.526	0.620	0.768	0.822
99%	0.533	0.629	0.778	0.832

Exhibit 8.11 R^2 values for robust portfolios (box uncertainty) with various confidence levels for a 1-year estimation period

Confidence	Value of λ			
	0.01	0.02	0.06	0.1
1%	0.408	0.423	0.327	0.263
10%	0.410	0.431	0.352	0.286
20%	0.417	0.446	0.376	0.305
30%	0.423	0.456	0.400	0.329
40%	0.430	0.468	0.429	0.363
50%	0.436	0.480	0.463	0.406
60%	0.443	0.492	0.500	0.458
70%	0.453	0.507	0.537	0.513
80%	0.464	0.524	0.574	0.565
90%	0.479	0.547	0.608	0.609
95%	0.494	0.564	0.626	0.624
99%	0.519	0.591	0.644	0.623

of a portfolio is increased. For both the ellipsoid and box cases, the increasing pattern shown when rebalancing the optimal allocation every three years also appears when rebalancing every year.

Finally, the analysis is repeated with a different set of factors. In addition to the three factors originally established by Fama and French, they also published a five-factor model that adds two additional factors, which explain returns related to profitability and investment.[22] Thus, the additional regression analysis is performed using the returns of the five factors from 1985 to 2014. Since only monthly returns are available for the five factors, the portfolios are optimized using daily returns but monthly performances are used for the regression. The outcomes when using a three-year estimation period are summarized in Exhibits 8.12, 8.13, and 8.14, and the increasing pattern of correlation with factor movements is still evident. Similar to Exhibits 8.5, 8.7, and 8.9, the robust portfolios are shown to have higher R^2 values than mean-variance portfolios. Increasing the robustness of a portfolio also reveals the same dependency pattern as

Exhibit 8.12 R^2 values for mean-variance and robust portfolios (five factors and three-year estimation)

λ	Mean-variance	Robust Ellipsoid (90% confidence)	Robust Box (90% confidence)
0.01	0.244	0.366	0.286
0.02	0.335	0.519	0.396
0.04	0.392	0.678	0.522
0.06	0.383	0.753	0.581
0.08	0.358	0.795	0.611
0.1	0.331	0.822	0.624

Exhibit 8.13 R^2 values for robust portfolios (ellipsoid uncertainty) with various confidence levels (five factors and three-year estimation)

Confidence	Value of λ			
	0.01	0.02	0.04	0.06
1%	0.326	0.456	0.595	0.664
10%	0.336	0.474	0.621	0.695
20%	0.341	0.482	0.631	0.707
30%	0.345	0.487	0.639	0.715
40%	0.348	0.492	0.645	0.721
50%	0.351	0.496	0.651	0.727
60%	0.354	0.501	0.657	0.732
70%	0.357	0.506	0.662	0.738
80%	0.361	0.511	0.669	0.745
90%	0.366	0.519	0.678	0.753
95%	0.370	0.526	0.685	0.759
99%	0.379	0.537	0.698	0.771

Exhibit 8.14 R^2 values for robust portfolios (box uncertainty) with various confidence levels (five factors and three-year estimation)

Confidence	Value of λ			
	0.01	0.02	0.04	0.06
1%	0.242	0.333	0.392	0.384
10%	0.248	0.335	0.395	0.395
20%	0.244	0.336	0.401	0.407
30%	0.248	0.339	0.406	0.418
40%	0.252	0.340	0.413	0.434
50%	0.255	0.346	0.426	0.455
60%	0.260	0.351	0.443	0.482
70%	0.266	0.360	0.463	0.511
80%	0.274	0.373	0.488	0.543
90%	0.286	0.396	0.522	0.581
95%	0.297	0.416	0.546	0.605
99%	0.323	0.456	0.583	0.631

Exhibit 8.15 R^2 values for mean-variance and robust portfolios (five factors and two-year estimation)

λ	Mean-Variance	Robust Ellipsoid (90% confidence)	Robust Box (90% confidence)
0.01	0.252	0.399	0.317
0.02	0.302	0.535	0.414
0.04	0.304	0.686	0.527
0.06	0.277	0.761	0.570
0.08	0.248	0.804	0.583
0.1	0.223	0.830	0.582

presented in Exhibits 8.13 and 8.14. The patterns are also observed when using a shorter estimation period; Exhibits 8.15, 8.16, and 8.17 report the findings when using a 2-year estimation period.

As shown throughout the analyses presented in this section, the relationship between portfolio robustness and factor dependency is clear regardless of the uncertainty set for the expected return (interval or ellipsoidal uncertainty sets), the estimation periods (one, two, or three years), the number of factors considered (three or five), and the risk-aversion level (various values of λ). All of the results support the fact that robust portfolios are more dependent on factor movements than classical mean-variance portfolios and also that the dependency on factors increases as the robustness of a portfolio is increased.

Exhibit 8.16 R^2 values for robust portfolios (ellipsoid uncertainty) with various confidence levels (five factors and two-year estimation)

Confidence	Value of λ			
	0.01	0.02	0.04	0.06
1%	0.354	0.464	0.586	0.649
10%	0.366	0.485	0.618	0.689
20%	0.372	0.494	0.631	0.704
30%	0.376	0.500	0.640	0.714
40%	0.380	0.505	0.647	0.722
50%	0.383	0.511	0.654	0.730
60%	0.386	0.516	0.661	0.736
70%	0.389	0.521	0.668	0.743
80%	0.393	0.527	0.676	0.751
90%	0.399	0.535	0.686	0.761
95%	0.404	0.543	0.694	0.769
99%	0.412	0.556	0.709	0.782

Exhibit 8.17 R^2 values for robust portfolios (box uncertainty) with various confidence levels (five factors and two-year estimation)

Confidence	Value of λ			
	0.01	0.02	0.04	0.06
1%	0.252	0.303	0.305	0.278
10%	0.255	0.304	0.317	0.293
20%	0.259	0.312	0.327	0.312
30%	0.262	0.318	0.342	0.332
40%	0.267	0.325	0.359	0.359
50%	0.273	0.334	0.382	0.393
60%	0.280	0.347	0.410	0.432
70%	0.288	0.363	0.442	0.476
80%	0.299	0.383	0.480	0.522
90%	0.317	0.414	0.527	0.570
95%	0.332	0.440	0.557	0.597
99%	0.361	0.486	0.593	0.620

8.5   FACTOR MOVEMENTS AND ROBUST PORTFOLIOS

As explained at the beginning of this chapter, portfolio dependency on factor movements is valuable for understanding the overall risk of a portfolio. If increasing robustness increases factor dependency, then replacing a mean-variance optimal portfolio with its robust counterpart will increase the dependency on factor movements.

Sections 8.3 and 8.4 provided evidence that applying robust optimization to portfolio selection changes the factor exposure of the optimal portfolio. Since the factor exposure increases for robust portfolios, it means that robust portfolios are more sensitive to movements in the major factors. For example, if the returns of the size factor are very volatile during an investment period, it is likely that robust portfolio returns will also be more volatile during that period. Based on these findings, one might argue that robust portfolios are more robust because they are betting more on factor movements. The properties of robust portfolios are further discussed in the next two chapters to understand how robust portfolios achieve their robustness.

8.6   ROBUST FORMULATIONS THAT CONTROL FACTOR EXPOSURE

Even though portfolio managers can protect the uncertainty risk by using robust formulations based on the mean-variance model, they will not be able to maintain control of portfolio factor exposures because, as discussed throughout this chapter, portfolios formed from robust optimization tend to have higher dependency on factors when compared to classical mean-variance portfolios. It is, however, possible to reformulate robust portfolio problems to reach a certain level of exposure to factor movements. Here, two approaches based on a factor model are discussed.[23]

Suppose a factor model for returns $r \in \mathbb{R}^N$ is written as

$$r = Bf + \varepsilon$$

where $B \in \mathbb{R}^{N \times M}$ is the factor loading, $f \in \mathbb{R}^M$ encompasses the returns for M factors, and $\varepsilon \in \mathbb{R}^N$ is the error term, which is uncorrelated with the factors. Then, using the factor model, the return of a portfolio ω_0 can be expressed as

$$\omega_0' r = \omega_0' Bf + \omega_0' \varepsilon.$$

Then, the mean and variance of the portfolio return becomes

$$E(\omega_0' r) = E(\omega_0' Bf + \omega_0' \varepsilon) = \omega_0' B \cdot E(f)$$

$$Var(\omega_0' r) = Var(\omega_0' Bf + \omega_0' \varepsilon) = \omega_0' B\Sigma_f B' \omega_0 + \omega_0' \Sigma_\varepsilon \omega_0$$

where $\Sigma_f = Var(f)$ and $\Sigma_\varepsilon = Var(\varepsilon)$. As a measure of how much portfolio ω_0 invests in factors, we can use the amount of return invested in factors, $\omega_0' B$, or the proportion of variance dependent on factors

$$\frac{Var(\omega_0' Bf)}{Var(\omega_0' r)} = \frac{\omega_0' B\Sigma_f B' \omega_0}{\omega_0' \Sigma \omega_0}.$$

Therefore, controlling the level of factor loading by incorporating these values into the constraints will result in portfolios that possess the same level of factor dependency as ω_0.

One way to achieve a certain factor exposure is to add an additional constraint to match the factor loading with a target exposure portfolio ω_0. The expected return of the target portfolio ω_0 is $\omega_0' B \cdot E(f)$, where $\omega_0' B$ is the part of the return that depends on the factors. Thus, if a portfolio ω satisfies element-wise equality $\omega_0' B = \omega' B$, it will have the same exposure to factors as portfolio ω_0. Including this constraint to the robust formulation finds a robust portfolio while controlling the factor loading. An example is shown as follows:

$$\min_\omega \max_{\mu \in U(\hat{\mu})} \frac{1}{2}\omega' \Sigma \omega - \lambda \mu' \omega$$

$$\text{s. t. } \omega' \iota = 1$$

$$\omega' B = \omega_0' B$$

where $U(\hat{\mu})$ is the uncertainty set of the expected return for this robust portfolio problem.

Since an exact equality may be too restrictive, the constraint can be modified as the following to set a feasible range for the factor loading:

$$\min_\omega \max_{\mu \in U(\hat{\mu})} \frac{1}{2}\omega' \Sigma \omega - \lambda \mu' \omega$$

$$\text{s. t. } \omega' \iota = 1$$

$$\omega_0' B - \varepsilon \leq \omega' B \leq \omega_0' B + \varepsilon$$

where the vector ε sets the element-wise allowed distance from the target factor exposure.

Another approach is to concentrate on the variance of returns rather than the mean returns. If the returns of a portfolio are heavily influenced by the returns of factors, the portion of the variance expressed as $\omega'B\Sigma_f B'\omega$ will be greater than the portion of the variance arising from the idiosyncratic risk of individual asset movements expressed as $\omega'\Sigma_\varepsilon\omega$. So from the following equality, a portfolio ω will have the same factor exposure as portfolio ω_0,

$$\frac{\omega'B\Sigma_f B'\omega}{\omega'\Sigma\omega} = \frac{\omega_0'B\Sigma_f B'\omega_0}{\omega_0'\Sigma\omega_0}.$$

While this equality constraint will set the factor dependency of portfolio ω to that of portfolio ω_0, adding this constraint to a portfolio problem will make it non-convex. A simple modification is to first find the portfolio ω_{max} that has the maximum value of $\dfrac{\omega'B\Sigma_f B'\omega}{\omega'\Sigma\omega}$ and prohibit the optimal portfolio from being too close to ω_{max}. The distance from ω_{max} is necessary because robust portfolios have the tendency to increase factor exposure. Revised robust portfolio formulations such as the following will help maintain the portfolio factor exposure close to a desired level:[24]

$$\min_{\omega}\ \max_{\mu\in U(\hat{\mu})}\ \frac{1}{2}\omega'\Sigma\omega - \lambda\mu'\omega$$

$$\text{s. t.}\ \omega'\iota = 1$$

$$(\omega_{max} - \omega_0)'(\omega - \omega_0) = 0.$$

Exhibit 8.18 graphically shows how the additional constraint affects the factor dependency of a portfolio; the optimal portfolio will lie on the line

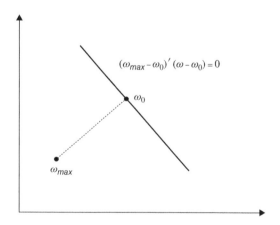

Exhibit 8.18 Graphical representation of constraint based on portfolio variance

perpendicular to the direction between ω_{max} and ω_0. As a result, the optimal robust portfolio ω will not be near the extreme portfolio ω_{max}, which has maximum exposure to factor returns.

The higher factor dependency of robust portfolios may not be an attractive attribute for portfolio managers since factor exposures in many cases reflect risk exposures. Thus, tilted factor exposures may result in either underestimating or overestimating the risk associated with an investment portfolio. With the revised formulations demonstrated in this section, robust portfolio optimization can be used to achieve robust performance as well as expected risk exposures. Experiments with historical returns confirm the robustness and the controlled factor exposures of portfolios when adding extra constraints on factor exposure.

KEY POINTS

- Factors explain the major movements in the market.
- Identifying factors and managing a portfolio's exposure to the factors are important for managing the overall risk of a portfolio.
- A widely known factor model for stock markets is the Fama-French three-factor model, the three factors being: market return, market capitalization (size), and book-equity to market-equity ratio.
- Robust portfolio optimization with an ellipsoidal uncertainty set for the expected return can be shown analytically, under structural assumptions, to increase the dependency on factor movements.
- Observing robust portfolios constructed using ellipsoidal and box uncertainty sets both show empirically that higher robustness leads to higher factor exposures. The pattern is observed regardless of the investment setting such as the estimation period and the risk-aversion level.
- The higher dependency on factors of robust portfolios requires additional analysis when considering robust counterparts of mean-variance portfolios in order to effectively manage portfolio risk.
- By adding further constraints on factor exposure to robust formulations, the level of factor exposure can be managed while also achieving improvement in robustness.

NOTES

1. We first introduced multifactor models in Chapter 2, where the model was written in matrix form.
2. Although factor models have the same form as a linear regression, there are fundamental differences between the two. In linear regression, the independent

variables, or explanatory variables, are all observed variables. For example, if one were to test a linear relationship between the returns of stocks and the unemployment rate, one might use linear regression, where the independent variable is the unemployment rate. However, the factors of a factor model are unobserved variables. In other words, a factor model would try to find whether stock returns can be explained by a few hidden factors. Another key assumption of factor models is that the errors, or residuals, are uncorrelated with one another. A comparison between a factor model and a linear multiple regression model is explained in Chapter 12 in Frank J. Fabozzi, Sergio M. Focardi, Svetlozar T. Rachev, and Bala G. Arshanapalli, *The Basics of Financial Econometrics: Tools, Concepts, and Asset Management Applications* (Hoboken, NJ: John Wiley & Sons, 2014).

3. The industry classifications are from the data library of Kenneth R. French (http://mba.tuck.dartmouth.edu/pages/faculty/ken.french/data_library.html), and returns of the five industries are also retrieved from this data library.

4. Although not discussed here, principal components analysis is a statistical tool for data reduction, which is also used for explaining the returns in the equity market. Principal components analysis, including the details of principal components, is discussed in Ian Jolliffe, *Principal Component Analysis* (Springer, 2002).

5. Factor analysis and principal components analysis, along with a comparison between the two, are explained in Chapter 12 in Fabozzi, Focardi, Rachev, and Arshanapalli, *The Basics of Financial Econometrics: Tools, Concepts, and Asset Management Applications*.

6. A comparison among fundamental, macroeconomic, and statistical factor models is explained in Gregory Connor, "The Three Types of Factor Models: A Comparison of Their Explanatory Powers," *Financial Analysts Journal* 51, 3 (1995), pp. 42–46.

7. The three factors are identified in Eugene F. Fama and Kenneth R. French, "Common Risk Factors in the Returns on Stocks and Bonds," *Journal of Financial Economics* 33, 1 (1993), pp. 3–56.

8. The fourth factor, momentum, is tested in Mark M. Carhart, "On Persistence in Mutual Fund Performance," *Journal of Finance* 52, 1 (1997), pp. 57–82.

9. Of course, asset management firms may have their own proprietary factor models.

10. In addition to the long-term factors, there are medium fundamental factors for investment horizons of one month and one year (Analyst Sentiment, Short Interest, Regional Momentum, Industry Momentum, and Downside Risk) and trading factors (Volatility Skew, News Sentiment, Seasonality, Short-term Reversal, and 1-Day Reversal).

11. The derivation for the ellipsoid model was discussed in section 6.5. The only difference here is the inclusion of $\frac{1}{2}$, which does not affect the outcome but is included for simplifying mathematical computations for the analysis.

12. This section is based on the analytical findings reported in Woo Chang Kim, Jang Ho Kim, and Frank J. Fabozzi, "Deciphering Robust Portfolios," *Journal of Banking and Finance* 45 (2014), pp. 1–8.
13. The proof in Box 8.1 was originally introduced in Lemma 1 in Kim, Kim, and Fabozzi, "Deciphering Robust Portfolios."
14. The rest of the KKT conditions are not included here since we focus on how the optimal ω of (8.4) satisfies conditions (8.3). This is also the case in (8.7).
15. The full proof is provided in Proposition 1 in Kim, Kim, and Fabozzi, "Deciphering Robust Portfolios."
16. The complete derivation based on the problem given by (8.11) is presented in Propositions 4.3, 4.4, and 4.5 in Kim, Kim, and Fabozzi, "Deciphering Robust Portfolios."
17. This section is based on the empirical study by Woo Chang Kim, Jang Ho Kim, So Hyoung Ahn, and Frank J. Fabozzi, "What Do Robust Equity Portfolio Models Really Do?" *Annals of Operations Research* 205, 1 (2013), pp. 141–168.
18. Returns of the 49 industry portfolios are those that are available from the data library of Kenneth R. French.
19. Since we are studying the properties of robust portfolios, we do not distinguish between estimation and evaluation periods (i.e., we focus on in-sample results). For example, the first optimal portfolio is constructed using returns during 1985 to 1987, and the returns of that optimal portfolio are calculated during 1985 to 1987.
20. Although the analyses presented here follow the same framework as in Kim, Kim, Ahn, and Fabozzi, "What Do Robust Equity Portfolio Models Really Do?", the experiment in this chapter includes up-to-date results using the most recent 30 years of data and analyses using five factors.
21. The interval uncertainty set, or box uncertainty set, is introduced in section 6.4 along with MATLAB functions for finding optimal robust portfolios.
22. The five-factor model is introduced in Eugene F. Fama and Kenneth R. French, "A Five-Factor Asset Pricing Model," *Journal of Financial Economics* 55, 1 (2015), pp. 389–406. Among several variations, the five factors identified as 2×3 used for our experiment and the factor returns are retrieved from the data library of Kenneth R. French (http://mba.tuck.dartmouth.edu/pages/faculty/ken .french/data_library.html).
23. The formulations for controlling factor exposure are introduced in Woo Chang Kim, Min Jeong Kim, Jang Ho Kim, and Frank J. Fabozzi, "Robust Portfolios that Do Not Tilt Factor Exposure," *European Journal of Operational Research* 234 (2014), pp. 411–421.
24. Additional variations of the constraint based on portfolio variance are illustrated in section 2 of Kim, Kim, Kim, and Fabozzi, "Robust Portfolios that Do Not Tilt Factor Exposure."

CHAPTER 9

Composition of Robust Portfolios

Robust portfolios' having higher dependency on factor movements compared to traditional mean-variance portfolios, as discussed in the previous chapter, is a portfolio-level observation. This characteristic explains how overall portfolio returns can be better explained by factor returns and how factor exposure enhances a portfolio manager's understanding of the overall risk of a portfolio. In this chapter, analyses on robust equity portfolios are continued at the stock level. Observing how robust portfolio optimization allocates weights to individual stocks will provide further understanding of robust portfolios in equities. Stock-level analyses will focus on the following.[1]

- Composition based on investment styles
- Composition based on momentum
- Composition based on industries
- Composition based on stock betas

9.1   OVERVIEW OF ANALYSES

For analyzing stock-level observations, various datasets are considered. Retrieving meaningful information by looking at individual weights of a portfolio constructed from a universe of thousands of stocks will be difficult. The datasets used for constructing portfolios divide the entire U.S. stock market into different groups. For example, the U.S. stock market can be divided into 10 industries, about 40 sectors, or more than 100 subsectors. By tracking the weights given to the subsectors, which are considerably fewer in number than the total number of stocks, a portfolio manager can focus on how robustness affects the allocation to each of the subsectors. Furthermore, the characteristics of each subsector will help a portfolio manager understand characteristics that robust portfolios tend to favor.

The three datasets that we use are:[2]

- *100 funds formed on size and book-to-market ratio*: The funds constructed are intersections of 10 portfolios formed on size and 10 portfolios formed on book-equity-to-market-equity ratio. These 100 funds include all stocks in the NYSE, AMEX, and NASDAQ, with data for market equity and book equity, and are formed at the end of June every year.

- *10 momentum funds*: All stocks in the NYSE, AMEX, and NASDAQ are grouped into 10 funds every day based on their prior returns (return from previous 12 months to 2 months).
- *49 industry funds*: All stocks in the NYSE, AMEX, and NASDAQ are grouped into 49 industry funds based on the four-digit Standard Industrial Classification (SIC) code. The stocks are regrouped at the end of every June.

The source for the three datasets is the Kenneth R. French Data Library.[3] All the datasets provide daily returns. Each dataset will provide additional information on the composition of robust portfolios, because each dataset is constructed based on unique factors and rules.

Our main focus is to look at the allocations directly, examining any change in composition as portfolio robustness is increased. If robust portfolios are consistently investing more in certain types of stocks, the finding will be useful for understanding the effect of increased robustness. Similarly to Chapter 8, we study how robust portfolios constructed using interval and ellipsoidal uncertainty sets on expected stock returns compare with classical mean-variance portfolios. We also compare robust portfolio composition with that of global minimum-variance (GMV) portfolios.[4] Checking the composition of the GMV portfolio will also be insightful because the GMV portfolio can be considered an extreme case of robust portfolio construction in which the uncertain expected returns of stocks are not considered.[5] Thus, the GMV portfolio is robust since it contains no uncertain components.

When constructing these portfolios, a restriction on weights is imposed. If optimal portfolios are compared without any weight constraints, classical mean-variance portfolios contain very large weights allocated to a few stocks, whereas GMV and robust portfolios only invest very small portions in any single stock. The few large weights (in positive and negative directions) of mean-variance portfolios not only add minimal information in addition to the obvious aggressiveness of the classical approach, but also do not portray a realistic investment situation because large exposures are avoided to reduce large risks. Therefore, the portfolios compared in this chapter restrict the minimum allocation in any fund to be −100% and the maximum allocation in any fund to be 100%.

The composition of portfolios is investigated for the 30-year period 1985 to 2014. Optimal portfolios are formed each year from daily returns during that year. As a result, the experiment creates 30 mean-variance portfolios, 30 GMV portfolios, and so forth for a given level of risk aversion. These 30 optimal allocations for each portfolio type are searched for any meaningful patterns. Portfolios are optimized for several risk-aversion levels (denoted by the parameter λ) to confirm the consistency of any observations.[6] The various risk-aversion levels lead to portfolios with annualized volatility ranging from 5% to 40%. Finally, when formulating robust portfolios, a confidence level of 90% is set for both robust optimization approaches.

9.2   COMPOSITION BASED ON INVESTMENT STYLES

The two factors, *size (market capitalization)* and *book-to-market ratio* of firms, divide equities into four major asset classes: *large-cap value, large-cap growth, small-cap value,* and *small-cap growth*.[7] Thus, we begin our analyses by checking whether robust portfolio optimization tilts the portfolio's exposure in these four asset classes. The daily returns of 100 funds formed on size and book-to-market ratio are used where the 100 funds represent stock-level returns, each with a unique level of size and book-to-market ratio. Since the 100 funds are grouped based on the two factors, it allows us to present a clear understanding of the allocation among the four asset classes obtained on the basis of the two factors. Furthermore, the number of funds is large enough to look for patterns in the diversification levels of portfolios, as well as additional portfolio attributes based on composition.

Exhibit 9.1 shows the average portfolio weights when the value of λ is set to 0.01 for the four approaches: classical mean-variance, GMV, robust optimization with box uncertainty set, and robust optimization with ellipsoidal uncertainty set. The most noticeable observation is that the average weights of mean-variance portfolios deviate the most. This is expected because classical mean-variance portfolios are concerned the least about risk and uncertainty and thereby lead to a more aggressive allocation. A more interesting finding is that the average weights of GMV portfolios deviate more than the average weights of robust portfolios, even though GMV portfolios aim at reducing risk without considering portfolio returns. The average weights of robust portfolios tend to stay relatively close to 0%. These observations are also evident in Exhibit 9.2, which plots the average portfolios' weights when the value of λ is set to 0.05. The weights of GMV portfolios are the same as in Exhibit 9.1 because the formulation for GMV portfolios is unaffected by risk-aversion levels. In Exhibit 9.2, mean-variance portfolios have average weights that tend to deviate more because a higher value of λ represents an investor who is willing to take more risk. Nonetheless, even with the higher value of λ, robust portfolios still do not put much weight on average to any single allocation.

The attributes of the portfolios shown in Exhibits 9.1 and 9.2 are also confirmed numerically in Exhibit 9.3 where the average standard deviation

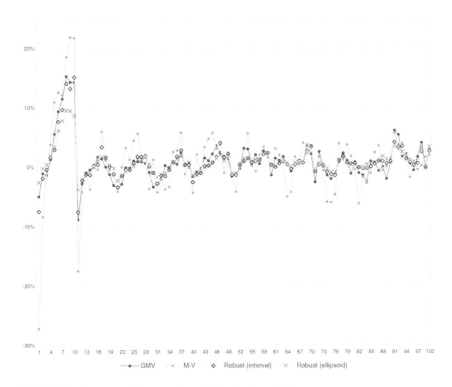

Exhibit 9.1   Average allocation in 100 funds ($\lambda = 0.01$)

of weights is first compared. For each approach, the standard deviation of the 100 weights is computed each year, and the average among those values is listed in the third column. Mean-variance portfolios have the highest average standard deviation followed by GMV portfolios. Robust portfolios tend to have less average standard deviation, with the ellipsoid method having the lowest deviation on average. The average number of non-zero weight allocations as well as the average number of negative-weight allocations (i.e., short positions) are also compared in the last two columns of the exhibit. For counting non-zero allocations, allocations with an absolute weight of at least 0.01% were counted (i.e., weights greater than 0.01% and weights less than −0.01%). As shown in Exhibit 9.3, mean-variance portfolios have the highest non-zero allocations and the highest negative allocations. This result may not be intuitive because the more robust or risk-averse portfolios may allocate weight in all candidate investments to achieve high diversification, but the observation is consistent throughout various values of λ. One explanation for this observation could be the tendency of robust portfolios to reduce short positions. When comparing the average of only positive weights

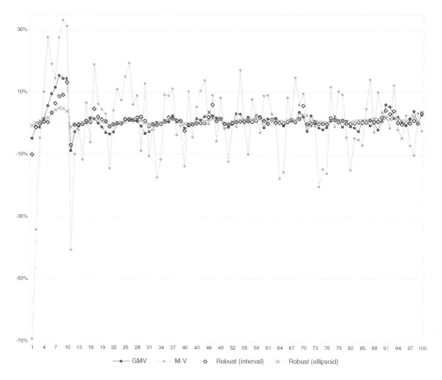

Exhibit 9.2 Average allocation in 100 funds ($\lambda = 0.05$)

Exhibit 9.3 Details on average weights allocated in 100 funds

Value of λ	Portfolio Formulation	Avg Standard Deviation of Weights	Avg of Positive Weights	Avg of Negative Weights	Avg Number of Non-Zero Allocations	Avg Number of Negative Allocations
0.01	GMV	7.8%	6.3%	−5.0%	98.5	45.6
	Mean-Variance	15.4%	12.6%	−11.1%	99.5	48.6
	Robust (interval)	6.2%	4.4%	−2.4%	96.2	48.4
	Robust (ellipsoid)	4.2%	3.5%	−1.7%	92.1	42.9
0.05	GMV	7.8%	6.3%	−5.0%	98.5	45.6
	Mean-Variance	49.9%	41.5%	−41.5%	99.8	48.7
	Robust (interval)	6.6%	2.9%	−1.1%	86.3	37.9
	Robust (ellipsoid)	2.3%	1.8%	−0.7%	89.6	25.0
0.1	GMV	7.8%	6.3%	−5.0%	98.5	45.6
	Mean-Variance	66.8%	57.6%	−59.1%	100.0	48.5
	Robust (interval)	7.8%	2.5%	−1.1%	72.4	23.4
	Robust (ellipsoid)	1.8%	1.4%	−0.5%	90.9	15.3

and the average of only negative weights, mean-variance and GMV port-folios show similar values, whereas robust portfolios only allocate half of their positive positions into negative positions as shown in Exhibit 9.3. The average weights in the fifth column (average of negative weights) for robust portfolios have magnitudes that are about half of the average weights in the fourth column (average of positive weights).

Finally, the compositions based on the four major asset classes in equities are presented in Exhibit 9.4. The largest positive allocations and the small-est negative allocations of mean-variance portfolios confirm the aggressive exposures of the traditional approach discussed earlier. All approaches show the largest allocations in small-cap value stocks and the second largest alloca-tions in large-cap value stocks. This reveals how all portfolios are investing primarily in value stocks with a small-cap bias. The four approaches also agree on the smallest weights: All portfolios allocate the smallest weight (the largest negative allocations unless no negative allocations) in small-cap growth stocks. The apparent distinction is how mean-variance portfolios invest in large-cap growth stocks. Although other portfolios allocate positive weights but small relative to other asset classes, mean-variance portfolios take a short position in large-cap growth. These short positions will allow the mean-variance portfolios to invest more heavily in value stocks.

Another remarkable finding is the similarity between GMV and robust portfolios. Exhibit 9.5 graphically expresses the first four rows of allocations in Exhibit 9.4. The similarity between GMV and robust portfolios are more

Exhibit 9.4 Allocation in small-cap growth, small-cap value, large-cap growth, and large-cap value

Value of λ	Portfolio Formulation	Small-Cap Growth	Small-Cap Value	Large-Cap Growth	Large-Cap Value
0.01	GMV	−17.8%	73.0%	20.4%	24.4%
	Mean-Variance	−38.2%	108.5%	−8.5%	38.2%
	Robust (interval)	−27.5%	80.9%	16.6%	30.0%
	Robust (ellipsoid)	−13.2%	59.1%	19.2%	34.9%
0.05	GMV	−17.8%	73.0%	20.4%	24.4%
	Mean-Variance	−100.9%	201.9%	−78.9%	77.9%
	Robust (interval)	−19.2%	70.9%	17.9%	30.4%
	Robust (ellipsoid)	3.7%	41.6%	20.7%	34.0%
0.1	GMV	−17.8%	73.0%	20.4%	24.4%
	Mean-Variance	−146.1%	247.7%	−102.1%	100.5%
	Robust (interval)	−19.3%	70.0%	18.6%	30.8%
	Robust (ellipsoid)	8.7%	38.3%	20.8%	32.1%

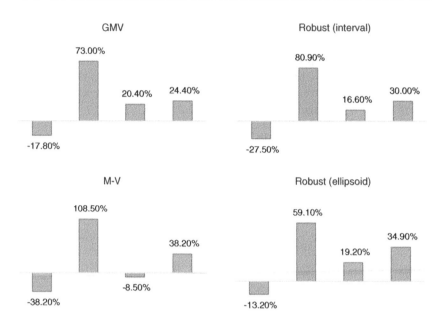

Exhibit 9.5 Allocation in small-cap growth, small-cap value, large-cap growth, and large-cap value ($\lambda = 0.01$)

apparent in Exhibit 9.5 as they allocate about 60% to 80% in small-cap value, about 25% to 35% in large-cap value, about 15% to 20% in large-cap growth, and about −30% to −10% in small-cap growth. The comparable compositions are not completely unexpected; as mentioned earlier in this chapter, the GMV formulation is robust because it does not incorporate expected returns that contain uncertainty. Nonetheless, it provides further justification for analyzing the attributes of robust portfolios in conjunction with the GMV portfolio.

9.3 COMPOSITION BASED ON ADDITIONAL FACTORS

In the previous section, we investigated the decomposition of portfolio weights based on the two most common factors that divide stocks into large-cap or small-cap and value or growth. Since there are additional factors in the equity market, in this section the analysis is extended in order to identify any additional properties of robust portfolios.

Momentum describes a trend of a given stock. If a stock has been performing well recently, then its momentum will be positive. On the other hand, if the price of a stock has been decreasing in recent periods, the momentum of that stock will be negative. The information becomes useful to portfolio managers when assuming that recent trends will continue in the near future. For example, if a stock's price has been continuously increasing in the last 10 to 12 months, it is likely that the stock will continue to rise during the next few months unless the underlying business of the company goes through changes that can affect the trend of the stock.

For studying portfolio composition based on momentum, the 10 momentum funds described earlier in this chapter are used for representing the entire U.S. equity market. Descriptive statistics of the returns of the 10 momentum funds are shown in Exhibits 9.6 and 9.7. From the correlation among the 10 momentum funds listed in Exhibit 9.6, we see that funds with similar levels of momentum have high correlation. In fact, funds that are adjacent in the momentum scale have correlations around 0.9. But the two funds that are the furthest, namely the lowest momentum stocks and the highest momentum stocks, have correlation less than 0.6.

In Exhibit 9.7, the annualized return of the 30-year period from 1985 to 2014 and average daily returns indicate how the momentum is a good predictor of stock movements because stocks categorized as having the highest momentum exhibited the highest returns. However, standard deviation suggests that the two extremes—stocks with highest momentum and stocks with lowest momentum—might not be too attractive due to high volatility. A very high momentum for a stock could be signaling further high returns, but it could also mean that the stock is near the end of its increasing trend (i.e., the stock price has peaked). Hence, when combining the views of return and risk, the fourth to eighth momentum funds seem to be the most attractive. Not surprisingly, optimal portfolios invest more in these funds with relatively high expected return along with low standard deviation.

Exhibit 9.6 Correlation among the 10 momentum funds

	Low	2	3	4	5	6	7	8	9	High
Low	1									
2	0.89	1								
3	0.85	0.92	1							
4	0.81	0.89	0.92	1						
5	0.78	0.87	0.90	0.92	1					
6	0.74	0.83	0.87	0.91	0.92	1				
7	0.70	0.79	0.84	0.88	0.90	0.92	1			
8	0.66	0.75	0.80	0.85	0.87	0.91	0.93	1		
9	0.64	0.72	0.77	0.81	0.84	0.87	0.90	0.92	1	
High	0.59	0.62	0.65	0.70	0.72	0.75	0.79	0.83	0.88	1

Panel A. Annualized Return

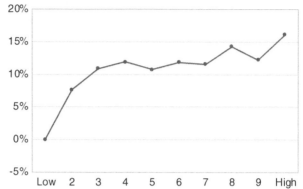

Panel B. Average Daily Return

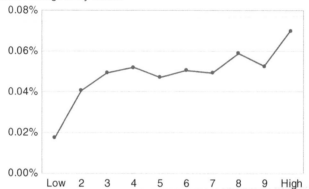

Panel C. Standard Deviation

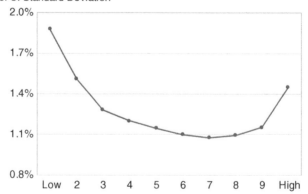

Exhibit 9.7 Descriptive statistics of the 10 momentum funds

Exhibits 9.8 and 9.9 graph average allocations of GMV, mean-variance, and robust portfolios among the 10 momentum funds when the value of λ is set to 0.01 and 0.1, respectively. The average weights shown in Exhibit 9.8 are all similar since even the mean-variance investor is highly risk averse in this case. It is, however, still apparent that robust portfolios do not allocate too much in any single fund; the weights tend to be closer to 0% and show lower deviation in the 10 weights. In Exhibit 9.9, which shows the more aggressive case for mean-variance portfolios, the average weights tend to deviate more in order to exploit funds that can result in a higher expected

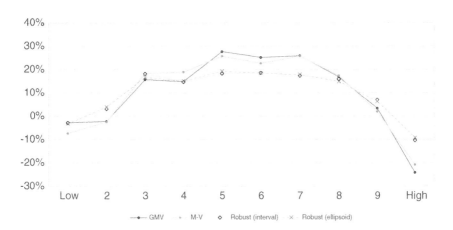

Exhibit 9.8 Average allocation in 10 momentum funds ($\lambda = 0.01$)

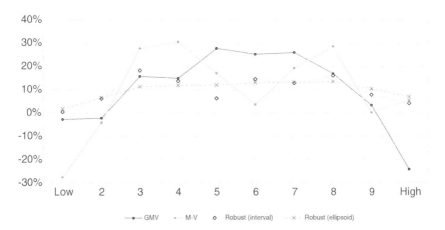

Exhibit 9.9 Average allocation in 10 momentum funds ($\lambda = 0.1$)

portfolio return. Even though the value of λ is also higher for robust formulations, robust portfolios tend to more evenly distribute their weights and also avoid negative allocations on average. In summary, when the value of λ is 0.1, GMV portfolios take a short position in the stocks with the highest momentum, traditional mean-variance portfolios take a short position in the stocks with the lowest momentum, and robust portfolios almost evenly distribute their allocation. These patterns are observed when the value of λ is greater than about 0.03, which is around when mean-variance portfolios allocate less to the highest momentum stocks and more to the lowest momentum stocks. By focusing on only 10 funds, the difference between GMV and robust portfolios becomes even more evident. We continue the investigation by focusing next on 49 industry funds, which allows us to look at results when investing in not as many as 100 funds but also not as few as 10 funds.

The 49 industry funds divide the U.S. equity market into 49 groups based on their industry classification. The 49 industries are listed in Exhibit 9.10 and a summary of the results is detailed in Exhibit 9.11. The overall behavior of portfolios is similar to the experiment when using 100 funds formed on the basis of size and book-to-market ratio. Traditional mean-variance portfolios are the most aggressive in allocating weights, showing the highest standard deviation of weights with the most exposure in long and short positions. In contrast, robust portfolios tend to be the most conservative as the shows average weight that are closest to zero.

9.4   COMPOSITION BASED ON STOCK BETAS

The final analysis on the composition of robust portfolios we investigate in this chapter is whether allocations are impacted by beta, sensitivity to excess market return, of individual stocks. In the previous chapter, robust portfolios were shown to be more sensitive to changes in major factors. Here, we study if the sensitivities of individual stocks reveal additional characteristics of robust portfolios. The two datasets from sections 9.2 and 9.3, excluding the momentum funds since there are only 10 funds, are explored, and we begin by finding the beta of each fund. The value of beta for a fund is estimated from the returns of the fund and the excess market returns. Then the weights of the portfolios are compared with the betas of the funds.

Exhibit 9.12 is similar to Exhibits 9.1 and 9.2, but the weights are sorted in ascending order of beta. The grey area in each of the three graphs plots the betas of the 100 funds. Mean-variance portfolios, especially for higher values of λ, certainly show considerable deviation in weights regardless of a fund's beta. In contrast, the other portfolios tend to invest more in low-beta funds than other funds with higher beta. As denoted numerically in

Exhibit 9.10 List of 49 industries

1. Agriculture	2. Food Products	3. Candy & Soda	4. Beer & Liquor	5. Tobacco Products	6. Recreation	7. Entertainment
8. Printing and Publishing	9. Consumer Goods	10. Apparel	11. Healthcare	12. Medical Equipment	13. Pharmaceutical Products	14. Chemicals
15. Rubber and Plastic Products	16. Textiles	17. Construction Materials	18. Construction	19. Steel Work, etc.	20. Fabricated Products	21. Machinery
22. Electrical Equipment	23. Automobiles and Trucks	24. Aircraft	25. Shipbuilding, Railroad Equipment	26. Defense	27. Precious Metals	28. Non-Metallic and Industrial Metal Mining
29. Coal	30. Petroleum and Natural Gas	31. Utilities	32. Communications	33. Personal Services	34. Business Services	35. Computers
36. Computer Software	37. Electronic Equipment	38. Measuring and Control Equipment	39. Business Supply	40. Shipping Containers	41. Transportation	42. Wholesale
43. Retail	44. Restaurants, Hotels, Motels	45. Banking	46. Insurance	47. Real Estate	48. Trading	49. Other

Exhibit 9.11 Details on average weights allocated in 49 industry funds

Value of λ	Portfolio Formulation	Avg Standard Deviation of Weights	Avg of Positive Weights	Avg of Negative Weights	Avg Number of Non-Zero Allocations	Avg Number of Negative Allocations
0.01	GMV	10.4%	8.4%	−5.9%	48.7	21.4
	Mean-Variance	12.2%	9.7%	−7.8%	48.6	21.0
	Robust (interval)	7.6%	5.7%	−2.5%	47.7	20.8
	Robust (ellipsoid)	5.8%	5.2%	−2.3%	48.1	19.6
0.05	GMV	10.4%	8.4%	−5.9%	48.7	21.4
	Mean-Variance	32.2%	26.5%	−23.6%	48.8	23.7
	Robust (interval)	7.5%	3.8%	−0.7%	42.6	13.2
	Robust (ellipsoid)	3.2%	3.2%	−1.1%	47.2	10.7
0.1	GMV	10.4%	8.4%	−5.9%	48.7	21.4
	Mean-Variance	50.3%	42.4%	−40.4%	48.9	23.9
	Robust (interval)	8.5%	3.3%	−0.5%	36.5	8.4
	Robust (ellipsoid)	2.6%	2.8%	−0.9%	47.6	8.5

Exhibit 9.13, even though the beta of robust portfolios is higher compared to mean-variance portfolios, the correlation between portfolio weights and betas is lower for robust portfolios than mean-variance portfolios. The third column of Exhibit 9.13 shows that the average portfolio beta and the higher values for robust portfolios are consistent with the findings reported in the previous chapter: Robust portfolios have higher exposure to factor movements. More importantly, robust portfolios demonstrate lower correlation (larger in the negative direction) as shown in the last column of Exhibit 9.13, which means that robust portfolios allocate more weight to low-beta funds compared to the traditional mean-variance approach. While GMV portfolios also exhibit a low correlation between allocation in funds and beta of funds, robust portfolios are the only ones that are characterized by having the low correlation as well as large portfolio beta. The situation is similar when observing portfolios investing in 49 industry funds. Exhibit 9.14 confirms the behaviors of robust portfolios as they have higher portfolio beta and a tendency to invest more in low-beta funds when compared to mean-variance portfolios. This unique attribute observed for robust portfolios could be why they result in more robust performance, and we next demonstrate how to explore this attribute.

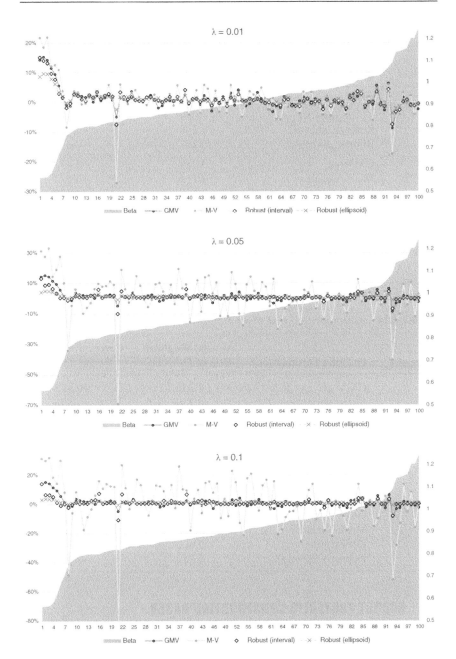

Exhibit 9.12 Average allocations in 100 funds sorted by beta (primary axis: weight, secondary axis: beta)

Exhibit 9.13 Allocation and beta of 100 funds

Value of λ	Portfolio Formulation	Average Weighted Beta of Portfolio	Correlation between Weight and Beta
0.01	GMV	0.088	−0.473
	Mean-Variance	0.084	−0.241
	Robust (interval)	0.208	−0.511
	Robust (ellipsoid)	0.297	−0.670
0.05	GMV	0.088	−0.473
	Mean-Variance	0.114	−0.073
	Robust (interval)	0.449	−0.320
	Robust (ellipsoid)	0.586	−0.661
0.1	GMV	0.088	−0.473
	Mean-Variance	0.170	−0.050
	Robust (interval)	0.533	−0.219
	Robust (ellipsoid)	0.679	−0.609

Exhibit 9.14 Allocation and beta of 49 industry funds

Value of λ	Portfolio Formulation	Average Weighted Beta of Portfolio	Correlation between Weight and Beta
0.01	GMV	0.236	−0.475
	Mean-Variance	0.259	−0.386
	Robust (interval)	0.368	−0.537
	Robust (ellipsoid)	0.423	−0.620
0.05	GMV	0.236	−0.475
	Mean-Variance	0.359	−0.131
	Robust (interval)	0.586	−0.330
	Robust (ellipsoid)	0.671	−0.535
0.1	GMV	0.236	−0.475
	Mean-Variance	0.487	−0.066
	Robust (interval)	0.666	−0.218
	Robust (ellipsoid)	0.759	−0.434

9.5 ROBUST PORTFOLIO CONSTRUCTION BASED ON STOCK BETA ATTRIBUTES

An ultimate goal of analyzing the attributes or characteristics of portfolios constructed from robust portfolio optimization would be to use those attributes for constructing robust portfolios without necessarily solving robust optimization problems in order to reduce complexity. Since a few characteristics of robust portfolios were empirically observed in this chapter, we conclude the chapter by illustrating their use in improving the robustness of portfolios.[8]

The main idea behind the strategy is to focus on the worst returns. Thus, the broad approach is very similar to robust portfolio optimization. It begins by setting a trading period for which returns of candidate stocks as well as a comprehensive market index can be collected. By focusing on the returns of the market index, the trading days of the collected data are divided into N groups. The first group will contain data during the lowest market return days, and the last group will contain data during the highest market return days. For each of the N groups, two metrics are computed: the average market return during the days in the group and the optimal mean-variance portfolio weights using the stock returns during the days in the group. So far, the steps lead to N mean returns and N optimal portfolio weight vectors. Note that there are a total of N weights that correspond to a single stock, one from each optimal portfolio. In other words, for a single candidate stock, the first optimal portfolio constructed from the first group will have allocations to the stock, the second optimal portfolio constructed from the second group will also have allocations to the stock, and so forth. The next step is to continue focusing on each stock separately and calculating the correlation between the N weights for the stock (one from each of the N optimal portfolios) and the N mean returns. The correlation shows whether optimal portfolios allocate more to the stock as the market performs better. Hence, the stock with the lowest correlation indicates that optimal portfolios invest more in the stock as the market performs worse. Finally, the robust portfolio is created by equally weighting 25% of the total number of candidate stocks with the lowest correlation. This algorithm is graphically summarized in Exhibit 9.15.

The algorithm simplifies a few steps through proxy measures. First, the worst-case information is collected by searching the trading days that recorded the lowest returns as measured by a broad-based market index. Second, instead of estimating stock betas, the approach finds the correlation between the weight allocated in optimal mean-variance portfolios and market returns. Whereas a low stock beta represents stocks that have relatively low returns when the market is performing well, a low value of correlation used in the proposed approach represents stocks that are not favored in the optimal portfolio when the market is moving up.

When comparing the attributes of robust portfolios observed in sections 9.2, 9.3, and 9.4, the proposed simple algorithm focuses on the worst-case information, which is comparable to the worst-case optimization. Finding the low correlation between optimal portfolio allocations and market

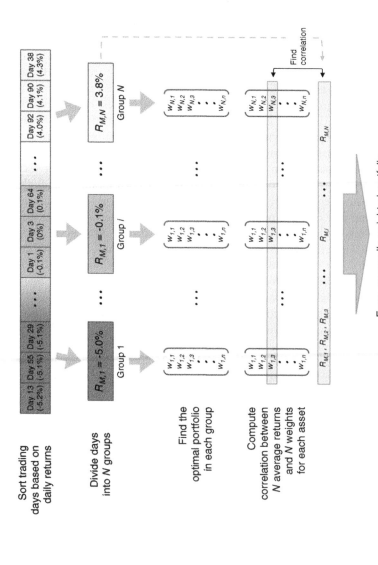

Exhibit 9.15 Rule-based robust portfolio algorithm

Source: Jang Ho Kim, *Understanding Robust Optimization by Analyzing Robust Portfolios* (doctoral dissertation, KAIST, 2014).

Exhibit 9.16 Investment performance with various estimation periods from 1973 to 2011

	Market Index	Equally Weighted Portfolio	Mean-Variance Portfolios				Robust Portfolios (Proposed)			
			2 yrs	3 yrs	4 yrs	5 yrs	2 yrs	3 yrs	4 yrs	5 yrs
Return	11.5%	13.4%	8.8%	8.3%	10.3%	10.7%	12.7%	14.8%	14.3%	15.2%
Volatility	15.5%	16.2%	22.5%	21.3%	19.3%	18.5%	16.3%	16.3%	15.9%	16.1%
Sharpe ratio	0.37	0.46	0.14	0.13	0.24	0.27	0.42	0.55	0.53	0.58
Max draw-down	50.5%	55.2%	72.7%	76.6%	79.9%	71.7%	51.4%	48.0%	50.3%	47.3%
VaR at 95%	−7.3%	−6.9%	−9.7%	−9.8%	−8.6%	−7.9%	−6.6%	−6.1%	−5.8%	−5.7%
CVaR at 95%	−10.0%	−10.6%	−15.7%	−14.7%	−13.2%	−12.0%	−11.0%	−10.3%	−10.4%	−10.2%

returns is similar to the tendency of robust portfolios allocating more to low-beta stocks. Building a portfolio with only 25% of candidate stocks reflects how robust portfolios overall invest in fewer stocks than traditional mean-variance portfolios. Moreover, creating an equally weighted portfolio will help in achieving a high portfolio beta because the portfolio only takes long positions. Since most stocks have positive beta, the weighted average of betas will be relatively high with the weights and betas all being positive.

The performances of the portfolios are reported in Exhibit 9.16.[9] The portfolios compared here invest in 40 industries as classified by the Datastream Industry Classification Benchmark (ICB) at level 4, and returns are evaluated from 1971 to 2011. For classical mean-variance portfolios and robust portfolios constructed from the proposed rule-based algorithm, various estimation periods are used to check the consistency in performance. For example, an estimation period of two years demonstrates a situation where historical returns during the most recent two years are considered for estimating the optimal portfolio for the following year. The robust portfolios clearly exhibit much better performance than classical mean-variance portfolios for all measures. Furthermore, when at least three years for an estimation period is considered, the proposed robust portfolios also outperform the market index as well as the equally weighted portfolio. Exhibit 9.17 compares the wealth of the portfolios from 1996 to 2011 by plotting the logarithm of wealth beginning with a value of one. The mean-variance and robust portfolios with a three-year estimation period

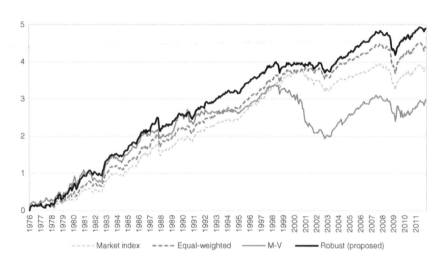

Exhibit 9.17 Log wealth of portfolios from 1976 to 2011 (wealth starting from one)

are shown. The superior performance of the robust portfolio demonstrates how attributes of robustness can lead to additional approaches for finding dominant portfolios.

KEY POINTS

- By extending the portfolio level analysis on factor exposure, the behavior of robust equity portfolios at the stock level provides details on the composition of robust portfolios.
- When forming portfolios that invest in 100 funds with unique size and book-to-market ratio levels, mean-variance portfolios show the highest deviation in weights, and robust portfolios show the lowest deviation.
- Robust portfolios invest in fewer funds and do not hold as many short positions as mean-variance portfolios. These observations are confirmed with portfolios investing in 49 industries.
- GMV and robust portfolios reveal similar allocations in the four major asset classes for equities: large-cap value, large-cap growth, small-cap value, and small-cap growth stocks.
- Optimal allocation of robust portfolios show the most evenly distributed weights compared to classical mean-variance and GMV portfolios when tested with 10 momentum funds as candidate assets.
- Even though robust portfolios show higher portfolio beta, they reveal a tendency to allocate more in low-beta investments.
- The properties of robust portfolios constructed from robust optimization can be used as the basis for formulating additional robust portfolio strategies.

NOTES

1. Composition of robust equity portfolios based on investment styles and stock betas are based on analyses in Jang Ho Kim, Woo Chang Kim, and Frank J. Fabozzi, "Composition of Robust Equity Portfolio," *Finance Research Letters* 10, 2 (2013), pp. 72–81.
2. Although the dataset used in our analyses are simply portfolios (e.g., 10 momentum portfolios, 49 industry portfolios, etc.), we will refer to them as *funds* in this chapter to minimize any confusion between funds which we refer to as investment candidates and optimal portfolios which represent optimal allocations in the funds.
3. http://mba.tuck.dartmouth.edu/pages/faculty/ken.french/data_library.html
4. The GMV portfolio is introduced in section 2.4 of Chapter 2.

5. Recall that in our formulation of robust portfolio optimization that we assume the covariance matrix of stock returns contains no uncertain elements.
6. To review how risk aversion is incorporated into robust portfolio optimization, see Chapter 6 and the use of parameter λ.
7. Size and book-to-market ratio are two of the three Fama-French factors introduced in Chapter 8.
8. The portfolio construction method presented in this section is discussed in more detail in Woo Chang Kim, Jang Ho Kim, John M. Mulvey, and Frank J. Fabozzi, "Focusing on the Worst State for Robust Investing," *International Review of Financial Analysis* 39 (2015), pp. 19–31. Note that the algorithm was introduced to demonstrate the value of worst-case information and not as a complete investment strategy.
9. Details of these results along with performances in the U.K. and Japanese markets are discussed in Kim, Kim, Mulvey, and Fabozzi, "Focusing on the Worst State for Robust Investing."

CHAPTER 10

Robust Portfolio Performance

In this chapter we show how to evaluate the performance of portfolios and also investigate how robust portfolios perform compared to other conventional approaches. In this book, we have introduced multiple strategies for constructing portfolios: classical mean-variance portfolios, global minimum-variance (GMV) portfolios, equally weighted portfolios, and robust portfolios. Investors select portfolio models and their parameters based on the objective and constraints of the investment. Consequently, there is no one portfolio strategy that is ultimately better than others. Likewise, there is no one measure of performance that can fully represent the performance of portfolios. For example, an aggressive investment strategy may have high expected return but, at the same time, have very volatile returns. Thus, the primary purpose of this chapter is to:

- Introduce common measures of portfolio return and risk
- Demonstrate the implementation of performance measures using MATLAB
- Present historical performance of various portfolio optimization methods
- Investigate the advantage of robust portfolio optimization by analyzing historical performance
- Present a measure of robustness based on robust optimization formulations

10.1   PORTFOLIO PERFORMANCE MEASURES

Holding Period Return

The simplest way to measure the return of an investment is to calculate the percentage change of its total value during the investment horizon, also known as the holding period. For an equity portfolio, the *holding period return*, denoted by $r_{0,T}$ to represent the return from time 0 to time T, is written as:

$$r_{0,T} = \frac{(P_T - P_0) + D_{0,T}}{P_0}$$

where P_0 and P_T are portfolio values (or price of an equity) at times 0 and T, respectively, and $D_{0,T}$ is any dividend received during times 0 to T. The return of a portfolio is often expressed only by a change in portfolio value,

$$r_{0,T} = \frac{P_T - P_0}{P_0} = \frac{P_T}{P_0} - 1.$$

The holding period return can be explained by returns in shorter time periods. Consider a portfolio that is invested for three months ($T = 3$). The monthly returns of the portfolio are

$$r_{0,1} = \frac{P_1}{P_0} - 1, \; r_{1,2} = \frac{P_2}{P_1} - 1, \; r_{2,3} = \frac{P_3}{P_2} - 1.$$

Given the monthly returns, the total return during the three months becomes

$$r_{0,3} = (1 + r_{0,1})(1 + r_{1,2})(1 + r_{2,3}) - 1 = \frac{P_1}{P_0}\frac{P_2}{P_1}\frac{P_3}{P_2} - 1 = \frac{P_3}{P_0} - 1$$

and the above will hold for all values of T. Based on this approach, the holding period return is implemented in MATLAB as shown in Box 10.1.

Box 10.1 FUNCTION FOR COMPUTING HOLDING PERIOD RETURNS

```
% ================================================================
% holdingperiodreturn.m
%
% Compute the holding period return given portfolio returns
%
% Input:
%   pfoReturns: matrix where each column is a return series
%               for a single portfolio
% Output:
%   periodReturns: row vector of holding period returns for
%                  each portfolio
% ================================================================
function periodReturns = holdingperiodreturn( pfoReturns )

    % Holding period return by multiplying (1+return) for
    % each period
    periodReturns = prod(1 + pfoReturns) - 1;
end
```

Annual Return (Annualized Return)

The holding period return is a straightforward calculation of return during an investment horizon. However, when analyzing performance of multiple portfolios, each portfolio may have a different holding period. Naturally, it is advised to compare performance for a given historical period or find average performance during identical lengths. A common practice is to represent portfolio performance in annual terms. In other words, even though the holding period for an investment may be shorter or longer than one year, its *annual return* shows the average rate of return for a year.

Consider a portfolio invested for one month with a holding period return r_H (i.e., return during the one-month period). With the assumption that monthly return of the portfolio will consistently be r_H during the next 12 months, the annual return r_A becomes

$$r_A = r_{0,12} = (1 + r_{0,1})(1 + r_{1,2}) \cdots (1 + r_{11,12}) - 1 = (1 + r_H)^{12} - 1.$$

Instead, if the holding period of a portfolio is two years, then the following will hold

$$(1 + r_A)(1 + r_A) = (1 + r_{0,1})(1 + r_{1,2}) \cdots (1 + r_{23,24}) = 1 + r_{0,24}$$

and therefore the annual return is

$$r_A = (1 + r_{0,24})^{1/2} - 1 = (1 + r_H)^{1/2} - 1.$$

The same applies to other holding periods, and in general for a y-year investment horizon, the annual return is computed as

$$r_A = (1 + r_H)^{1/y} - 1$$

where r_H is the portfolio return during the y-year period. The annual return of a portfolio is found using MATLAB as shown in Box 10.2.

The calculation for the annual return involves computing the geometric mean. The geometric mean is used for measuring portfolio performance because the value reflects compounding effects. This means that return in one period affects the amount invested in the following period. For example, if the return in the first period is 50% and return in the second period is −50%, the geometric mean for a single-period return is

$$((1 + 0.5)(1 - 0.5))^{1/2} - 1 = -13.4\%.$$

Box 10.2 FUNCTION FOR COMPUTING ANNUAL RETURNS

```
% ================================================================
% annualreturn.m
%
% Compute the annual return for the given portfolio returns
%
% Input:
%    pfoReturns: matrix where each column is a return series
%                for a single portfolio
%    totalYears: investment horizon in years for pfoReturns
% Output:
%    annualReturns: row vector of annual returns for each
%                   portfolio
% ================================================================
function annualReturns = annualreturn( pfoReturns, totalYears )

      % Annual return using geometric mean
      annualReturns = prod(1 + pfoReturns) .^ (1 / totalYears) - 1;
end
```

This is because the investor holds more than the initial invested amount at the end of the first period, so the loss in the second period amounts to more than half of the principal investment. This is a more accurate way of representing performance compared to the arithmetic mean, which, in this case, is $(50\% - 50\%)/2 = 0\%$.

An interesting case is when returns are continuously compounded. In this case, return between two periods, $t-1$ and t, is expressed as

$$P_t = P_{t-1}e^{r_{t-1,t}}$$

and the return becomes

$$r_{t-1,t} = \ln\left(\frac{P_t}{P_{t-1}}\right) = \ln(P_t) - \ln(P_{t-1}).$$

For multiple periods, the return is decomposed as

$$r_{0,T} = \ln\left(\frac{P_T}{P_0}\right) = \ln\left(\frac{P_1}{P_0}\frac{P_2}{P_1}\cdots\frac{P_T}{P_{T-1}}\right)$$

$$= \ln\left(\frac{P_1}{P_0}\right) + \ln\left(\frac{P_2}{P_1}\right) + \cdots + \ln\left(\frac{P_T}{P_{T-1}}\right)$$

$$= r_{0,1} + r_{1,2} + \cdots r_{T-1,T}$$

where $r_{t-1,t}$ is each a continuously compounded return. When $T = 12$, $r_{0,T}$ is the annual return and can be computed as the following,

$$r_A = r_{0,12} = r_{0,1} + r_{1,2} + \cdots r_{11,12} = 12 \left(\frac{1}{12} \sum_{i=1}^{12} r_{i-1,i} \right) = 12 \cdot \bar{r}_M,$$

where $\bar{r}_M$ is the average monthly return. Therefore, the annual return becomes 12 times the average monthly return. This derivation is valuable because $r \approx \ln(1 + r)$ for values of r close to zero. Hence,

$$\ln \left(\frac{P_t}{P_{t-1}} \right) = \ln \left(1 + \left(\frac{P_t}{P_{t-1}} - 1 \right) \right) \approx \frac{P_t}{P_{t-1}} - 1$$

and the annualizing formula for continuously compounding can be applied to simple returns when the returns are assumed to be close to zero.

Volatility (Standard Deviation)

The first two measures of performance indicate how much is earned from an investment, and higher values are more attractive for investors. Nonetheless, high returns normally result in high risk. Return alone is not enough for comparing portfolio performance, and there are many ways for measuring risk because avoiding a large loss is often more important than realizing a large gain.

The basic indicator for risk is *volatility*. The volatility of a portfolio quantifies deviation in portfolio returns with its standard deviation,

$$\sigma(r) = \sqrt{\frac{1}{T-1} \sum_{i=1}^{T} (r_i - \bar{r})^2}$$

where T is the number of periods for which the portfolio return is collected, $r \in \mathbb{R}^T$ is the portfolio return during T periods, r_i is the portfolio return from time $i - 1$ to time i, and $\bar{r} = \frac{1}{T} \Sigma_{i=1}^T r_i$ is the arithmetic mean of returns.

Similar to annual returns, volatility is also normally reported as an annualized value. If the volatility of monthly returns is σ_M, the annualized volatility is estimated as

$$\sigma_A = \sqrt{12} \cdot \sigma_M.$$

This simple conversion is derived from the assumption that annual return is the sum of independent and identically distributed monthly returns. Annualized volatility of portfolio returns can be computed as shown in Box 10.3.

Box 10.3 FUNCTION FOR COMPUTING PORTFOLIO VOLATILITY

```
% ================================================================
% volatility.m
%
% Compute the volatility of returns for the given portfolio
% returns
%
% Input:
%   pfoReturns: matrix where each column is a return series for
%               a single portfolio
%   numPeriodsYear: number of periods in a year (e.g., 12 for
%                   monthly returns)
% Output:
%   vol: row vector of volatilities for each portfolio
% ================================================================
function vol = volatility( pfoReturns, numPeriodsYear )

    % Annual volatility of returns
    vol = std(pfoReturns) .* sqrt(numPeriodsYear);
end
```

Sharpe Ratio

Even though both return and risk characterize fundamental aspects of performance, the measures introduced above either display the level of return or the level of risk. Nobel Prize laureate William Sharpe developed a measure for risk-adjusted performance.[1] The *Sharpe ratio* computes the expected excess return of a portfolio for every unit of volatility it takes,

$$\text{Sharpe ratio} = \frac{E(r) - r_f}{\sigma(r)}$$

where $r \in \mathbb{R}^T$ is portfolio returns and $r_f \in \mathbb{R}$ is the risk-free rate. It can be also expressed as

$$\frac{E(r) - E(r_f)}{\sigma(r)} = \frac{E(r - r_f)}{\sigma(r)}$$

where $r_f \in \mathbb{R}^T$ represents a change in the risk-free rate during the T-period, and the last numerator clearly shows that the expected excess return is computed. The theoretical development of the Sharpe ratio uses the arithmetic mean for finding the expected excess return, but the geometric mean is also used when performance is evaluated. Box 10.4 demonstrates several approaches for finding the Sharpe ratio.

Box 10.4 FUNCTION FOR COMPUTING SHARPE RATIOS

```
% ================================================================
% sharperatio.m
%
% Compute the Sharpe ratio for the given portfolio returns
%
% Input:
%   pfoReturns: matrix where each column is a return series
%               for a single portfolio
%   riskFreeRate: risk-free rate (either a single value or a
%                 vector)
%   numPeriodsYear: number of periods in a year (e.g., 12 for
%                   monthly returns)
%   totalYears: investment horizon in years for pfoReturns
% Output:
%   sharpeRatio: row vector of Sharpe ratios for each
%                portfolio
%   annualSharpeRatio: row vector of annualized Sharpe ratios
%                      for each portfolio using geometric mean
%                      for computing excess return
% ================================================================
function [sharpeRatio, annualSharpeRatio] = sharperatio( ...
        pfoReturns, riskFreeRate, numPeriodsYear, totalYears )

    % Total number of periods and number of portfolios in the
    % input data
    [nTime,numPfo] = size(pfoReturns);

    % Create a vector of risk-free rate if a single value is
    % given
    if(length(riskFreeRate) == 1)
        riskFreeRate = riskFreeRate * ones(nTime,1);
    end

    % Use arithmetic mean for computing excess return
    sharpeRatio = mean(pfoReturns - repmat(riskFreeRate, ...
                  1,numPfo)) ./ std(pfoReturns);

    % Use geometric mean for computing annual excess return
    excessReturn = prod(1 + pfoReturns - repmat(riskFreeRate, ...
                   1,numPfo)) .^ (1/totalYears) - 1;
    vol = std(pfoReturns) .* sqrt(numPeriodsYear);
    annualSharpeRatio = excessReturn ./ vol;
end
```

Furthermore, it is worth mentioning that the Sharpe ratio is not time-horizon independent. The Sharpe ratio for T periods, S_T, is estimated from the Sharpe ratio for one period, S_1, as

$$S_T = \frac{T \cdot (\text{excess return for one period})}{\sqrt{T} \cdot (\text{volatility for one period})} = \sqrt{T} \cdot S_1.$$

Alpha and Beta

Portfolio risk is also measured by *beta*, which quantifies risk that is generated from exposure to the market and hence known as *systematic risk*. Beta is also called nondiversifiable risk because it is the portion of risk that cannot be diversified away based on the modern portfolio theory. The notion of beta arises from the capital asset pricing model (CAPM),

$$E(r) = r_f + \beta(E(r_m) - r_f)$$

where r is the return for a stock or a portfolio, r_m is the market return, and r_f is the risk-free rate. From CAPM, the beta of a portfolio becomes

$$\beta = \frac{\text{cov}(r, r_m)}{\text{Var}(r_m)}.$$

Portfolios with beta greater than one indicate portfolios with more market risk than the market portfolio.

Empirically, beta is also computed from a linear regression,

$$r - r_f = \alpha + \beta(r_m - r_f) + \varepsilon$$

where α is the intercept and ε is the error term. In fact, the value of α in the above regression is another popular measure for portfolio performance, normally referred to as *alpha*. According to CAPM, the value of α should be zero if an asset is fairly priced. But when a market index such as the S&P 500 is used for the market portfolio, empirical tests reveal that alpha is not necessarily zero for many assets. One major goal of portfolio managers is to achieve positive alpha.

The method for empirically obtaining alpha and beta from a given portfolio return series is included in Box 10.5.

Tracking Error

Most performance metrics present absolute performance of portfolios. Sometimes, relative performance is of greater interest, such as the excess

Box 10.5 FUNCTION FOR COMPUTING PORTFOLIO ALPHA AND BETA

```
% ================================================================
% portfolioalphabeta.m
%
% Compute portfolio alpha and beta for the given portfolio
% returns
%
% Input:
%   pfoReturns: matrix where each column is a return series
%                 for a single portfolio
%   indexReturns: return vector of a benchmark index
%   riskFreeRate: risk-free rate (either a single value or a
%                 vector)
% Output:
%   alphas: row vector of portfolio alphas for each portfolio
%   betas: row vector of portfolio betas for each portfolio
% ================================================================
function [alphas, betas] = portfolioalphabeta( pfoReturns, ...
                          indexReturns, riskFreeRate )

    % Total number of periods and number of portfolios in the
    % input data
    [nTime,numPfo] = size(pfoReturns);

    % Find alpha and beta from linear regression
    alphas = zeros(1, numPfo);
    betas = zeros(1, numPfo);
    for i = 1:numPfo
        coeffs = regress(pfoReturns(:,i) - riskFreeRate, ...
            [ones(nTime,1), indexReturns - riskFreeRate]);
        alphas(i) = coeffs(1);
        betas(i) = coeffs(2);
    end
end
```

return over the risk-free rate because the risk-free rate can be achieved without taking any risk and also without applying any optimization strategy. In fact, most portfolio managers regularly assess their performance relative to a benchmark. Standard benchmarks include market indices such as the S&P 500 and the Wilshire 5000 Total Market Index or indices that focus on specific sectors. Portfolio performance against a benchmark is especially important if the portfolio is actively managed.

Tracking error shows how closely a portfolio follows a given benchmark. It is calculated as the standard deviation of the difference between returns of a portfolio and a benchmark,

$$\text{Tracking Error} = \sqrt{\text{Var}(r_i - r_{b,i})}$$

where $r_b \in \mathbb{R}^T$ is the benchmark return. Basically, tracking error is the standard deviation of *active return* because active return denotes the portfolio return in excess of the benchmark,

Active return = portfolio return − benchmark return.

Similar to the volatility of portfolio returns, an investor seeking a portfolio with low risk will prefer a low tracking error in general because a portfolio with high tracking error will likely deviate much from its benchmark. Thus, a passive investor will certainly reduce tracking error when performance is evaluated relative to a benchmark. Box 10.6 shows how MATLAB is used for computing the tracking error of a portfolio.

Box 10.6 FUNCTION FOR COMPUTING TRACKING ERRORS

```
% ================================================================
% trackingerror.m
%
% Compute the tracking error for the given portfolio returns
%
% Input:
%    pfoReturns: matrix where each column is a return series
%                for a single portfolio
%    indexReturns: return vector of a benchmark index
% Output:
%    trackingErrors: row vector of tracking errors for each
%                    portfolio
% ================================================================
function trackingErrors = trackingerror( pfoReturns, ...
   indexReturns )

    % Total number of portfolios in the input data
    numPfo = size(pfoReturns,2);

    % Compute tracking error from standard deviation
    trackingErrors = std(pfoReturns - repmat(indexReturns,1, ...
       numPfo));
end
```

Information Ratio

The significance of performance against a benchmark has led to a measure for risk-adjusted return very similar to the Sharpe ratio. The *information ratio* is evaluated by dividing the excess portfolio return over the benchmark by the tracking error,

$$\text{Information ratio} = \frac{E(r - r_b)}{\sigma(r - r_b)}$$

where r_b is the benchmark return. Information ratio is higher for portfolios that closely follow the benchmark but have higher expected returns. As shown in Box 10.7, information ratio combines steps for implementing the tracking error and the Sharpe ratio.

Box 10.7 FUNCTION FOR COMPUTING INFORMATION RATIOS

```
% ================================================================
% informationratio.m
%
% Compute the information ratio for the given portfolio
% returns
%
% Input:
%   pfoReturns: matrix where each column is a return series
%               for a single portfolio
%   indexReturns: return vector of a benchmark index
% Output:
%   infoRatios: row vector of information ratios for each
%               portfolio
% ================================================================
function infoRatios = informationratio( pfoReturns, ...
   indexReturns )

   % Total number of portfolios in the input data
   numPfo = size(pfoReturns,2);

   % Compute tracking error and then information ratio
   trackingErrors = std(pfoReturns - repmat(indexReturns,1, ...
      numPfo));
   infoRatios = mean(pfoReturns - repmat(indexReturns,1, ...
      numPfo)) ./ trackingErrors;
end
```

Sortino Ratio

Another return-risk that is widely used is the *Sortino ratio*.[2] In contrast to the information ratio, the Sortino ratio uses downside deviation as a measure of risk. Volatility of portfolio returns assumes symmetric upside and downside deviation. It also considers downside as well as upside deviation to be undesirable. On the other hand, *downside deviation*, also known as semi-deviation, addresses this drawback by only including bad volatility:

$$\text{Downside deviation} = \sqrt{\frac{1}{T-1}\sum_{i=1}^{T}(\min(0,\ r_i - r_{MAR}))^2}$$

where r_{MAR} is the minimum acceptable return or the desired target return, which is typically set to the risk-free rate or 0%.

The Sortino ratio is written as:

$$\text{Sortino ratio} = \frac{E(r) - r_{MAR}}{(\text{Downside deviation})_{MAR=r_{MAR}}}$$

and the convention is to use the same level of minimum acceptable return for both excess return and downside deviation. However, it is not uncommon to report the Sortino ratio with excess return over the risk-free return and deviation of negative returns,

$$\frac{E(r) - r_f}{(\text{Downside deviation})_{MAR=0\%}}.$$

We illustrate the former case of setting the same level of r_{MAR} for both return and risk in Box 10.8.

Maximum Drawdown

The variance or standard deviation of returns provides an average deviation value. Even though an average is a good representation of how volatile the return is, the maximum deviation is just as important because investors may be more concerned about one large loss than frequent small deviations.

Drawdown is computed for a specific time horizon. Drawdown at time T measures a decline from its previous peak during its investment horizon:

$$DD_T = \max\left(0,\ \max_{t\in(0,T)}\left(-\frac{P_T - P_t}{P_t}\right)\right) = \max\left(0,\ \max_{t\in(0,T)}\left(\frac{P_t - P_T}{P_t}\right)\right)$$

Box 10.8 FUNCTION FOR COMPUTING SORTINO RATIOS

```
% ================================================================
% sortinoratio.m
%
% Compute the Sortino ratio for the given portfolio returns
%
% Input:
%    pfoReturns: matrix where each column is a return series
%                for a single portfolio
%    mar: level of minimum acceptable return (MAR)
% Output:
%    sortinoRatios: row vector of Sortino ratios for each
%                   portfolio
% ================================================================
function sortinoRatios = sortinoratio( pfoReturns, mar )

    % Sortino ratio with MAR = mar
    pfoReturnsMAR = pfoReturns;
    pfoReturnsMAR(pfoReturns > mar) = 0;
    sortinoRatios = (mean(pfoReturns) - mar)./ std(pfoReturnsMAR);
end
```

where P_t is the value of the portfolio at time t. In Exhibit 10.1, the vertical black lines indicate trading days with positive drawdown. It clearly shows how drawdown is calculated from the most recent peak. *Maximum drawdown* denotes the largest drawdown, and it finds the maximum loss that can incur during a given period. Mathematically, it is expressed as

$$\mathrm{MDD}_T = \max_{\tau \in (0,T)} (\mathrm{DD}_\tau) = \max_{\tau \in (0,T)} \left(0, \ \max_{t \in (0,\tau)} \left(\frac{P_t - P_T}{P_t} \right) \right).$$

Even though drawdown and maximum drawdown may be presented simply as a change in value, they are mostly written as a percentage change from the peak. From the previous formula, the maximum drawdown in Exhibit 10.1 occurs on December 30, 2013. The MATLAB implementation for maximum drawdown from return data is shown in Box 10.9.

Value-at-Risk

Similar to maximum drawdown, *value-at-risk* (VaR) also attempts to find the worst-case loss of an investment.[3] But, in contrast, VaR is a probabilistic approach. VaR at 95% represents the minimum level of loss that is only

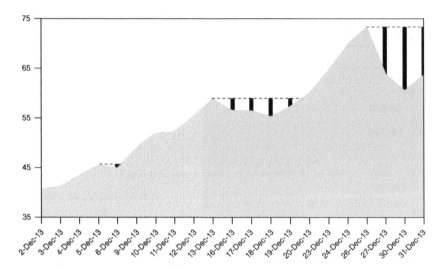

Exhibit 10.1   Stock price of Twitter, Inc. (TWTR) during December 2013 (positive drawdown shown as black bars)

Box 10.9 FUNCTION FOR COMPUTING MAXIMUM DRAWDOWNS

```
% ===============================================================
% maxdrawdown.m
%
% Compute the maximum drawdown for the given portfolio returns
%
% Input:
%   pfoReturns: matrix where each column is a return series
%               for a single portfolio
% Output:
%   maxDrawdowns: row vector of maximum drawdowns for each
%                 portfolio
% ===============================================================
function maxDrawdowns = maxdrawdown( pfoReturns )

    % Total number of periods and number of portfolios in the
    % input data
    [nTime, numPfo] = size(pfoReturns);

    % Compute the wealth path of the investment
    % (assume wealth of first day is 1)
```

```
wealth = cumprod([ones(1,numPfo); 1+pfoReturns(2:end,:)]);

% Find the maximum drawdown from the wealth path
drawdown = zeros(nTime,numPfo);
for i = 1:nTime
    drawdown(i,:) = 1 - wealth(i,:) ./ max(wealth(1:i,:));
end
maxDrawdowns = max(drawdown);
end
```

exceeded with, at most, 5% probability. In other words, VaR_α is the lowest loss l such that the portfolio loss l_p exceeds l with probability at most $1 - \alpha$:

$$\text{VaR}_\alpha = \min\{l \mid P(l_p > l) \leq 1 - \alpha\}.$$

For portfolio weights $\omega \in \mathbb{R}^N$ and random stock returns $r \in \mathbb{R}^N$, the VaR is

$$\text{VaR}_\alpha = \min\{l \mid P(-r'\omega > l) \leq 1 - \alpha\}.$$

Since VaR is a level of loss, it is represented as a positive value in the previous equations, whereas loss is a negative return in most cases.

There are several ways to compute VaR. By assuming a probability distribution of returns, VaR can be found from the confidence interval of the distribution. Moreover, VaR can be estimated from the appropriate quantile based on historical or simulated portfolio returns as demonstrated in Box 10.10.

Conditional Value-at-Risk

Aside from the computational shortcomings of VaR, such as it not being a coherent risk measure, there is another reason why VaR can be misleading: VaR does not reflect large losses at the left end of its tail. *Conditional value-at-risk* (CVaR), or *expected shortfall*, overcomes this drawback by computing the expected return of scenarios that are worse than the VaR level. By extending the notation used for defining VaR, we arrive at the following formula for CVaR:

$$\text{CVaR}_\alpha = E(l \mid l \geq \text{VaR}_\alpha).$$

It is also written using portfolio returns as

$$\text{CVaR}_\alpha = \frac{1}{1 - \alpha} \int_{-r'\omega \geq \text{VaR}_\alpha} (-r'\omega)p(r)dr$$

Box 10.10 FUNCTION FOR COMPUTING VaR

```
% ===================================================================
% valueatrisk.m
%
% Compute the value-at-risk (VaR) given portfolio returns
%
% Input:
%    pfoReturns: matrix where each column is a return series
%                for a single portfolio
%    alpha: level of confidence (widely used values are 0.9,
%           0.95, and 0.99)
% Output:
%    valueAtRisks: row vector of value-at-risks for each
%                  portfolio
% ===================================================================
function valueAtRisks = valueatrisk( pfoReturns, alpha )

    % Find the value for VaR from the proper quantile
    valueAtRisks = quantile(pfoReturns, 1 - alpha);
end
```

where $p(r)$ is the probability distribution of random portfolio return r, and computed in MATLAB from return data as included in Box 10.11.

10.2 HISTORICAL PERFORMANCE OF ROBUST PORTFOLIOS

Portfolio Strategies

For the remainder of this chapter, we evaluate historical performance of a number of portfolio strategies.[4] The main purpose is to present how robust portfolios perform compared to more conventional approaches. Most of the basic methods have been discussed earlier in this book, and they are summarized in Exhibit 10.2.

The movement of a market index is a representation of how the market behaves, and market indices are usually benchmarks for evaluating portfolio performance. Thus, we also use a composite index as the main benchmark (*Index*). Another diversified portfolio is the equally weighted portfolio (*EqW*); this portfolio allocates $1/N$ weight to all N assets. Equally investing in all assets is a strategy that does not solve a portfolio selection problem but is known to be more attractive than some involved methods.

Box 10.11 FUNCTION FOR COMPUTING CVaR

```
% ================================================================
% condvalueatrisk.m
%
% Compute the conditional value-at-risk (CVaR) given portfolio
% returns
%
% Input:
%   pfoReturns: matrix where each column is a return series
%               for a single portfolio
%   alpha: level of confidence (widely used values are 0.9,
%          0.95, and 0.99)
% Output:
%   condVaRs: row vector of conditional value-at-risks for
%             each portfolio
% ================================================================
function condVaRs = condvalueatrisk( pfoReturns, alpha )

    % Total number of portfolios in the input data
    numPfo = size(pfoReturns,2);

    % Find VaR from the proper quantile and then CVaR
    valueAtRisks = quantile(pfoReturns, 1 - alpha);
    condVaRs = zeros(1,numPfo);
    for i = 1:numPfo
        condVaRs(i) = mean(pfoReturns(pfoReturns(:,i) <= ...
            valueAtRisks(i), i));
    end
end
```

Exhibit 10.2 Description of conventional portfolios

(1) Index:	Passive strategy that invests in the composite index of the market
(2) EqW:	Equally weighted portfolio of all candidate assets
(3) GMV:	Global minimum variance portfolio
(4) MV10:	Mean-variance optimal portfolio with annual volatility of 10%
(5) MV20:	Mean-variance optimal portfolio with annual volatility of 20%

The global minimum variance portfolio (*GMV*) is a portfolio within the Markowitz framework that has minimum risk. Selecting GMV portfolios shows how portfolios perform when neglecting information on expected return. We also check the performance of mean-variance efficient portfolios. Among many portfolios on the efficient frontier, we select portfolios that limit the estimated annual portfolio volatility to 10% and 20% (*MV10* and *MV20*, respectively). During periods of high market volatility when GMV has annual standard deviation greater than 10%, the strategy for MV10 is to invest in GMV for that period.

As the main focus is to analyze the performance of robust methods, we hold a total of 10 portfolios based on robust portfolio optimization with structural variations. Our robust strategies consider uncertainty in the expected return and the modifications are caused by how the uncertainty set is defined, and they are listed in Exhibit 10.3.[5] By investigating a long list of robust portfolios, we will be able to arrive at a general understanding of how robust optimization influences portfolio performance. For simplicity, we refer to each strategy by its abbreviation.

Data Description and Rebalancing Method

In this analysis, we simulate portfolios that invest in the global stock market. An investor planning to achieve global diversification considers investing in the following 25 country indices: Australia. Brazil, Canada, Chile, China, Germany, Hong Kong, India, Indonesia, Italy, Japan, Korea, Malaysia, Mexico, Russia, Singapore, South Africa, Spain, Sweden, Switzerland, Taiwan, Thailand, Turkey, United Kingdom, and the United States.

Exhibit 10.4 plots the value of investing internationally as proxied by the major stock market index for each of the 25 countries. The exhibit

Exhibit 10.3   Description of robust portfolio strategies

(1) RB10: (2) RB20:	robust portfolios with box uncertainty set and the same level of risk-averse coefficient as MV10 and MV20, respectively
(3) RE10: (4) RE20:	robust portfolios with ellipsoidal uncertainty set where $\Sigma_\mu = \frac{1}{T}\Sigma$ and with the same level of risk-averse coefficient as MV10 and MV20, respectively
(5) REf10: (6) REf20:	robust portfolios with ellipsoidal uncertainty set where Σ_μ is from the factor model and with the same level of risk-averse coefficient as MV10 and MV20, respectively
(7) RE10d: (8) RE20d:	robust portfolios the same as RE10 and RE20, respectively, but with Σ_μ as a diagonal matrix
(9) REf10d: (10) REf20d:	robust portfolios the same as REf10 and REf20, respectively, but with Σ_μ as a diagonal matrix

Exhibit 10.4 Wealth of investment in major stock market indices (in logarithm)

demonstrates how some markets are more correlated with each other, whereas some other markets move independent of the major global movements. The wealth for investing in each country in Exhibit 10.4 begins from one, and the logarithm of wealth is plotted for comparison purposes. We continue to plot portfolio values in logarithms throughout this chapter.

All strategies used for this experiment, as summarized in Exhibits 10.2 and 10.3, have a one-month rebalancing period. In other words, the portfolio selection problem is solved at the beginning of each month, and the position is held until the beginning of the following month when a new allocation is optimized.

When a portfolio is rebalanced, past asset returns are used as estimates for finding the optimal portfolio for each strategy. We denote this period of past returns used for estimating the inputs of the portfolio selection problem as the estimation period. In our experiment, we observe daily portfolio performance from estimation periods of three, six, and 12 months. For a three-month estimation period, daily returns during the previous three months are collected at every rebalancing time.

Performance from 1981 to 2013

We study the long-term performance of portfolios from 1981 to 2013. Investigating investments for more than 30 years is meaningful because the investment horizon includes a number of notable market downturns. We confirm that robust portfolio optimization leads to robust performance and, as a result, is an attractive investment strategy. We next summarize the key findings on portfolio performance and also graphically present the outcome in Exhibits 10.5 to 10.8. All performance measures except beta,

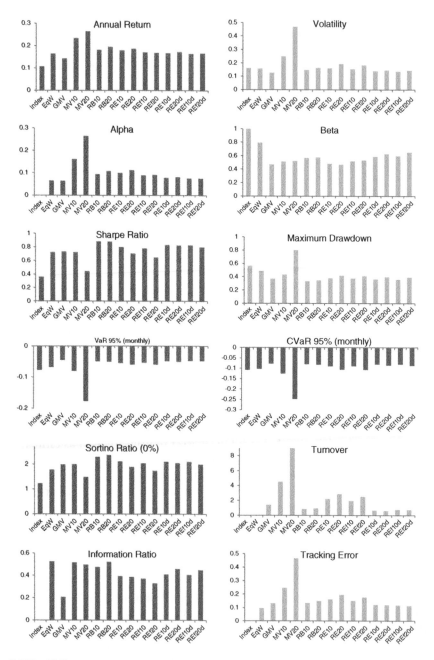

Exhibit 10.5 Summary of monthly performance from 1981 to 2013 with three-month estimation

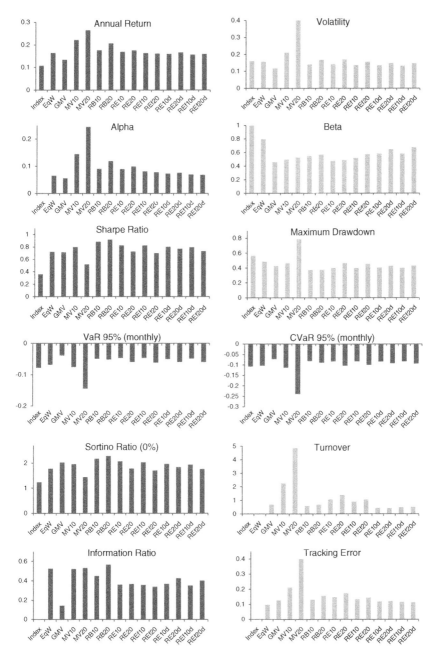

Exhibit 10.6 Summary of monthly performance from 1981 to 2013 with six-month estimation

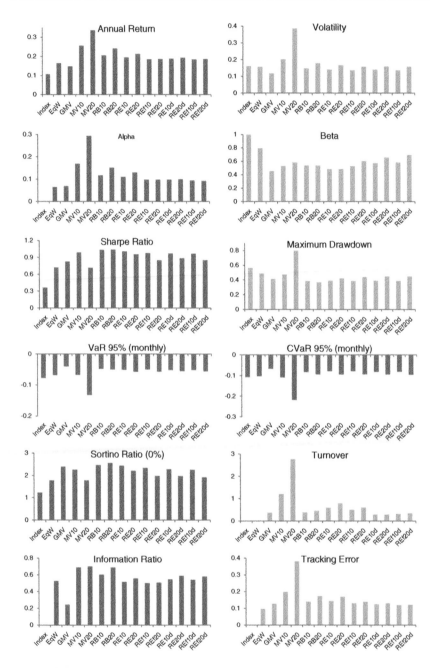

Exhibit 10.7   Summary of monthly performance from 1981 to 2013 with 12-month estimation

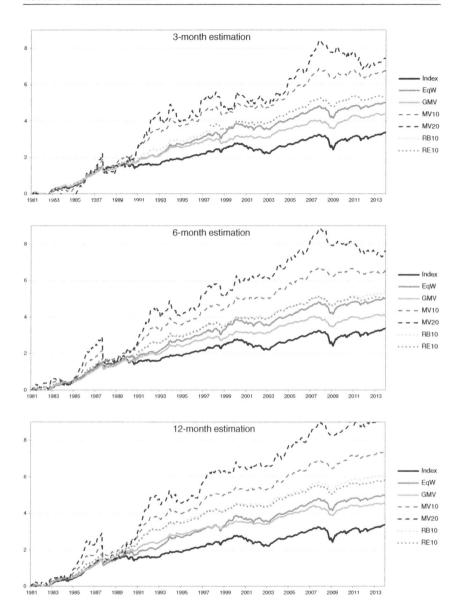

Exhibit 10.8   Wealth from investment from 1981 to 2013 (in logarithm)

maximum drawdown, and turnover are compared and presented as annualized values. Our six principal findings are summarized below:

- *MV has the highest returns but R is better than Index, EqW, and GMV*: When investing in 25 country indices from 1981 to 2013, mean-variance portfolios produce the highest return based on holding period return, annual return, and alpha. Mean-variance portfolios put more emphasis on expected return compared to other strategies and thus result in a larger gain for a long investment horizon. Although robust portfolios are not a close second, robust models bring in additional return compared to investing in the index, equally weighted portfolio, and the GMV portfolio. Robust portfolio models based on mean-variance optimization still include the expected portfolio return in its formulation, which is where the advantage comes from.

- *R has much lower risk than MV and is comparable to Index, EqW, and GMV*: The high return of mean-variance portfolios comes at a price; mean-variance portfolios display significantly higher portfolio risk as measured by the standard deviation of returns (annual volatility). Furthermore, robust portfolios are only as volatile as the fully diversified investments, the index, and the equally weighted portfolio. Robust portfolio optimization also forms portfolios that are not much riskier than GMV portfolios.

- *R has smaller worst-case loss than MV and is comparable to Index, EqW, and GMV*: The patterns found in volatility are matched by the measures for worst case loss, namely maximum drawdown, VaR, and CVaR. Mean-variance portfolios are the least attractive due to the large loss in worst cases. But robust portfolios, which are built to prepare for worst cases, prevent critical worst-case damage compared to the market index and the equally-weighted strategy. Even though the GMV portfolio seems to be the favorite, the GMV portfolio reduces its worst-case loss because it is also a robust portfolio that excludes uncertainty arising from the expected return estimates.

- *R has the highest Sharpe ratio and Sortino ratio*: Constructing portfolios from robust optimization leads to investment with the overall highest Sharpe ratio. While mean-variance portfolios outperform robust portfolios in terms of return, the low risk of robust portfolios delivers larger risk-adjusted returns. Because the trade-off between return and risk is important, the high Sharpe ratio of robust portfolios when calculated from either arithmetic or geometric means will be very appealing to investors. Comparably, robust portfolio returns exhibit superior Sortino ratio for minimum acceptable returns of 0% and 5%. Again, robust methods reveal the advantage of seeking extra return while controlling variability.

- *Low turnover is another advantage of R*: There is a substantial difference in turnover between mean-variance and robust portfolios. Robust models with box uncertainty sets or ellipsoidal uncertainty sets with diagonal estimation error covariance matrix have turnover no greater than the turnover of the GMV portfolio. The low turnover of robust portfolios becomes more beneficial in practice because transaction cost and market impact are not considered in this analysis.
- *R has very low tracking error compared to MV*: When a composite index is considered as a benchmark, the high tracking error of mean-variance portfolios reflects how easily portfolios can underperform the benchmark index. In comparison, robust portfolios more closely follow movements of the benchmark. Due to the small tracking error of robust portfolios, mean-variance portfolios do not always have dominant information ratio.

To summarize, for an investor with the sole purpose of maximizing portfolio return, mean-variance portfolios will be the best choice. Nonetheless, an investor who also worries about loss will select robust models. Robust portfolios let investors avoid large volatility, large worst case loss (e.g., maximum drawdown, VaR, and CVaR), large turnover, and large tracking error against a composite index. More importantly, robust portfolios exhibit high Sharpe ratio and Sortino ratio, which result in their being ranked above mean-variance portfolios as well as other strategies when return and risk are both considered.

The advantage of robust portfolio optimization is clearly shown in Exhibit 10.8. Regardless of the estimation period, robust portfolios lie above the index, equally weighted portfolio, and GMV portfolio, and the wealth curve of robust models displays the least fluctuation. Even though more wealth can be eventually acquired from mean-variance optimal portfolios, the wealth path is evidently the most unstable and highly dependent on the estimation data.

Performance during the Global Financial Crisis

We now switch to an investment horizon with extreme turbulence. More specifically, we concentrate on the most recent financial crisis, which began in 2007. To analyze portfolios during a market crash and also recovery, we collect performance from 2007 to 2012, a six-year period. Furthermore, we use a different set of data that focuses on the U.S. stock market: data that divide stocks in NYSE, AMEX, and NASDAQ into 49 industries as categorized in Exhibit 10.9.[6]

Exhibit 10.9 The 49 industry classifications

Agriculture	Defense
Food Products	Precious Metals
Candy & Soda	Non-Metallic and Industrial Metal
Beer & Liquor	Mining
Tobacco Products	Coal
Recreation	Petroleum and Natural Gas
Entertainment	Utilities
Printing and Publishing	Communication
Consumer Goods	Personal Services
Apparel	Business Services
Healthcare	Computers
Medical Equipment	Computer Software
Pharmaceutical Products	Electronic Equipment
Chemicals	Measuring and Control Equipment
Rubber and Plastic Products	Business Supplies
Textiles	Shipping Container
Construction Materials	Transportation
Construction	Wholesale
Steel Works, etc.	Retail
Fabricated Products	Restaurants, Hotels, Motels
Machinery	Banking
Electrical Equipment	Insurance
Automobiles and Trucks	Real Estate
Aircraft	Trading
Shipbuilding, Railroad Equipment	Other

Due to the elevated volatility during this period, the GMV portfolio has above 10% annual standard deviation for many estimation periods. Thus, instead of forming MV10 and MV20, we construct MV20 and MV30, which are mean-variance optimal portfolios with annual volatility of 20% and 30%, respectively.

Exhibits 10.10 and 10.11 summarize performance while focusing mainly on risk measures. While robust methods do not display promising returns or dominant risk-adjusted performance during this period, robust portfolios are arguably exposed to minimal risk. Especially, in Exhibit 10.12, it is undeniable that mean-variance portfolios are much more uncertain than the movement of the market index. On the other hand, robust portfolios have the highest minimum value while consistently staying above the market.

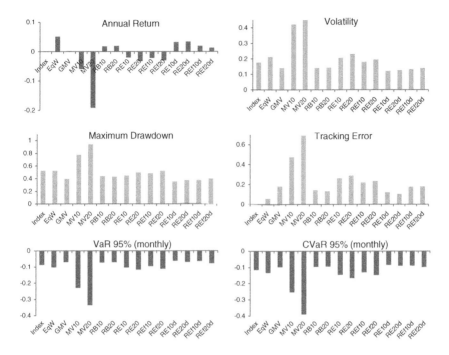

Exhibit 10.10   Summary of weekly performance from 2007 to 2012 with six-month estimation

10.3   MEASURING ROBUSTNESS

As the final remark for this chapter, we present one approach based on the concepts of robust optimization for measuring the robustness of portfolios.[7] A robustness measure will allow portfolio managers to compare robustness when selecting an optimal portfolio.

The robustness of a function can be checked by observing the variation in the function value while changing the value of the uncertain parameter. The smaller the variation in the function value, the more robust the function becomes. Measuring the robustness of a portfolio can be performed using a similar framework. If the value of a portfolio shows minimal fluctuation, then the portfolio will be classified as being robust. Thus, in mean-variance portfolio optimization, it is reasonable to say that a portfolio is robust if the value of the portfolio is stable with respect to the mean vector and the covariance matrix.

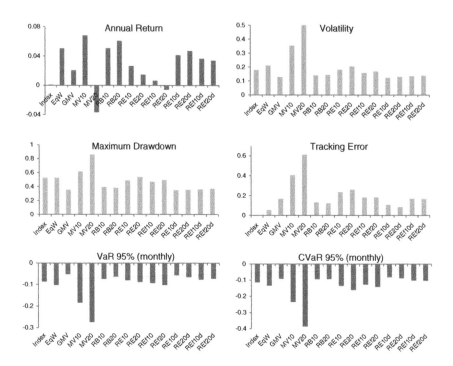

Exhibit 10.11   Summary of weekly performance from 2007 to 2012 with 12-month estimation

Suppose the only uncertain parameter is the vector of mean returns μ. Then the value of a portfolio ω can be expressed as $f(\omega, \mu)$. If the possible values of μ are known, the variation in portfolio value can be easily computed. However, since the distribution of future returns are difficult to estimate, the idea of defining uncertainty sets in robust optimization can be incorporated. Suppose the uncertainty set $U(\hat{\mu})$ is defined around an estimated value $\hat{\mu}$. Then, the following measures the maximum possible deviation from the estimate μ:

$$\max_{\mu \in U(\hat{\mu})} |f(\omega, \hat{\mu}) - f(\omega, \mu)|. \tag{10.1}$$

Hence, portfolios that have small objective values for the equation given by (10.1) are the more robust ones because the maximum possible deviation is small. On the other hand, portfolios with large objective values are the more uncertain portfolios. The formulation given by (10.1) can be used as the basic framework for measuring robustness.

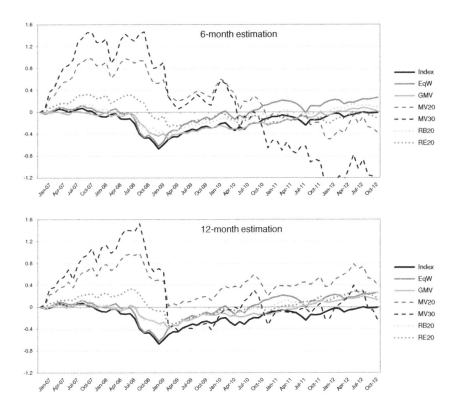

Exhibit 10.12 Wealth from investment from 2007 to 2012 (in logarithm)

Many measures are possible for denoting the value of a portfolio; numerous performance measures can represent the value of a portfolio as we have already presented in this chapter. One choice for the portfolio value would be to use the value of the objective function of the portfolio problem since it reflects the objective of a mean-variance investor. An example is to let

$$f(\omega, \mu) = \frac{1}{2}\omega' \Sigma \omega - \lambda \mu' \omega,$$

which expressed the trade-off between risk and return. By using the ellipsoidal uncertainty set, the problem given by (10.1) becomes

$$\max_{\mu \in U_\delta(\widehat{\mu})} \left| \frac{1}{2}\omega' \Sigma \omega - \lambda \widehat{\mu}' \omega - \frac{1}{2}\omega' \Sigma \omega + \lambda \mu' \omega \right| \tag{10.2}$$

where

$$U_\delta(\widehat{\mu}) = \{ \mu | (\mu - \widehat{\mu})' \Sigma_\mu^{-1} (\mu - \widehat{\mu}) \leq \delta^2 \}.$$

Further calculation shows that the problem given by (10.2) is equivalent to the following:

$$\max_{\mu \in U_\delta(\widehat{\mu})} \lambda |(\mu - \widehat{\mu})' \omega| = \delta \lambda \sqrt{\omega' \Sigma_\mu \omega}.$$

Therefore, the robustness of a portfolio can be measured by calculating $\delta \lambda \sqrt{\omega' \Sigma_\mu \omega}$ when an ellipsoidal uncertainty set is assumed, where smaller values indicate higher robustness. As briefly summarized, the concept of maximum deviation along with uncertainty sets allows portfolio managers to measure the level of robustness of a portfolio and compare robustness among various portfolios.

KEY POINTS

- Performance measures such as holding period return, annual return, and alpha indicate how much is earned from an investment.
- Since high risk can lead to large losses, many measures of risk quantify various aspects of risk: volatility, beta, drawdown, tracking error, VaR, and CVaR.
- In order to measure the trade-off between return and risk, risk-adjusted returns of a portfolio are presented as a ratio: Sharpe ratio, information ratio, and Sortino ratio.
- Additional measures of performance, such as turnover, also reveal factors that affect performance of portfolios.
- Investigating historical performance in the global stock market from 1981 to 2013 shows that robust portfolios allow investors to control risk and uncertainty while seeking extra return.
- Within the U.S. stock market, robust portfolios managed to minimize fluctuation during the recent financial crisis while mean-variance portfolios resulted in volatile performance along with the market.

NOTES

1. The Sharpe ratio is introduced in William F. Sharpe, "Mutual Fund Performance," *Journal of Business* 39, 1 (1966), pp. 119–138; and also explained in William F. Sharpe, "The Sharpe Ratio," *Journal of Portfolio Management* 21, 1 (1994), pp. 49–58.
2. The downside deviation and Sortino ratio are discussed in Frank A. Sortino and Robert van der Meer, "Downside Risk," *Journal of Portfolio Management* 17, 4 (1991), pp. 27–31; and Frank A. Sortino and Lee N. Price, "Performance

Measurement in a Downside Risk Framework," *Journal of Investing* 3, 3 (1994), pp. 59–64.

3. Recall that VaR and CVaR were introduced in Chapter 3.
4. Results presented here are more thoroughly analyzed in Jang Ho Kim, Woo Chang Kim, Do-gyun Kwon, and Frank J. Fabozzi, "Robust Equity Portfolio Performance," Working paper, 2015.
5. Defining various uncertainty sets is explained in Chapter 6.
6. Details for the 49 industry portfolios can be found in the online data library of Kenneth R. French.
7. The main ideas presented here are based on section 2 of Woo Chang Kim, Min Jeong Kim, Jang Ho Kim, and Frank J. Fabozzi, "Robust Portfolios that Do Not Tilt Factor Exposure," *European Journal of Operational Research* 234 (2014), pp. 411–421.

CHAPTER 11

Robust Optimization Software

Throughout the book, we have used MATLAB to illustrate how portfolio optimization can be efficiently solved using programming languages. In particular, the step-by-step process for solving robust portfolio optimization was demonstrated in Chapter 6. While MATLAB allows one to solve a complex conic optimization problem, one must reformulate the original problem to a form that can be efficiently solved (e.g., reformulate the ellipsoidal uncertainty problem into a second-order cone program) before running the optimization function with proper arguments in MATLAB. Likewise, the reformulation step is also necessary when using CVX, because these tools provide great computational strength but not the capability to generate a new problem that incorporates parameter uncertainty. There are, however, software packages with features for solving robust optimization problems that allow users to easily define uncertainty sets and provide functions that automatically reformulate a given problem into tractable form. In this chapter, we discuss the following three optimization tools that can help solve robust portfolio optimization:

- YALMIP
- ROME (Robust Optimization Made Easy)
- AIMMS (Advanced Integrated Multidimensional Modeling Software)

11.1   YALMIP

YALMIP is a modeling toolbox for MATLAB and contains functions for various optimization classes.[1] YALMIP provides functions built precisely for robust optimization, and it also performs reformulation so that a given uncertain problem can be efficiently solved. Therefore, only two preliminary steps are needed for incorporating uncertainty in YALMIP: declaring uncertain variables and defining uncertainty sets for those variables. YALMIP is especially suitable if MATLAB is being considered as the primary tool for constructing robust portfolios because YALMIP runs in the MATLAB environment, and it is available as a free software.[2]

Basic Structure

Once YALMIP is installed, its commands can be freely used in MATLAB code. We demonstrate the basic structure of YALMIP with a simple linear programming problem:

$$\max_{x,y} x + 2y$$

$$\text{s.t.} \quad 2x + 5y \leq 10$$

$$5x + y \leq 20 \tag{11.1}$$

$$x, y \geq 0.$$

The most important YALMIP functions are *sdpvar* and *optimize*. The sdpvar function defines decision variables, either as a vector or a matrix:

$$\text{x\_vector} = \text{sdpvar(n, 1);}$$

$$\text{y\_matrix} = \text{sdpvar(n, n)}$$

for any value of n. The decision variables in (11.1) can be expressed as a single vector of length two:

$$\text{x} = \text{sdpvar(2, 1)}$$

where variable y in (11.1) is now represented by the second element of vector x.

The variables declared can then be used for setting the objective function and constraints. The objective and constraints for the problem (11.1) are written as the following in YALMIP:

$$\text{objective} = -[1, 2] * \text{x;}$$

$$\text{constraints} = [2 * \text{x(1)} + 3 * \text{x(2)} <= 10, \ 5 * \text{x(1)} + \text{x(2)} \leq 20, \ \text{x} >= 0]$$

where a negative sign is inserted in the objective because the given problem is searching for a maximum value. While setting the objective function is straightforward, the constraints take the form of a row vector in which each element is an expression for a single constraint. Setting the objective and constraints separately, as shown earlier, is critical because the *optimize* function takes the two as arguments; the optimization is solved by the following command:

$$\text{optimize(objective, constraints).}$$

Box 11.1 shows a MATLAB script that finds the optimal solution of the problem given by (11.1) using YALMIP. The YALMIP commands are freely integrated in MATLAB.

Box 11.1 YALMIP EXAMPLE FOR SOLVING A SIMPLE LINEAR PROGRAM

```
% ================================================================
% yalmip_example.m
%
% MALTAB script for solving a simple linear programming
% problem using YALMIP
%    max  (x + 2y)
%    s.t. (2x + 5y) <= 10
%         (5x + y)  <= 20
%          x, y >= 0
% ================================================================
% Declare variables
x = sdpvar(2, 1);

% Define the objective function
objective = -[1, 2] * x;

% Set constraints
constraints = [2*x(1) + 5*x(2) <= 10, 5*x(1) + x(2) <= 20, ...
  x >= 0];

% Solve the model and get optimal values
optimize(constraints, objective);

disp(value(x));
```

Uncertain Variables

In YALMIP, robust optimization is solved by adding additional constraints reflecting the desired uncertainty set. For example, if a variable z is uncertain but known to be within an interval between -1 and $+1$, then the following extra constraint can be added:

$$z\_constraints = [-1 <= z <= 1, uncertain(z)].$$

Note how the last part specifies that the variable is uncertain. The *optimize* command can still be used for solving problems with uncertainty as long as the first argument includes constraints that reflect uncertainty. Suppose the problem given by (11.1) contained some uncertainty. More specifically, if one of the constants in the first inequality constraint were uncertain, the problem can be written as

$$\max_{x,y} x + 2y$$

$$\text{s.t.} \quad 2x + zy \le 10$$

$$5x + y \le 20 \tag{11.2}$$

$$x, y \ge 0.$$

with an uncertain component z. If we know that the value of z lies between 4 and 6, we can find the optimal robust solution through robust optimization by defining a box uncertainty set for z. Box 11.2 demonstrates how the uncertain linear program can be solved using YALMIP.

Box 11.2 YALMIP EXAMPLE FOR SOLVING A SIMPLE UNCERTAIN LINEAR PROGRAM

```
% ================================================================
% yalmip_uncertain_example.m
%
% MALTAB script for solving a simple linear programming
% problem with uncertainty using YALMIP
%     max   (x + 2y)
%     s.t. (2x + z*y) <= 10
%          (5x + y)   <= 20
%           x, y >= 0
%     where z is uncertain but known to be 4 <= z <= 6
% ================================================================
% Declare variables
x = sdpvar(2, 1);
z = sdpvar(1, 1);

% Define the objective function
objective = -[1, 2] * x;

% Set constraints
constraints = [2*x(1) + z*x(2) <= 10, 5*x(1) + x(2) <= 20, ...
  x >= 0];
z_constraints = [4 <= z <= 6, uncertain(z)];

% Solve the model and get optimal values
optimize([constraints, z_constraints], objective);

disp(value(x));
```

Another function worth mentioning is the *robustify* function in YALMIP. Like the optimize function, the robustify function takes constraints and objective function as the first two arguments. But, instead of solving the optimization problem, it returns the robust counterpart of the original problem. The function returns constraints and objective function reflecting the robust counterpart,

[rc_objective, rc_constraints] = robustify(objective, constraints).

In other words, the inputs of *robustify* are the original problem, and the outputs are its robust counterpart. The robust solution can also be found by solving the robust counterpart using the *optimize* function:

optimize(rc_objective, rc_constraints).

Examples

The two main robust portfolio optimization problems that have been discussed in this book are the formulations that incorporate uncertainty in mean returns through a box uncertainty set or an ellipsoidal uncertainty set, both introduced in Chapter 6. Here, we replicate the MATLAB functions for solving these two formulations using YALMIP.

First, the optimal portfolio for the box uncertainty formulation, as described in section 6.4, can be found from the function presented in Box 11.3, which is comparable to Boxes 6.7, 6.8, and 6.9 in Chapter 6. The only difference from solving the certain version is when setting the constraints. As shown in Exhibit 11.1, nearly identical robust portfolios are

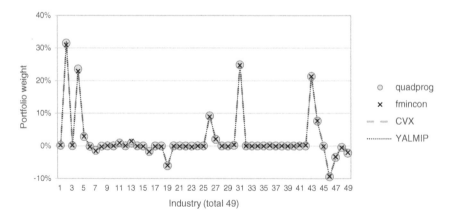

Exhibit 11.1 Comparison of optimal robust allocations for box uncertainty

Box 11.3 FUNCTION THAT SOLVES THE ROBUST PROBLEM WITH A BOX UNCERTAINTY SET USING YALMIP

```
% ================================================================
% robustboxyalmip.m
%
% Find the optimal robust portfolio with box uncertainty using
% YALMIP
%
% Input:
%   returns: matrix of stock returns (each column represents
%            a single stock)
%   lambda: value of the risk-seeking coefficient
%   alpha: confidence level of the uncertainty set
% Output:
%   optPortfolio: optimal mean-variance portfolio (a column
%                 vector)
% ================================================================
function optPortfolio = robustboxyalmip( returns, lambda, ...
  alpha )

    [nDays,n] = size(returns);
    mu = mean(returns)';
    sigma = cov(returns);

    % Compute delta (use confidence interval of mean for
    % normal distribution)
    z = norminv(1 - (1 - alpha) / 2, 0, 1);
    delta = z * sqrt(var(returns))' / sqrt(nDays);


    % ---------------------- YALMIP ------------------------
    w = sdpvar(n, 1);
    mu_true = sdpvar(n, 1);

    objective = w' * sigma * w - lambda * mu_true' * w;
    constraint = [sum(w) == 1, ...
        mu - delta <= mu_true <= mu + delta, uncertain(mu_true)];

    optimize(constraint, objective);
    optPortfolio = value(w);
end
```

found regardless of whether CVX, YALMIP, or only MATLAB functions are used; the graph shows optimal allocations when forming a portfolio of 49 industries using monthly returns during 2005 to 2014 for the four approaches. The correlation of portfolio weights among the four approaches are greater than 0.99, confirming how different tools can be used for solving the same robust optimization problem.

Second, a function for solving the ellipsoidal formulation is shown in Box 11.4, which is comparable to Boxes 6.10 and 6.11 in section 6.5 in Chapter 6. The correlation of portfolio weights was again greater than 0.99, regardless of the function chosen to find the optimal portfolio with ellipsoidal uncertainty.

11.2 ROME (ROBUST OPTIMIZATION MADE EASY)

ROME, or Robust Optimization Made Easy, is a toolbox for solving robust optimization.[3] As indicated by its name, its primary focus is on robust optimization. Hence, the software package provides many examples on defining uncertainty sets and solving robust optimization problems. Similar to YALMIP, ROME is also a free toolbox that runs in the MATLAB environment.

Basic Structure

Within MATLAB code, the commands *rome_begin* and *rome_end* denote the start and the end of a ROME block, respectively. After calling *rome_begin* to enter the ROME environment, a new ROME model object is created. Then, decision variables, objective function, and constraints are defined for the model object. Once all the details of the model are declared, solving the model requires one additional command, the *solve* function.

Revisiting the simple linear programming problem given in (11.1), Box 11.5 shows how the optimal solution is found within the ROME environment.

Uncertain Variables

When declaring a variable in ROME, one option is to specify the variable as uncertain:

$$variable\_name = \text{newvar}(variable\_size,'uncertain').$$

This is the first step in constructing a model with uncertainty; the next step is to define the uncertainty set for the uncertain variable. The box

Box 11.4 FUNCTION THAT SOLVES THE ROBUST PROBLEM WITH AN ELLIPSOIDAL UNCERTAINTY SET USING YALMIP

```
% ==============================================================
% robustellipsoidyalmip.m
%
% Find the optimal robust portfolio with ellipsoid uncertainty
% using YALMIP
%
% Input:
%    returns: matrix of stock returns (each column represents
%             a single stock)
%    lambda: value of the risk-seeking coefficient
%    alpha: confidence level of the uncertainty set
% Output:
%    optPortfolio: optimal mean-variance portfolio (a column
%                  vector)
% ==============================================================
function optPortfolio = robustellipsoidyalmip( returns, ...
  lambda, alpha )

    [nDays,n] = size(returns);
    mu = mean(returns)';
    sigma = cov(returns);
    sigmaMu = sigma / nDays;
    sqrtSigmaMu = sqrtm(sigmaMu);


    % Compute delta
    delta = sqrt(chi2inv(alpha,n));


    % --------------------- YALMIP -----------------------
    w = sdpvar(n, 1);
    mu_true = sdpvar(n, 1);

    objective = w' * sigma * w - lambda * mu_true' * w;
    constraint = [sum(w) == 1, ...
        (mu_true-mu)'/(sigmaMu)*(mu_true-mu) <= delta, ...
        uncertain(mu_true)];

    optimize(constraint, objective);
    optPortfolio = value(w);
end
```

Box 11.5 ROME EXAMPLE FOR SOLVING A SIMPLE LINEAR PROGRAM

```
% ================================================================
% rome_example.m
%
% MALTAB script for solving a simple linear programming
% problem using ROME
%    max  (x + 2y)
%    s.t. (2x + 5y) <= 10
%         (5x + y)  <= 20
%          x, y >= 0
% ================================================================
% Begin ROME
rome_begin;

% Create a new ROME model
h = rome_model('Example');

% Declare variables
newvar x y;

% Define the objective function
rome_maximize(x + 2*y);

% Set constraints
rome_constraint(2*x + 5*y <= 10);
rome_constraint(5*x + y <= 20);
rome_constraint(x >= 0);
rome_constraint(y >= 0);

% Solve the model and get optimal values
h.solve;
x_val = h.eval(x);
y_val = h.eval(y);

% End ROME
rome_end;
```

uncertainty set, or simply the interval for an uncertain variable, can be easily set by the *rome_box* command,

rome_box(*uncertain_variable_name, lower_bound, upper_bound*).

More complex uncertainty sets such as ellipsoids can be set using the *rome_constraint* function; add additional constraints stating how the uncertain variable must lie within a specified set.

Box 11.6 exhibits how the uncertain linear programming problem given by (11.2) is solved using ROME commands. Note that the uncertain variable z is declared with the keyword *uncertain* and the intervals are set by the *rome_box* function.

Example

Robust optimization can be applied to various portfolio problems for increasing robustness. One simple example is to find the optimal allocation of a no-shorting portfolio that will maximize return when individual stock returns are expected to be within an interval. In addition to defining the intervals, a budget uncertainty set limits the maximum amount of total deviation because it is unlikely that all stocks will have their worst possible return at the same time. Mathematically, the problem can be written as:[4]

$$
\max_{\omega} \min_{z \in \mathcal{U}_\Gamma} \sum_{i=1}^{n} (\mu_i + \sigma_i z_i)\omega_i
$$

$$
\text{s.t. } \omega' \iota = 1
$$

$$
\omega \geq 0
$$

(11.3)

where ω is the portfolio weights, μ_i is the expected return of stock i, and ι is the vector of ones. Thus, the objective is to find the portfolio with maximum return, where the stock return r_i is not certain but rather expressed as

$$
r_i = \mu_i + \sigma_i z_i,
$$

which shows how it can deviate from its expected return μ_i where σ_i is a measure of the uncertainty of the return. The uncertainty set in (11.3) is expressed as

$$
\mathcal{U}_\Gamma(z) = \{z \mid ||z||_\infty \leq 1, ||z||_1 \leq \Gamma\}.
$$

The maximum deviation in return for each stock is σ_i, while the total maximum deviation is Γ. The implementation of the budget uncertainty for this portfolio problem is shown in Box 11.7.

Box 11.6 ROME EXAMPLE FOR SOLVING A SIMPLE UNCERTAIN LINEAR PROGRAM

```
% ================================================================
% rome_uncertain_example.m
%
% MALTAB script for solving a simple linear programming
% problem with uncertainty using ROME
%     max   (x + 2y)
%     s.t.  (2x + z*y) <= 10
%           (5x + y)  <= 20
%            x, y >= 0
%     where z is uncertain but known to be 4 <= z <= 6
% ================================================================
% Begin ROME
rome_begin;

% Create a new ROME model
h = rome_model('Example');

% Declare variables (along with uncertainty set for uncertain
% variables)
newvar x y;
newvar z uncertain;
rome_box(z, 4, 6);

% Define the objective function
rome_maximize(x + 2*y);

% Set constraints
rome_constraint(2*x + z*y <= 10);
rome_constraint(5*x + y <= 20);
rome_constraint(x >= 0);
rome_constraint(y >= 0);

% Solve the model and get optimal values
h.solve;
x_val = h.eval(x);
y_val = h.eval(y);

% End ROME
rome_end;
```

Box 11.7 ROME EXAMPLE ON ROBUST PORTFOLIO OPTIMIZATION WITH A BUDGET UNCERTAINTY SET

```
% ================================================================
% Source: http://www.robustopt.com/examples/price_of_robustness
% _example/price_of_robustness.m
%
% Suppose the following variable values are set before calling
% ROME:
%    n: number of stocks
%    mu: mean return of stocks
%    sigma: deviation in stock returns
%    gamma: budget of uncertainty
% ================================================================
% Begin ROME
h = rome_begin;

% Uncertainty set
newvar z(n) uncertain;
rome_box(z, -1, 1);
rome_constraint(norm1(z) <= gamma);

% Returns relations with uncertain factors
r = mu + sigma.*z;

% Portfolio weights
newvar x(n) nonneg;

% Objective
rome_maximize(r'*x); % Note that r is uncertain and depends on z.
                     % The objective should be interpreted as
                     % max{y : y<= r(z)'x for z in uncertainty
                     % set}

% Constraint
rome_constraint(sum(x)==1);

% Solve
h.solve;
obj = h.objective;
xx = h.eval(x);

% End ROME
rome_end;
```

11.3　AIMMS

The final software package we cover in this chapter is AIMMS (Advanced Integrated Multidimensional Modeling Software).[5] AIMMS is a development environment for creating applications that support analytic decisions. It provides advanced computational techniques and also the capacity to solve various optimization models. Although AIMMS is very different from the MATLAB environment, it offers a versatile modeling language and also supports graphical user interface and integration with databases and other applications.

AIMMS is also well suited for forming robust portfolios because its robust optimization add-on automatically generates a reformulation of an uncertain problem for finding the optimal robust solution. Indicating the uncertain parameters with the possible realizations is sufficient for AIMMS to optimize the robust counterpart of the given problem. Parameters in AIMMS can be specified with its property being *uncertain*, and its *region* attribute allows setting the uncertainty set as a box, an ellipsoid, or a convex hull.

KEY POINTS

- YALMIP is a modeling toolbox for MATLAB and contains functionality to solve robust optimization. In addition to solving robust optimization by defining the uncertain variables, it contains a function for creating robust counterparts.
- ROME is also a toolbox for solving robust optimization in the MATLAB environment. ROME allows users to declare uncertain variables and define uncertainty sets.
- Both YALMIP and ROME automatically reformulate uncertain optimization problems for finding optimal robust solutions. Furthermore, both tools are easy to learn for MATLAB users and available for free.
- AIMMS is a modeling environment with strengths in solving optimization problems, including features to efficiently solve robust optimization problems after reformulating uncertain problems.

NOTES

1. For an overview of YALMIP, see Johan Löfberg, "YALMIP: A Toolbox for Modeling and Optimization in MATLAB," *Computer Aided Control Systems Design, 2004 IEEE International Symposium on*, IEEE (2004), pp. 284–289. More details along with recent updates are available at http://users.isy.liu.se/

johanl/yalmip/. How to solve robust optimization with YALMIP is explained in Johan Löfberg, "Automatic Robust Convex Programming," *Optimization Methods and Software* 27, 1 (2012), pp. 115–129.

2. Installation is another advantage since it only requires unzipping the YALMIP zip file and adding the necessary paths in MATLAB.

3. An overview of ROME is provided by Joel Goh and Melvyn Sim, "Robust Optimization Made Easy with ROME," *Operations Research* 59, 4 (2011), pp. 973–985, and a detailed users' guide is available at http://www.robustopt .com/references/ROME_Guide_1.0.pdf

4. The approach was first introduced in Dimitris Bertsimas and Melvyn Sim, "The Price of Robustness," *Operations Research* 52, 1 (2004), pp. 35-53, and the implementation in ROME is accessible at http://www.robustopt.com/examples/ price_of_robustness_example/price_of_robustness.m

5. A complete AIMMS user's guide is available at http://www.aimms.com/aimms/ download/manuals/aimms_user.pdf and description on solving robust optimiza- tion is found at http://www.aimms.com/aimms/download/manuals/aimms3lr_ robustoptimization.pdf

About the Authors

Woo Chang Kim is an associate professor of the Industrial and Systems Engineering Department at Korea Advanced Institute of Science and Technology (KAIST). The author of many papers in portfolio management and financial optimization, Woo Chang serves on the editorial boards for several journals, including *Journal of Portfolio Management*, *Optimization and Engineering*, and *Quantitative Finance Letters*. He was a founding member of DPT Capital Management, LLC, a hedge fund based in Princeton, New Jersey. Woo Chang earned a doctorate in operations research and financial engineering from Princeton University, and an M.S. and a B.S. in industrial engineering from Seoul National University.

Jang Ho Kim is an assistant professor of industrial and management systems engineering at Kyung Hee University. Previously, he was a visiting assistant professor of finance in the College of Business at James Madison University. Jang Ho received a doctorate in industrial and systems engineering from KAIST where he gained research interest in robust portfolio optimization. Prior to earning his doctorate, he worked in the electronic trading unit of Bank of America Merrill Lynch. He holds an M.Eng. and a B.S. in computer science, both from Cornell University.

Frank J. Fabozzi is editor of the *Journal of Portfolio Management*. He is a professor of finance at EDHEC Business School and a senior scientific adviser at the EDHEC-Risk Institute. A CFA holder, Frank is a trustee for both the BlackRock closed-end fund complex and the equity-liquidity fund complex. Frank is the CFA Institute's 2007 recipient of the C. Stewart Sheppard Award and the CFA Institute's 2015 recipient of the James R. Vertin Award. Frank was inducted into the Fixed Income Analysts Society Hall of Fame in November 2002. He has authored and edited numerous books on portfolio management.

About the Companion Website

The main quantitative approaches in this book are presented with MATLAB examples, allowing readers to easily implement portfolio problems in MATLAB or similar modeling software. The companion website provides the MATLAB codes that appear in the chapter boxes. To access the code, go to www.wiley.com/go/robustequitypm, password wiley16.

Printed and bound by CPI Group (UK) Ltd, Croydon, CR0 4YY

23/04/2025

14660999-0001